POP IDOLS AND PIRATES

For Frances, who made it all possible

Pop Idols and Pirates

Mechanisms of Consumption and the
Global Circulation of Popular Music

CHARLES FAIRCHILD
University of Sydney, Australia

ASHGATE

Published by
Ashgate Publishing Limited
Gower House
Croft Road
Aldershot
Hampshire GU11 3HR
England

Ashgate Publishing Company
Suite 420
101 Cherry Street
Burlington, VT 05401-4405
USA

Ashgate website: http://www.ashgate.com

British Library Cataloguing in Publication Data
Fairchild, Charles, 1967–
    Pop idols and pirates : mechanisms of consumption and the global circulation
    of popular music. – (Ashgate popular and folk music series)
    1. Music trade – Social aspects 2. Popular music – Social aspects
    3. Piracy (Copyright) I. Title
    306.4'842

Library of Congress Cataloging-in-Publication Data
Fairchild, Charles, 1967–
    Pop idols and pirates : mechanisms of consumption and the global circulation
of popular music / Charles Fairchild.
        p. cm.—(Ashgate popular and folk music series)
    Includes bibliographical references (p.   ) and index.
    ISBN 978-0-7546-6383-6 (alk. paper)
    1. Music trade—Social aspects. 2. Popular music—Social aspects. 3. Piracy (Copyright)
I. Title.

    ML3790.F34 2008
    338.4'778163—dc22

2007044477

ISBN 978-0-7546-6383-6

Printed and bound in Great Britain by MPG Books Ltd, Bodmin, Cornwall.

Contents

General Editor's Preface   vii
Acknowledgements   ix

Introduction: Industrial-Strength Strawmen   1

Part I   All of the In-between

1   The Acts and Spaces of Consumption   17

2   The Medium and Materials of Popular Music   35

Part II   Bridging the Distance between Production and Consumption

3   Power and Property: CDs, MP3s, and SoundScan   55

4   Mediating and Manufacturing the Investment in Desire   75

Part III   The Spectacle as Consumption Environment

5   Constructing the "Idol" Empire   95

6   Building the Authentic Celebrity: The Structure of a Spectacle   103

7   Becoming Who You Are: The Content of a Spectacle   123

Conclusion: Why "Idol"?   155

Bibliography   159
Index   179

General Editor's Preface

The upheaval that occurred in musicology during the last two decades of the twentieth century has created a new urgency for the study of popular music alongside the development of new critical and theoretical models. A relativistic outlook has replaced the universal perspective of modernism (the international ambitions of the 12-note style); the grand narrative of the evolution and dissolution of tonality has been challenged, and emphasis has shifted to cultural context, reception and subject position. Together, these have conspired to eat away at the status of canonical composers and categories of high and low in music. A need has arisen, also, to recognize and address the emergence of crossovers, mixed and new genres, to engage in debates concerning the vexed problem of what constitutes authenticity in music and to offer a critique of musical practice as the product of free, individual expression.

Popular musicology is now a vital and exciting area of scholarship, and the *Ashgate Popular and Folk Music Series* presents some of the best research in the field. Authors are concerned with locating musical practices, values and meanings in cultural context, and draw upon methodologies and theories developed in cultural studies, semiotics, poststructuralism, psychology and sociology. The series focuses on popular musics of the twentieth and twenty-first centuries. It is designed to embrace the world's popular musics from Acid Jazz to Zydeco, whether high tech or low tech, commercial or non-commercial, contemporary or traditional.

Professor Derek B. Scott
Professor of Critical Musicology
University of Leeds

Acknowledgements

I began working on this book shortly after my arrival in Australia after a seven year hiatus from academic work. At many points in time my absence from academia appeared to be permanent. So when I started the process of teaching and research which would result in this book, I was not at all confident I would succeed. There have been many people who convinced me otherwise. First and foremost is my partner Frances Clarke. She remains the most ardent and convincing of my advocates. There were many friends and colleagues who helped me acclimate to a strange country and an often mysterious tertiary education system. Stephen Robertson, whose help in preparing for my job interview and, later, the classroom was invaluable. Ian Maxwell was in many ways a key institutional sponsor of the ideas contained in this book. His expertly conceived subject "Performing Australia" was the first venue in which my ideas on the "Idol" phenomenon were expressed. His enthusiasm, feedback, and support helped shape these ideas into their current form. Kurt Iveson provided crucial support and many insightful suggestions for several draft chapters, especially those on the music industry. Readers from Context, Popular Music, Popular Music and Society, and M/C Journal have lent a hand in shaping this work. Thanks to all for taking the time and making the effort.

Introduction

Industrial-Strength Strawmen

> The power to record sound was one of the three essential powers of the gods in ancient societies, along with that of making war and causing famine (Jacques Attali).[1]

By way of illustrative example, let's think back to the world of 1980. It is by now, in many respects, an unimaginable world. There were no mobile phones, no text messages, and no emails. There was only the occasional music video on free-to-air television, no MP3s, and no DVDs. CDs were still in the lab, soon to escape, Pandora-like, to bedevil the very industry that pushed their universal adoption so vigorously. Cable television was rare, there was no internet outside of the Pentagon and a network of elite universities, the idea of a home computer was almost mystical, the average VCR weighed about ten kilos, and most things musical were analog. Given the overwhelming changes to the stuff of popular culture in the intervening years, it should not be a surprise that the circulation of those profitable slices of sound known as compact disc digital recordings has become a process fraught with both grave threats and surprising opportunities. The mediation of meaning and control over the circulation of popular music between the moments of production and consumption has become more difficult for the music industry than it has been for a long time. The foundational changes in our entertainment options have produced what many in the music industry have perceived as a rolling series of crises which have been met with a range of creative efforts which have produced both successes and failures that have been breathtaking. At the core of these crises is the increasingly problematic management of the relationships between the entertainment industry and its consumers. These relationships have become much more specific and complicated in recent years. The music industry in particular has been compelled to react to several interrelated crises provoked by the rapid globalization of popular culture, the digitalization of music, and the ever more extensive commercialization of public culture by waging some very significant battles with its own consumers, struggles viewed by many as central to the industry's survival as a central mediator in the circulation of popular music.[2]

---

1   Attali (1985:87).

2   I will be using the term "music industry" in the generic sense implying neither unity of purpose nor centrality of structure. Some argue that the term of art should be "music industries." However, this argument is based on the assumption that the term "music industry" implies the above noted characteristics (Williamson and Cloonan, 2007). There is no necessary reason for this. For example, when one uses the term "oil industry" it is reasonable and common to assume this term includes companies that make money from the rendering and distribution of oil, including companies that build oil rigs or sell petrol. Similarly, I will be using the terms music industry and "entertainment industry" when talking about companies that make

Yet much of what is written about the music industry presumes either a generic or only occasionally problematic relationship between the moments of production and consumption, or more precisely, that relationship has been problematized in very specific and limited ways. The primary form of connection between the music industry and its consumers is most often described in terms of the relationships between musicians and fans with the industry lurking in the background, intervening without any apparent guiding purpose other than a convenient marriage of pleasure and profit. Descriptions of those who control the means of production assume a paradoxical cast, positing an industry that is both beastly and beneficent (Wallis and Malm, 1984; Robinson, 1991; Negus, 1999; Gebesmair and Smudits, 2001; Anderson, 2006). Works which analyze the market in music more broadly tend to be economic analyses dealing with resolutely mighty issues (Leyshon et al., 2005; Burkart and McCourt, 2004). While these efforts are invaluable to understanding the music industry, they rarely link the material facts of mechanisms of consumption to the material facts of music. In contrast, this book focuses on all that happens in-between the musician and the fan in an effort to better understand how the links between the two are produced and maintained. Within the academic study of popular music, conceiving of all the activity after the product is complete, but prior to the act of consumption, as a coherent object of study doesn't quite fit into most existing research paradigms. It fits neither with the theoretical assumptions of cultural populism nor with associated methodologies which track consumer desire, musician creativity, and industry mendacity.[3] For an academic musicologist, this research agenda might seem almost perversely anti-musical. Yet it is clear that all that lies in-between the musician and the fan has become inordinately visible in recent years. Despite the vital and growing body of literature documenting and theorizing the evolution of the mechanisms of consumption created through the activities of the advertising, marketing, public relations, and promotions industries, industries which have been growing in scale, scope, and power since the early twentieth century, the field has yet to be seriously exploited by scholars of popular music (Ewen, 1996; Carey, 1995; Nelson, 1989; Turner et al., 2000). The many specific, situated intermediations that lie between fans and "their" music are overripe for analysis precisely because of the crises so many intermediaries have been facing for the last few years (Jones, 2000 and 2002; Negus, 2002; Nixon and du Gay, 2002).

This book presents two interrelated cases of crisis and opportunity: the music industry's struggles over piracy and the "Idol" phenomenon. The handling of both reveals explicit attempts to control and justify the ways in which the music industry makes money from music. The battles over piracy have been fought with a collection of campaigns consisting of argument and coercion intended to demonstrate and enforce the "right" way to consume music. From these complicated and often

---

money from selling us music or entertaining us. I recognize an obvious and significant overlap between these complex, multi-tiered industries.

3   I am following McGuigan's use of the term "cultural populism," not as a pejorative, but as a description of the tradition within cultural studies that examines popular culture through the experience of ordinary people within the context of everyday life (McGuigan, 1992).

contradictory campaigns we can draw out a reasonably clear picture of what many within the music industry imagine their industry to be. In a complementary way, "Idol" works to demonstrate the joy and pleasure that result from consuming popular music the "right" way. By creating a series of intertwined relationships with consumers through multiple sites of consumption, incorporating television, radio, live performance, text messaging, traditional advertising campaigns, and all manner of internet-based systems of communication and "fan management," the producers of "Idol's" various iterations model and facilitate an ideal relationship between musicians and audiences. Instead of focusing on selling CDs, the music industry's digital Achilles' heel, "Idol" gives us a familiar narrative framework which takes the form of a seamlessly integrated cross-media platform through which the music industry can display its expanded palette of products and venues for consumption. When understood in specific relation to the battles against piracy, "Idol," and the emerging promotional cultures of the music industry it embodies, demonstrates how multiple sites of consumption and attempts to mediate and control the circulation of popular music are being used to combat the challenges facing the music industry.

The connections I am drawing between piracy and "Idol" may not seem immediately obvious, but the correlation between the two is considerable. The claims people have made about each phenomenon present virtually identical, if inverted, stories of freedom and disaster. Each phenomenon has been lauded as the pure, unfettered, democratic expression of the will of the people. Each phenomenon has also been routinely accused of killing music. Each phenomenon has been credited with introducing new music and real talent to more people, but also with destroying the livelihoods of musicians and damaging the aesthetic and economic health of the music industry. Both phenomena have been described as paragons of inventive, active consumption and as evil enterprises which delude and addle the minds of otherwise virtuous music lovers. Empirically or conceptually, all of these stories cannot be true, nor can they be reconciled with one another. Fortunately, I am not trying to prove their validity. Instead, I am examining the ways in which both piracy and "Idol" are both emblematic and symptomatic of struggles the music industry has been having with its own consumers for decades. These struggles were raging long before the MP3 was conjured out of the otherwise obedient compact disc and they will continue long after the demons of unfettered, illegal file sharing are exorcised from enough of us to matter. These struggles are not about "stealing music" or "communicating emotions" through music. They are about bridging the literal, unavoidable gap between the act of production and the act of consumption and doing so profitably. The complicated mechanisms for accomplishing this task are the subject of this book.

Piracy and "Idol" both arrived at the exact historical moment when the music industry was at the peak of its political and economic power, but was exhibiting vulnerability in what we might call its cultural reach; put simply, there were increasing numbers of consumers who acted as if the music industry wasn't necessary anymore. While the music industry was never as fragile as it often liked to appear, it still seemed to be easily shaken by the likes of Napster, Kazaa, and myriad competing demands on consumer spending that have been growing since the 1970s. The shrill rhetoric and furious condemnation directed at file trading music fans, the bulk of whom were doing little more than really enjoying "their" music, might have suggested an industry close to collapse. But these were mostly symptoms of an industry going through a particularly ugly transition. The intrepid captains of the music and entertainment industries managed the transition as well as might be expected. When things got tough, they flexed their legislative, economic, and communicative muscles in order to enshrine their economic oligopoly, insert draconian restrictions on intellectual property permanently into the law of dozens of countries, and repeatedly insist that their dominance was natural and just. In those arenas of greatest material consequence, such as the WTO's various secretive tribunals, the informal yet curiously binding deliberations of the World Economic Forum, the formally binding and globally influential decisions of the US Supreme Court, and every trade negotiation undertaken by the US government since the early 1980s, the music and entertainment industries have received just about everything they ever demanded (Drahos, 2002; Mann, 2000).

Finally, piracy and "Idol" both appeared at the tail end of one of the most remarkable revenue growth curves the music industry has ever experienced, an upward trajectory that lasted from 1982 until 1995. Underlying both the long boom and its eventual end were at least two dominant trends in the music and entertainment industries. The first was the near total encapsulation of the music industry within the larger structures and strategic priorities of the entertainment industry, a sprawling monster that now incorporates media production, content distribution, broadcasting networks, infrastructure development, and marketing which has resulted in consolidated conglomerates whose edges are increasingly difficult to identify. This first trend has led directly to the second, the now reflexive cross-media promotion of music in films, television shows, video games, on websites, and various fields of merchandising. Once used to push album sales, cross-media promotion has become an end in itself as sales of albums decreased and sales of just about everything else one can imagine more than took up the slack. "Idol's" producers in particular have capitalized on the role of recorded music as a sales catalyst for the entire entertainment industry and created a multi-platform marketing bonanza, combining the appeal of MTV, game shows, and the visceral soap opera inflections of reality television to create a success so total it has changed the rules for creating success in the music business.

The environments in which music is consumed have become the source of much angst and worry, but they have also become the objects of an unprecedented level of strategic planning. And this is the most important commonality between the piracy wars and "Idol": both are the offspring, one wanted, one not, of a very specific form of power that slides easily across economic, social, and political arenas. The music and entertainment industries express their power by trying to shape as many contexts of consumption as possible in order to reduce market risk to overall profitability as close to zero as possible. They do so in the most mundane and pervasive ways imaginable by thoroughly acknowledging the agency of consumers and then working with or around that agency to establish as many ways to profit from it as possible. Obviously, there are always market risks and the music industry's risks are probably greater than most. Their famously high failure rate tells us that this industry is not governed by simple calculations of per unit profit and loss. But the efforts these industries make in assiduously shaping their market relationships with consumers in the least risky ways possible are clearly worth the reward. Evidence of these efforts is difficult to ignore.

The Four Strawmen of Consumerism: Industrial Mendacity, Analytical Cynicism, Cultural "Democracy," and Consumer "Resistance"

There remains a distinct lack of recognition in popular music studies for the aims, scope, and consequences of these complex manifestations of market power. Arguments about the "real" character of the culture industries are rarely advanced through detailed analyses of how their markets are constructed and maintained, but through a series of familiar strawman arguments. Critics unearthing examples of industrial mendacity are called pessimistic, cynical, or disdainful. They are accused of denigrating popular culture by denying people their inalienable right to express their unique forms of human agency (Fiske, 1987:93). They are said to be caught in a cycle of shame and nostalgia for those rosy days of yore when families gathered around the piano or sat on the front porch singing the old songs without the aid of industrial mediation (Frith, 1988:11–13). They are called arrogant sophisticates who want to impose their values on the rest of us, incapable of recognizing the democratic genius of the market (Cowen, 1998; Twitchell, 1999). They are scolded and told that the cultural industries are not comprised of a simple top–down machinery dominated by industry moguls who "simply produce" products for audiences who "simply consume" them. Fans are not passive dupes who do what they are told (Grossberg, 1992:65; Solomon, 2003:10, 37; Anderson, 2006:xxi).

We are told that there are many creative and earnest people in the music industry who respect artists and embrace what they create (Negus, 1999). This benevolent industry allows us to experience the pleasure of music through its uniquely productive capacities. The music industry doesn't constrain artistic and consumer visions, desires, and choices, it helps us invest ourselves in its products. The music industry can only exist by respecting the "social and cultural needs of any given moment" (Anderson, 2006:xxix). While these claims are certainly true, or, more exactly, truisms, they are merely tired bromides of consumer capitalism that just happen to dovetail comfortably with the stern admonitions of academic populism. It seems oddly difficult for many to acknowledge the fact that the music industry is an industry like any other, less mendacious than many perhaps, but no less legally bound to place the profit motive above everything else like every other industry in the world (Bakan, 2004:36–7). Few seem particularly interested in the many varied, evolving, and inventive mechanisms through which the entertainment and music industries try to shape and facilitate "the social and cultural needs of any given moment" in order to profit from them. Those that do are accused of that cardinal sin of cultural studies, being a bunch of know-it-alls. As Thomas Frank has showed in extensive and humorous detail, the epithet "elitist" is no longer hurled at those running large industrial conglomerates. It is instead directed at their critics (Frank, 2000:252–306).

These criticisms are supported by two key misunderstandings. First, that the market in cultural goods is a representation of the "popular" will, and second, that any interpretations of cultural texts that differ from their intended meaning is a form of resistance or, more daringly, subversion. It has become increasingly unpopular for academics to criticize the constituent elements of the culture industries mostly because of these two misapprehensions (Ang, 2003:365). While some academics pine away in a populist fervor to produce theoretically sophisticated exegeses of consumer behavior and agency, the music and entertainment industries are far more ambivalent about the agents upon whom it relies to survive. It is most telling that the music industry's intermediaries can't decide whether the audience is their enemy or their savior. As increasing numbers of consumers have defected to the enemy in the war on piracy, a marked ambivalence has crept into the otherwise reflexive happy talk of the music industry. As market conditions became tougher, the supposed democratic essence of popular culture, and its enabling "genius of the market," began to emerge into a far more strict space of practice as corporate globalization became more deeply institutionalized in the everyday lives of more and more people. Far from some democratic utopia, what has evolved instead is a logic in which democracy is embodied in consumption and consumerism is a measure of citizenship (Garcia-Canclini, 2001). What has been exposed is the yawning gap between these two forms of agency so often rhetorically twinned.

Advocates of the active audience and resistant consumer are simply wrong when they argue that the glory of popular culture rests in its free and democratic essence.[4] Those studying so many individuated and sometimes glorified acts of interpretation do little to recognize, much less challenge, the consumerist paradigm, simply by taking existing market mechanisms for granted. They can only argue that the pleasures of popular culture are of a piece with freewill and democracy because they condone or disregard, by definition, how the entertainment industry conceives of us as consumers, and thus how it works, overlooking its fairly clear organizing principles, its oft-stated goals, and its plain, blatant will to power. Given this, there are several important questions that are crucial to understanding how acts of consuming popular music are shaped and directed before they happen. There are many ways of asking such questions, so I will try to be succinct. Is the consumption environment that envelopes popular music casually or even randomly constructed? Do we always encounter the products we desire unfettered and of our own accord? What music is made available, how is it made visible, how is it made to cross our paths, and how are our choices of what music to consume informed by what exists outside of us? To put it more dramatically, how is our will as consumers in part a product of the worlds of consumption in which we live?

It is important to note that I am taking for granted the important, but increasingly banal observation that people interpret the things they consume variously and in accordance with their lived experience. The extensive body of research tracking diverse forms of consumer behavior has rightly become an important part of the literature in

---

4   Chapter 8 of Frank (2000) and Chapter 8 of Gracyk (1996) provide two strong, distinct critiques of the populist and postmodernist strains of cultural analysis. Frank pays particular attention to a wide variety of claims of democracy in consumer culture.

studies of popular culture and the media, tempering cavalier assumptions about the nature of mass audiences and consumer desires. However, much of this work reaches its apogee through very thin claims about the consequences of consumption, positing that symbolic forms of resistance are inherent in varied readings of media texts. It is often simply presumed that "aberrant" readings of media texts have disobedient political effects both within and beyond the sphere of consumption.[5] But it is fairly easy to accept the evidence gathered by the more sophisticated and circumspect studies of consumer agency as far as that evidence goes. Nor is it a huge leap to couple that evidence with a defining interest in structural and political economic analysis of the cultural industries and embrace the conclusion that consumers can exert identifiable forms of definitional power over the meanings drawn from their experience of cultural texts, power that might even have some discernible resonance beyond their bedrooms, house parties, or car stereo systems. To put it simply, most people will more or less reach their own conclusions about most things in specific relation on the context in which they act. The volumes of both defensive and occasionally aggressive commentary on such issues have shaped debates over consumption in popular culture for far too long (see Born, 1993:266–92).

These interminable debates over the relationships between texts and their interpretation often miss the point. We are sentient beings who interpret the world in which we live in varied and idiosyncratic ways; we do this reflexively. The debate doesn't end here, it only starts here. As historian Walter Johnson has noted, lurking at the heart of these debates is an all too common conflation of the distinct categories of "humanity," "agency," and "resistance" (Johnson, 2003). This conflation marks every human act as the act of a resistant agent regardless of the context in which it occurs, rendering all contexts equal and equally irrelevant. This entangling of social categories has obscured the fact that any consumer, no matter how active and engaged, is still acting within a context pervaded by extensive and expansive corporate power. These are not contradictory constructions; they are complementary and mutually constitutive. Producers and consumers always act in a dynamic relationship with each other, acting towards some measure of benefit which is always mutual, always unequal, and always produced within identifiable and demonstrable productive logics which often contradict each other. Recognition of the wide range of forms of consumer activity is a necessary precondition to any detailed analysis of the kinds of relationships the music industry is intent on constructing. However, it is the area in-between consumers and producers, the contexts in which their dynamic relationships are made material, that remain in analytical shadow. And it is exactly these gnarly questions about the in-between contexts through which we act as consumers that are most often left to the side in much recent scholarship on popular music, displaced most often by the now familiar ritual of politely flogging Adorno and his heirs (Connell and Gibson, 2003:20, 59; Nunns, 2002:131–2; Toynbee, 2000:3–8; Potter, 1998:32, 36; Burnett, 1996:31–2; Negus, 1995:8–12, 37–9; Longhurst, 1995:3–14). The thoroughgoing critique presented by the Frankfurt School's standard-bearers still provokes so many fresh accusations of elitism that one might be forgiven for

---

5   For two detailed and provocative critiques of the active audience thesis, see Gibson (2000) and McGuigan (1992).

thinking their oddly modernist critique of human agency had not been given up for dead a long time ago.

Unfortunately, any thoroughgoing critiques of the cultural industries have been displaced by models of culture that posit a mostly correlative relationship between choice, freedom, consumerism, and democracy, a relationship said to be either facilitated by or embodied in what are presumed to be largely autonomous expressions of consumer agency. But expressions of consumer choice and freedom do not exist because the market is a democratic medium defined by the equitable distribution of transparently exercised power. Increased consumer freedom exists simply because cultural products circulate more voluminously than ever before, through channels of an exponentially increasing number and type; if you have enough money, you can get anything you want. But, as I argue throughout this book, our freedom to consume is clearly a problem for the entertainment industry insofar as they are continually trying to find new ways to solve it. This isn't exactly a recent problem. Numerous histories have documented the struggles over exactly how consumers can or should consume music showing how they have been endemic to the music industry (Mann, 2000; Coleman, 2005; Chanan, 1995).

The music and entertainment industries' ceaseless efforts at fine-tuning its mechanisms of consumption suggest that they seek to provide something other than mere choice or freedom. They rely heavily on extraordinarily expansive types of strategic planning provided by "trendspotters," "consumer psychologists," "futurists," or remarkably detailed demographic, ethnographic, or psychological research, research designed to ensure that the habits, attitudes, and activities of consumers are continually subject to microscopic interest (Hoggard, 2003; McIntyre, 2004b; Clements, 2005; Morris, 2005; Hills, 2006). Given this, it is hard to justify the casting of all manner of creative cultural agency as inherently democratic, as has been blandly asserted by a wide range of scholarship, its authors purporting to have discovered a nascent cultural democracy burgeoning everywhere from fanzines to karaoke clubs to blogs and chatrooms (Frith, 2002:241; Fenster, 2002:90; Drew, 2004:65; Toynbee, 2000:xviii, 10, 162). A small coterie of highly visible and unrestrained celebrants of commercial culture has even pushed these cultural studies axioms beyond their populist roots to present an even more reductive approach in their studies of popular culture and consumption. They produce a stilted neo-liberal model of consumption in which consumers are imagined as rational, self-contained units of economic freewill acting within a context that is so drained of any animating intent that one's range of choice is the only measure of the market's effectiveness, influence, or social function (Cowen, 1998; Twitchell, 1999). This fantasy is not confined to the ranks of economic libertarians as both free market acolytes and academic postmodernists come to nearly identical conclusions about the origins and consequences of consumer power (Fiske, 1987:93, 313). There is little to choose from in these supplementary visions of corporate and popular democracy. In each, the operational terms of democracy elide into the mere opportunity to do what you want, when you want. But can we really define as democracy the fact that we are more or less free to make up our own minds, make our own choices, ingest our own music, and use it how we wish? Surely there is more to democracy than this.

Instead of continuing a debate in which the acts of the consuming subject are imagined as autonomous from the social and economic structures that surround them, I want to turn my analysis in another direction. I want to examine the culture of consumption surrounding popular music as it is expressed through the ways in which the dynamic relationships created by the music industry with consumers are made material. It is in those moments when we participate most directly in our cultures of consumption that claims equating the free or democratic character of consumer culture with the limitless choice on offer can be most definitively neutered. Instead, we can deal with these issues by critically examining the ways in which all those circulating things are made visible to us and the complex ways in which they have been placed in front of us, seemingly all the time, as the direct result of a tremendous amount of strategic effort and planning.

Despite the fundamental changes in the material culture of popular music described throughout this book, the goal of the promotional culture of popular music has always been clear and stable regardless of the means used to achieve it: make the distribution and sale of music less risky, more predictable, and more profitable. It is not surprising that the music industry has based its collective, continued existence on this goal (McCourt and Rothenbuhler, 1997). What is crucial to our understanding of the worlds of consumption in which we live, is the core idea that our supposed democracy of things is problematic to those who produce, sell, and profit from the circulation and consumption of all these things; worse, it is growing increasingly problematic. Yet, they seem to feel the effort is the reward because they spend so much time and money on it. Yet, as advertisers and market researchers work harder to figure us out, their efforts are often met with decreasing clarity (Jinman, 2004a; Needham, 2003; Needham and Jinman, 2003).

Industrial failure, however, is not synonymous with consumer resistance. This "problem of freedom" is inherent in consumer culture. Industry executives can't simply tell us what to consume. We have opinions, desires, and feelings. The question for the music and entertainment industries is can we shape and direct the construction of desire and then profit from the consequences? A vast apparatus of manufactured visibility exists to put some things most blatantly before some of us at particular times in particular places. The music and entertainment industries imagine their consumers as an inherently dissatisfied public. They exist to satisfy as many of us in as many ways as they can as often as possible. The music press, the popular press, clever packaging, all manner of viral, virile, and invisible marketing campaigns, music videos, live performance, and all manner of discourses of social and cultural grandeur are constantly being produced continually asking us to buy more music. Why? Does anyone really think they have to convince us to buy music? They know we're going to buy it. What they want is for us to buy it from them and repeat the process as often as is necessary. They want to construct and maintain as many mutually beneficial relationships with as many of us as possible. This book is primarily about the shape, structure, and commercial aspirations of these relationships.

Throughout this book, I analyze these relationships through the ways in which they inextricably bind popular music and consumer culture together. I do so by presenting music as a materially specific form, a form that moves through the world in particular ways to which meanings are attached in particular ways. There are few works which problematize how the production, distribution, and consumption of music are linked by specific systems of economic and political power and even fewer which analyze how music moves within these systems of power. The few works on music consumption which consider music as a distinct material form give far more attention to the ways in which the relationships which link fans and artists are produced, facilitated, and presented. The forces in-between consumption and production which inform, shape, direct, and constrain the agency of those producing, distributing, and consuming music are marginal concerns at best. The recent focus on sociological and ethnographic realism in studies of popular music and consumption too often produces work which implicitly conflates the music industry with the people who work in it and consumer culture with consumers (Negus, 1999; Cavicchi, 1998; Malbon, 1999).

I have constructed this book by cleaving off almost everything that matters to most of us about music, but that is precisely the point. Whether we are aware of it or not, we are constituted as a coherent and cohering public by those who seek to take our money by creating what are necessary and mutually beneficial relationships. I do not seek to explain how or why everybody on the planet experiences music. I only want to start to examine the ways in which the experience of consuming music exists within contexts which I describe and examine through the ideas and forces which define and structure those contexts. We have seen a surfeit of scholarly rumination over the power of people, as individuals and as groups, to exert definitional power over their chosen texts and express their agency through all manner of collective action (see Jenkins et al., 2002). I am much more interested in how we helped to find those texts upon which we work our constructions and transformations of meaning in the first place. I am also interested in the places where we find these texts and the ways in which the contexts in which they are set inevitably shape and inform the acts and meaningful consequences of consumption itself. While the cultural studies literature is rife with beautifully realized reports and evocations surveying the contested terrain of textual meaning, the contemporary contests under examination here go much deeper than a semiotic or symbolic struggle for supremacy. At the heart of the contested terrain of popular culture are constant struggles over the material and social relationships which constitute it.

The Shape and Argument of This Work

This book is centered on the analysis of the ways in which the music industry has reacted to the three main challenges it is facing: rapidly evolving regimes of corporate globalization, ever more extensive commercialization of culture, and the sometimes reluctant digitalization of the content of its industry. There are a few key points underlying the range of analysis and argument in this book. First, there is a necessary and inherent distance between the production of popular music and its consumption. Second, music is a materially specific form that moves through the world in particular ways and to which meanings are attached in particular ways. The way it moves affects how we consume it and how we ascribe meaning to it. The music and entertainment industries are continually trying to bridge the gap between the production and consumption of popular music by attempting to shape and focus the ways in which music moves and acquires meaning. Their primary means of doing so are their continuing and contested attempts to establish the most profitable and least risky sorts of relationships with as many consumers as possible.

In Chapter 1, I establish the broad theoretical and analytical frame for the work as a whole by linking a critical theory of globalization to a particular understanding of the experience of consumer culture in everyday life. While the term globalization implies a sense of all-pervasiveness, the mechanisms through which globalization is enacted are designed and intended to work very specifically. They are rarely seen to work the same way everywhere, at all times. Instead, I argue that we can read globalization through more specific understandings of the ways in which it is experienced. I frame my analysis with the idea of the imperial condition in consumer culture. This condition is defined by the fact that consumers can exert power within systems of consumption only through the extent and quality of their participation in them. Using this idea I integrate the fundamental assumptions of "active audience" research with the perspectives of those engaged in political economic analysis of the entertainment industry by arguing that global consumer culture is constituted by our inherent, necessary, and active participation in systems of cultural production defined by power relationships over which we have little direct influence.

In Chapter 2, I move from crafting the theoretical tools used to analyze the contexts of consumption described in Chapter 1, to presenting those I will use to analyze the specifically musical content of this book. I put forward a concise and practical analytic framework for the kinds of broadly aesthetic analysis I present throughout the book. The central argument of this chapter is that popular music is an aesthetically neutral analytical category. By that I mean, there are few ontologically identifying properties that all forms of what we call popular music share, nor does the music industry rely on fixed and immutable definitions of what constitutes aesthetically successful music. Instead of relying only on an amorphous social category such as "popular music" as the basis for analysis, I use two key concepts to make clear the analytic differences between the ontological distinctions we can draw between different kinds of music and the social categories which are generally used to ascribe meaning to that music: the medium and materials of popular music (Gracyk, 1996). These concepts take into account the actual series of activities that go into creating the sounds and performative gestures we consume and the varied and evolving meanings that are attached to those sounds and performative gestures as they are experienced in particular contexts. These concepts deepen my descriptive analyses of music which follow and account for the social inscription of meaning in popular music specifically through an understanding of how these meanings are rooted in and produced by the complex of material facts, values, and practices that constitute the object of meaning in the first place.

The importance of the distinctions I make between medium and materials will grow throughout the course of this book. In Chapter 3, I examine the most obvious conflicts over the kinds of relationships the music industry has with its consumers, the battles over copyright and technology that always seem to dog the music industry, contests they have pursued with impressive vigor for decades. The relentless acquisition of intellectual property and the rights to use it are an unusually defining feature of the music industry. Few industries have pursued the acquisition and use of copyright as ruthlessly (Mann, 2000; Frith, 1993). I argue that a significant part of the contests over piracy is the concern expressed by the music industry about consumers experiencing their chosen musical materials through unofficial mediums such as BitTorrent or LimeWire. As I show, the music industry has responded to widespread illegal file sharing by setting out to redefine the terms through which the consumption of music is supposed to happen. In other words, the music industry has moved to codify their medium specifically through various attempts to shape the experience of consuming their materials.

Central to the music and entertainment industries' strategies are the specific models of globalization currently governing multilateral trade and investment regimes. These give pride of place to intellectual property, entrenching the restrictive American model of intellectual property law internationally and allowing the entertainment industry to more easily profit from intra-firm synergies, making their products inherently multi-format and cross-platform. Also, the music and entertainment industries have dramatically improved their ability to gather information on consumers. The advent of geodemographics, SoundScan, and other methods of data gathering have made these industries' systems of knowledge much more sensitive and specific. As such, the digitalization of music has actually made production, marketing, and distribution networks much more effective and efficient. More importantly, it has also forced costs down. When taken together, the music industry is in a much stronger position to take advantage of what business analysts call its "natural assets": music and musicians. Debates over piracy and copyright reveal a unified and coherent strategy despite the often conflicted and confused rhetoric emanating from industry representatives.

In Chapter 4, I argue that concepts such as brands, viral marketing, and the "attention economy" are tools used by many within the music and entertainment industries to try to reassert some measure of control over the mediums through which musical materials move. Paradoxically, the attention economy is a semi-happy accident. It was produced partly by the extraordinary din of the multitude of commercial messages we are confronted with daily and partly by the vertical integration of the entertainment industry allowing for cost-effective cross-promotion of various products. Marketers have been changing their practices to meet the challenges foisted on them by their own hand. Instead of relying only on fairly traditional forms of advertising, marketers have diversified the techniques used to craft media campaigns and reformulated their animating philosophies focusing more "building brand value" through the use of layered forms of communication through a variety of media channels to produce a presence or aura for a product that usually has little or nothing to do with the virtues of the product itself (McIntyre, 2004b).

Regardless of its founding impetus or continuing institutional imperatives, the attention economy highlights new methods for the creation and maintenance of consumer relationships. In order to sell their products, marketers need to find new ways to cut through the chatter of everyday life by creating dominant, pervasive, and unavoidable forms of chatter. The promotional cultures that surround the products of popular culture are increasingly defined by a cultural economy that values public attention as the prime commodity for which advertisers and cultural producers compete. The new wrinkles the attention economy is exhibiting, specifically in relation to digital technologies and the overwhelming complexity of our public culture, are reshaping the relationships between the music industry and its consumers. By comprehending the more detailed and interactive methods of market penetration, we can understand more clearly the ways in which popular music is sold and consumed through the more specific kinds of relationships these types of interactions help create. Again, we can see clearly the ways in which the music industry tries to construct and maintain consumer relationships through many varied attempts to create industry-controlled and dominated mediums though which their materials can and should travel. As I demonstrate in the final third of this book, these activities have had some interesting and sometimes surprising consequences.

Part III provides an extensive analysis of the first two series of Australian Idol. I argue that the "Idol" phenomenon is clearly shaped by strategies that bear all the distinct traces of a group of people struggling to exploit the challenges and opportunities described in the first two parts of this book. It is clear that the producers of "Idol's" various iterations have taken advantage of new methods of market penetration by using all manner of novel marketing techniques, the cost savings of extensive cross-promotion, and the market risk minimization possibilities inherent in their global brand franchising system. Given their undeniable success, "Idol's" producers often wax lyrical about their product being the future of popular music. This may be true, but not for the disingenuous reasons they most often give. As the show's creator, Simon Fuller, has made clear on repeated occasions, "Idol" is perfectly formed to fit the shape of the contemporary music industry. This is not for any particularly musical reasons, but because the show's producers have managed to capitalize on the increased ability of the marketing industry to target its pitches on the local level and on the multinational entertainment industry to make its products immediately available around the planet. Further, they have managed to blunt, for the moment, the threats of illegal or unofficial consumption by creating an impudent spectacle which has to be seen to be believed, not to mention consumed; the humble music pirate is of marginal import here. Instead, the producers of "Idol" have created a very specific medium through which their particularly crafted materials can travel.

I revisit the ideas of medium and materials in more detail and specificity throughout the last three chapters of this book, examining the forces which have allowed the "Idol" phenomenon to exist materially as well as conceptually. My analysis of the "Idol" phenomenon is closely related to the arguments made in the first half of the book, filling out the complexities and contradictions of this flamboyant form of actually-existing globalization. There is a direct connection between imbroglios over internet piracy and the "Idol" phenomenon; the globalization of popular culture has established both the social and technological basis for both. "Idol" is a spectacle founded on the creation and perpetuation of specific kinds of consumer relationships. Producers create contexts in which many kinds of audience participation flourish and compete, constantly offering more engaging and more focused forms of consumption. "Idol" is a nearly perfect reflection of the fact that the music industry has long been willing and capable to acknowledge and exploit the many creative ways consumers use music in everyday life. The many intertwined expressions of "Idol" demonstrate this clearly and forcefully.

The current literature on popular music and globalization is populated by work rife with intensely concentrated examples of syncretic, polysemic creativity trumping or co-opting global corporate power, many hewing very closely to familiar contests between "global capital" and "local creativity." I present a more subtle and insidious model. I argue that the very acts which are supposed to constitute consumer agency or resistance are not merely collusive with dominant global structures, but absolutely necessary to their function. "Idol" is a symbolic reflection of this fact, but its significance goes deeper than this. "Idol" is not simply a clever response to the challenges of global consumer culture. It is a constant reiteration of the basis on which the music industry manufactures consumer desire and defines its own success. The structures of feeling, which many in the industry have perceived to be resting on shaky foundations of late, are aggressively reconstituted in a familiar context through as many channels as possible as often as possible. As I argue throughout this book, globalization cannot be analyzed as if it is some celestial system detached from the myriad spaces and acts of consumption and communication which constitute it. The structure and intent behind "Idol", taken as a whole, is a prime example of actually-existing globalization. This glitzy and often ridiculous affair seems certain to find us through one or another of the myriad channels through which it courses, no matter how assiduously we may be trying to hide from it.

PART I
All of the In-between

Chapter 1

The Acts and Spaces of Consumption

Goods … are just physical tokens of a virtual regime (Hiromi Hosoya and Marus Schaffer).[1]

There is an inevitable distance between the production of cultural products and their consumption. This distance is not just metaphorical, it is literal. Overcoming this distance is no mean feat, but for both retailers and manufacturers, managing it has become a lot more complicated and exacting than it used to be. Between the mid 1970s and the mid 1990s, the ability of retailers and manufacturers to manage the flow of goods evolved significantly, producing more or less integrated systems of automated inventory management that greatly facilitated the spread of consumer capitalism worldwide. One of the first tangible signs of this system was the Universal Price Code (UPC), developed by a consortium of US retailers, distributors, and manufacturers. The now ubiquitous square of numerically identified black lines of varying widths on the back of most products has become "the thumbprint of a good by which its identity is asserted in the realm of information, the wheels by which its travels the infobahn" (Harvard Project on the City, 2002:158). The UPC is the practical embodiment of a system of information management that has had important consequences for the ways in which consumerism has developed around the world. First, automated inventory management systems led directly to an "explosion of inventory and store size." Prior to the introduction of these systems, the average size of US grocery stores had rested on a clear plateau for decades. After the introduction of the UPC, average store size doubled in a little under 15 years. The UPC system was organized and implemented by some of America's largest manufacturers and retailers who were able to convince competitors to use their systems of inventory management. Over time, businesses at all stages of the production chain were able to act in a far more cooperative and even collusive manner. The system confirmed a bias towards larger retailers who used the new system to grow dramatically. Second, these systems allowed businesses to use various kinds of coded information collected at the point of sale to "track consumer preferences and behavior almost in real time and react with unprecedented speed." Prices could be routinely altered throughout the day to enhance competitiveness and improve sales volume. Markets could be segmented with increasingly fine levels of detail based on an extensive range of demographic information gathered at the checkout counter. Consumers could be targeted and reached with far more efficiency and cost-effectiveness (Harvard Project on the City, 2002:157–8; Brown, 1997).

---

1 Harvard Project on the City (2002:158).

For celebratory commentators, the spread of consumerism has been achieved as the result of a kind of informal democratic referendum. Businesses merely responded to nascent consumer sentiment, we are told, focusing it through quality products offered at reasonable prices, disciplined through the correcting rod of market competitiveness, "liberating" the "natural" human predilection to consume (Twitchell, 1999:22, 272). But the inventory management systems described above were a response to stagnation, not success. Moreover, they were specifically designed to respond to a lack of knowledge about markets, not a surfeit of it. The logistical systems which now track unimaginably large numbers of objects around the world in real time were developed in the clubby atmosphere of ad hoc consortia, not in some imagined pit of competitive enterprise. They were inspired by the failure of that enterprise, directed by the one area of the economy one would assume had the easiest row to hoe, the food industry. The whole point of these systems was to reduce market risk and improve efficiency. But as with any system which produces exponentially increasing amounts of information, uncertainty and risk do not disappear, they are simply transformed (Winseck, 2002). Integrated systems of inventory management did make markets more efficient, but they also made them more crowded. And, while they helped producers, distributors, and retailers keep track of everything they produced and sold, they also increased markets to an intimidating size, making the management of what are euphemistically referred to as "global" markets much more difficult, but potentially, much more rewarding.

The Imperial Condition in Consumer Culture

Doug Henwood has observed that the word "globalization" was barely used in the US press in the early 1980s. It experienced a surge in popularity in the mid 1990s, along with its companion term "the new economy" which emerged from a similar obscurity a few years later (Henwood, 2003:4, 146–8). Despite the incorporation of globalization into the popular and academic lexicon, there are only a few specific commonalities to the many varied understandings of what the term means. Many of the attributes said to define globalization have been around for centuries while others have appeared and disappeared with alarming speed in recent years, such as the "frictionless" speed and efficiency supposedly inherent to the "new economy." As Henwood shows, at the heart of the lack of clarity regarding this allegedly universal phenomenon is a confusion of taxonomy in which the term globalization often "serves as a euphemizing and imprecise substitute for 'imperialism'" (ibid.).

As noted earlier, the music industry has three main challenges currently facing it: evolving regimes of globalization, ever more extensive commercialization of culture, and the sometimes reluctant digitalization of the content of its industry. The public statements of most within the industry do not explicitly acknowledge any link between these phenomena. If we are to judge from the actions of many of those in the music and entertainment industries, there is a clear understanding that these three aspects of contemporary consumer culture have provided significant challenges to many of their foundational assumptions. What links these phenomena is that each challenges traditional models of communication and connection on which the entertainment and music industries have relied to create and foster relationships with consumers in the past. As we will see in Chapters 3 and 4, this is in no small measure due to the efforts of these industries to exert specific kinds of control over the distribution and consumption of their products. We will see in Part III that these foundational changes to almost all aspects of the consumption and production of music have presented some remarkable opportunities for new ways of selling it. The "Idol" phenomenon is one such opportunity and we need a set of tools that can account for this vivid manifestation of globalization. Changes in the circulation and production of popular music over the last 30 or so years can help point us towards a distinct model of globalization that can account for how these changes have altered relationships between consumers and producers, conceptually and practically. It can also help us understand how those inside the entertainment and music industries have perceived these changes, altering their market strategies accordingly in order to shape and reshape acts and spaces of consumption

Central to the arguments which follow throughout this book is a concept I call the imperial condition in consumer culture, a concept based on a particular theorization of the role of media communication within the globalization of consumer culture. The dominant uses of the word globalization generally imply a sense of commonality or even universality. Work that bases an understanding of globalization on difference and localization (or more cleverly "glocalization") often presumes a broad, common set of processes, structures, and practices, arguing primarily about the contestation of textual meaning or struggles over how power affects the infrastructure of production and the experience of consumption (Parks and Kumar, 2003; Carroll and Carson, 2003; Tomlinson, 1991; 2003). Even interpretations of globalization that stress its complexity and contradictions still imply a broadly common logic joining its consequences, even if these consequences do not conform to expectations (see Appadurai, 1996). Instead, I will use a conception of globalization that regards the very possibility of some manner of "global culture" as illusory. I will argue that, in addition to the many existing concerns of globalization, we also need to analyze consumer culture in the ways in which it is continually reproduced through innumerable, specifically formed, and consummated relationships between producers and consumers. These relationships are constructed and maintained through myriad channels of communication. These channels are not only the obvious ones such as films or television shows or even the much lauded contestatory space of the internet. These channels also include everyday acts of consumption, the spaces in which these acts take place, and the mutually constitutive relationships which always exist between the two.

For example, if we consider the act of buying a CD in Sydney, an act I will explore in detail shortly, it is dependent on the existence and maintenance of channels of communication between Sydney and the world that are simply not reproducible elsewhere. The channels of communication that allow a consumer to buy a CD at the Virgin Megastore in Sydney's Central Business District (CBD) are threaded throughout a context resolutely defined by much wider forces: Australia's place within world trade and political systems, the fact that the dominant language is English making promotion of some products less complicated than others, the fact that US and British cultural production are proven safe bets, the fact that the

Australian music industry is dominated by branch offices of the big multinationals, and the country's remarkable level of general affluence all constitute the social ground upon which the range and availability of recorded music is based. These factors help determine the ways in which the Australian cultural economy is linked with the rest of the world. The character and quality of these connections informs the extent of the investment the multinational music industry is willing to make in Australia. Understood this way, "the global media" become more specific, still expansive in their reach, still displaying clear objectives, but producing particular consequences which can only be understood through an analysis of the contexts through which these consequences are produced, experienced, and understood. This chapter intends to draw out key aspects of the ways in which the acts and spaces of music consumption are evolving.

For this we have to understand the ways in which specific social and material facts are always inhered within media of communication producing particularities in the ways in which people use and experience them. These filters and funnels appear whether we are talking about the geographic "footprints" that define when and where satellites can be used, or the various legal constructs governing the consumption of film or television, or the technical and economic infrastructures which influence access to the internet. All of these technologies were once spoken of as if they were some kind of universal translators yet they display nothing more clearly than the multiplicity of experience they facilitate specifically because of the ways in which these networks of communication are shaped by the ways in which they are used. Unfortunately, not all users are created equal. We all have relative power based on our means, ability, and inclination to consume, as well as our history and perceived potential as consumers. When we understand communication as the process of establishing webs of social relations within which specific technologies function and through which we participate to produce meaning, then we can understand the kinds of contexts particular types of communication networks produce. To quote Angus (1998), communication technologies are "thoroughly imbued with the specific form of their socio-cultural context" in which they are set and which they help shape. As Angus notes, they are "perceptually and cognitively laden," helping to organize (not dictate) perception and meaning by producing a shaping context for the meanings of texts and the channels through which meanings are produced and circulated. The meaning of consumption is not limited to textual meaning, however contested, but is shaped by larger forces with specific consequences, intended or not, that have a powerful effect on the kinds of social relationships they produce and help maintain; these relationships are not relationships without our agency and participation.

Without theorizing it directly, the entertainment and music industries rely on an understanding of globalization based on this kind of particularistic use of media. They imagine their markets very literally as a massive collection of actions which they can monitor taken by people they can track and learn about through their actions as consumers. When we see media campaigns for particular products we often see straightforward television ads, press releases masquerading as "news," posters, street signs, stencils, newspaper and magazine articles, product placements in film and television programs, billboards and internet pop-ups, as well as endless rounds of celebrity gossip print campaigns in the tabloids. These innocent texts are far more strategic and specific than is immediately obvious. The entertainment industry is constantly shaping its messages to reach some of us in as many ways as possible. They are trying to make our participation not so much predictable as probable. The specific streams of communication of which we are the targets are not even established unless a carefully determined level of profitability is predicted, promised, or expected and they are not completed until evidence of our participation returns to its source. It is this literal and material system of contact that is constantly shaping and reshaping ideas on what should be produced, how it should be sold, and where it is most likely to be consumed most often. This is what Oscar Gandy calls a "constitutive system of knowledge" (Gandy, 1993:21). This system of knowledge defines the contours of consumer culture and has a significant impact on what things are produced and how they are consumed.

I define the imperial condition in popular culture, then, by our necessary participation in systems of cultural production over which we can exert power only through the extent and quality of our participation in them. The power of consumers does not extend to the ability to craft the governing structures and ideologies which shape and channel our participation for the benefit of those who do have this power. We do not draft the intellectual property laws grafted into international trade agreements nor do we decide how media regulations are interpreted or enforced. Our power as consumers lies in the benefits and pleasures we draw from consumption. This form of power is a central factor in the continuing maintenance of a set of social relationships created by the things we consume and the people who produce them. It is created largely as an intended, but problematic by-product of these relationships. These relationships pivot around acts of consumption whose outcomes are so difficult to predict with any measure of precision that a Herculean effort is made to take into account all aspects of the spaces in which those acts of consumption happen, even reshaping entire urban and suburban landscapes in the process, a process I will describe throughout this chapter (Harvard Project on the City, 2000). These connections are not formed by some panoptic eye in the sky but within a complex of social relations whose power dynamics are distinctly cast in favor of producers. This is a complex form of cultural seduction, the consummation of which is based on our desire, agency, and ability to participate in systems not of our making, but to which we undeniably contribute. The intent then, is not necessarily to structure our consciousness, but our agency, through the measured and measurable actions we take as consumers. The entertainment industry knows very well that it survives mostly on its ability to mortgage our attention, interests and expectations over time to form them into lasting mutually beneficial consumer relationships; it calls this meeting us halfway.

Globalization and the "Promotional Culture"

Complex regimes of planning and strategy within what Turner et al. (2000) call the "promotional culture" have become of paramount importance to the entertainment and music industries inspired by two undeniable facts of consumer culture. The first and most obvious fact is that the communications environment within which our consumer and advertising cultures work has grown exponentially more complex in recent years. Advertising practitioners and theorists alike are quite explicit about the challenges they face in breaking through the whirl of white noise their industry produces in order to capture and keep our attention and loyalty. Our collective lexicon fairly drips with new terms to describe their efforts: "branding," "the attention economy," "viral marketing," "coolhunting," and "peer-to-peer marketing" (Gladwell, 2001; Godin, 2001; Henry, 2003; Lee, 2004b; Rosen, 2000). Second, there are now more and more channels through which to produce, consume, and circulate content. Whether we are talking about mobile phones, chatrooms, blogs, video games, or the hundreds of broadcast channels surging through terrestrial and orbiting sources, the traditional models of communication connecting producers and consumers are much less dominant than they used to be. Account planners are now synergists, alchemists of consumerism working arduously across what were previously thought to be unrelated channels of communication planning communicative campaigns of a breadth and complexity that would stun their dark-suited Madison Avenue forebears (Elmer, 2004; Turow, 1997; 2000; McAllister, 1996).

This complexity is unavoidable, not simply because of new technologies, but because of a fundamental shift in the kinds of relationships the entertainment industry has with consumers. As noted, globalization holds out the promise of new markets, but some of these markets are far more valuable than others. Further, systems of market knowledge have become much more sensitive and thus far more capable of picking out desirable demographics from a far wider range of potential targets. They allow producers to pinpoint with unprecedented accuracy those most likely to buy their products. New demographic categories, such as "tweeners" or "challengers," have proliferated as a result. Target groups are definable by a much broader range of perceived and empirical characteristics than just age or level of disposable income, resulting in increasingly narrow bands of presumed consumer typologies (Henry, 2003; Lee, 2004a). New forms of media and inventive practices of media use have made consumers more "reachable" through a broader range of channels than ever before. New markets and uses for new formats of music are proliferating. In many respects, music is just one more collection of raw materials to be exploited by the entertainment industry. The extraordinarily profitable ringtone, video game, "song placement," and MP3 player industries have quite simply changed the rules for market creation, penetration, and perpetuation (Coultan, 2004; Emling, 2004; Gotting, 2003a; Lowe, 2003; Petradis, 2004).

As the tools the entertainment industry uses to understand and construct these new worlds of consumption become more and more finely tuned, strategists have been relying on an understanding of globalization that is more specific and material. The entertainment industry does not seem to rely on "global" concepts of globalization, if you will, but on an inchoate and imperfectly expressed understanding of globalization that takes into account material and literal flows of goods, messages, and meanings designed for very carefully targeted and defined groups of consumers. This flexible, practical and contextual understanding of globalization can help us understand how seemingly unrelated phenomena such as the ongoing battle over music piracy and the "Idol" phenomenon grow from the same communicative, technological, and cultural soil. Among the most consequential of "contested terrains" are the spaces in which acts of consumption actually happen.

Acts and Spaces of Consumption

Walk into a store that sells music, these stunning centers for consumable media that litter the landscape, and you cannot help but realize how you have been made into a tiny, but crucial atom of purchasing power right at the heart of a massive infrastructure of production and consumption like nothing the world has ever seen. They know you're coming and they know what you want to do. You want to purchase some pleasure, a little solidarity. You want to hear someone tell you about a life that you might recognize to be remarkably like your own. There's music playing, videos humming, staff helping, listening stations have been provided, all for your benefit, to help you find exactly what you want when you want it. If you can't find it at the store, go online. It is more than likely that someone somewhere will do their best to sell you almost any musical recording you want. The question is, how did you know where to find it? The other question is, how did you know you wanted it when you did?

There are many interesting ways to answer these questions. I will do so by analyzing the circulation of popular music as conceived by those who claim to be the most important and necessary circulators. There is an obvious absence in this analysis, the absence of the individual consumer, or rather a radical displacement of that consumer. I am analyzing the consumer as invented by the music and entertainment industries, lurking in the marketplace like a demographic cipher, a perpetual and expected presence. While it is clear that some of the more interesting examples of the circulation of recorded music happen in those informal networks that exist outside the formal retail industry, it is important to examine the formal infrastructure next to and within which informal networks exist, in whose contexts they function and against whose interests their participants sometimes act. I am doing so because the formal mainstream "musical economy" (Leyshon, 2005) has a significant amount of power to define the ground for music consumption and not simply because of the fairly straightforward economic facts of retailing. A central part of the entertainment industry's strategy for survival is to exert a defining influence on the musical economy generally. Even the most intrepid searcher for the most obscure CD will have to fight their way through a context they didn't create and don't control, but to which they undeniably and necessarily contribute.

This clear fact of life calls up one of the central acts I commit in this work: analyzing the cultural intermediations of the music industry as a system of power. We are all implicated in this system of power and we are all constituted as its objects. This is not to say we are obedient or passive, merely functional. We are constituted in specific ways by music producers, marketers, and retailers and the ways in which we appear necessary and useful to this industry tells us a lot about how it functions. As with any system of power, the control of information is central to its ability to reproduce itself. The maintenance of any system of power relies on "a constitutive field of knowledge, and the operation of power reveals both its possibilities and its limits" (Gandy, 1993:21). One of my primary goals is to examine this field of knowledge and its possibilities and limits in order to tease out the shape, goals, and function of this massive, unavoidable industry. Clever and often public-minded software developers and website designers and variously motivated thieves seem more interested in finding and consuming music without the aid of the industry of taste brokers, bringing litigation, legislation, and prosecution in their wake. This is the exact time to examine how that industry has been dealing with these nemeses. It is often at a moment of crisis when the desires, functions, and cultural work of an organized market appear most subtly and obviously. Further, while the ever-increasing amount of music piracy on the internet is often lauded as a paragon of consumer invention and creativity free of institutional constraint, why then are the most pirated and downloaded songs those created by the most popular artists? (Jones and Lenhart, 2004; Zuel, 2006). This is not as tautological as it might sound. Why do so many people steal music that is already very popular? I would argue that the pirating of what is already exceedingly popular music only highlights the need for different kinds of studies asking different kinds of questions. Here we have a remarkable case study in the removal of significant institutional and sometimes even economic constraints, and yet the reaction of many is to do more or less what the industry expects them to do, just not in the right way.

Other questions abound. Why did such massive and widespread violations of unambiguous copyright laws appear to catch the music industry completely off-guard? Why has the retail industry displayed an apparently sudden and extreme curiosity in how we enjoy ourselves in order to try and solve this vexing problem of freedom? (Harvard Project on the City, 2000:177–83). The contradictions implied here suggest other forces are at work. They suggest that the structures of feeling created by the music industry are strong and influential, but limited. They also suggest that metaphors equating consumer choice with democracy are misguided. The instigation for the structures of feeling produced by the music industry springs from that industry's own "constitutive field of knowledge," such as marketing campaigns and the data collected through the consumer surveillance that informs them. These mechanisms have a significant impact on us even when the music industry is the victim of so many ribald acts of unofficial consumption because they shape the contexts in which all acts of consumption, official and unofficial, occur. The music industry has produced such a specific and directed form of knowledge geared towards such a narrow range of desired outcomes for so long that it was only a matter of time before the limits of this knowledge would be demonstrated. It is the music industry's efforts to expand the limits of their systems of knowledge and power that concern me here.

As many have noted, consumption and shopping are constituted through the establishment and maintenance of social relationships through complex forms of communication (see Miller et al., 1998). When we shop we are brought into an extraordinarily complex web of social relationships that momentarily ties us to much larger forces. When we buy something, we enact our expected role in the economy of circulating things and establish a social relationship linking the chain between producers, distributors, marketers, and consumers. But we are not simply the end of a chain, but simultaneously the beginning of a new chain, or cycle into which we will be drawn repeatedly with each future purchase. The plain and unremarkable contours of our acts of consumption are important to explain literally. It seems painfully obvious to say it, but when we buy something, it is no longer there in the store or on the shelf in the warehouse. We have removed an object from the field of circulation and a fairly extensive, complicated, and uneven distribution and production system sets about at the exact moment of purchase to replace it. When the scanner rings up our purchase, a message is sent into the inventory control system which notes that a new object needs to go where the old one was. Sometimes it is a replica of what you have just bought, sometimes not, depending on the sales cycle in which your newly-acquired object and act of consumption were once enmeshed. But the "replacement" is neither a metaphorical nor literal replacement at all. Instead, the replacement is a different object and it already has a different and unique trajectory through the world of consumption. It has been inserted into a new context of consumption and it will have new destinations which it will reach in new ways. It has been inserted into a context that has changed because of its insertion, however slight or nearly invisible this change might appear to be. It has been precisely placed and will have idiosyncratic lines of movement. This is in part what makes studying the circulation of goods from any empirical ground extremely difficult; there are just so many things moving around out there. They exist in a context that is constantly changing in innumerable, almost imperceptible, but permanent ways.

Spaces of consumption are constituted by objects moving within spaces that are never quite the same from moment to moment. They are being continually altered by countless acts of consumption. To a significant degree, this holds true for items bought online, actual objects that is. The places in which we buy things, whether online or from "bricks and mortar" retailers, are reconstituted with every purchase we make. This is only partially true for the purchase of digital files on the internet. However, what is most important here is that every act of consumption produces new knowledge on the market for music and therefore alters the market within which each future purchase happens. This is the collective undeniable connection we make when we shop. Spaces of consumption are not randomly constructed, nor are the acts of consumption which occur within them, the autonomous, unproblematic acts of the freedom loving atoms of consumerism we are so often made out to be. At its end point, or more accurately the turn over point, each purchase alters and enhances the constitutive field of knowledge which defines and continually shapes its system of power. And with each purchase comes fresh intelligence for its continuous and evolving modes of operation (Elliott and Jankel-Elliott, 2003; Goss, 1995; Hackley, 2002).

The spaces of consumption in which we work our agency, our apparently awesome powers of interpretation and creativity as consumers, have been evolving at a stunning rate in recent years. In particular, surveillance of our buying habits and movement through these spaces has increased dramatically (Harvard Project on the City, 2002; Knight, 2004; McLaren, 1998:51). As mechanisms of consumption have been tuned in more specifically on individual consumers, the spaces in which we consume have been altered commensurately. The goals of the entertainment industry are a foundational shaping influence on these spaces and help guide the ways in which we move through and enact their practical meaning and function. These spaces are designed and fashioned for obvious goals, theirs and ours. However, it isn't the spaces of consumption themselves that are so carefully tuned, but the social relationships created within them. These relationships are the literal constitution of the spaces in which they occur. Spaces of consumption are constituted and produced by the more general social relationships of consumption. As Lefebvre noted, space is not a thing or a floating, transparent medium or container. It is a set of dynamic relations between things, systems, and people (Lefebvre, 1991:83). Further, social space is not a default space where relations are acted out within some pristine and permanent structure detached from their surroundings. That is to say, specific social relations create specific spaces and specific spaces shape the relations which are carried out within them, each acting in a dynamic relationship with the other. Social space is strategically produced as a consequence of larger social, political, cultural, and economic relations. But, as Lefebvre argues, social spaces are polyvalent. Although "it is a product to be used, to be consumed, it is also a means of production; networks of exchange and flows of raw material and energy fashion space and are determined by it" (ibid.:85). When we consider the spaces in which we act, whether as citizens exerting our rights, or as consumers expressing our purchasing power, or as human beings experiencing pleasure, the social spaces which both produce and are produced by these acts "cannot be separated either from the productive forces, including technology and knowledge, or from the social division of labour which shapes it, or from the state and the superstructures of society" (ibid.).

When we analyze the spaces in which the consumption of music is embedded we have to take into consideration a bewildering array of institutions stretching around the world. The spaces these institutions help produce are not accidental, although what actually happens within them is not necessarily predictable. Instead of producing an explanatory regime which claims to encompass the full range of such institutions and intentions, I would like to present an interpretation of the spaces of consumption in the form of a brief description of one of the flashest multimedia shops in Sydney's CBD as well as one of the tackiest. This description is not intended to be comprehensive, but demonstrative. The point here is not a full explanation of the entertainment retail industry, but a more subtle understanding of the actual terrain we are all constantly contesting. I want to examine one of the larger multimedia shops with the broadest intent within the urban space of Sydney's symbolic heart, but also one of the smaller ones that can clarify that intent by contrast. And I want to demonstrate how the globalization of the popular music industry looks when we participate in it most directly and tangibly.

Big and small multimedia shops are proliferating in Sydney's CBD despite numerous prognostications of their irrelevance and death. Instead of foreshadowing a well-prophesied death, they reflect the changing priorities of a music industry which is no longer a discrete and distinct entity. To understand the conduits through which we participate most directly with the global music industry, we can't imagine that industry as just one more social institution in which varying degrees of agency and autonomy are granted to performers, producers, musicians, and other participants. We can't analyze the producers of music as if they exist separately from the larger systems of knowledge and commerce in which they are inevitably enmeshed; this is simply not sufficient to any understanding how the music industry works.[2] Instead, we have to analyze the music industry as one part of the larger entertainment industry, the activities of which have spread well beyond the bounds of merely producing sounds and images. When considered this way, it is easier to see how musicians, producers, performers, and record labels are all deeply enmeshed with systems over which they have little direct control, but with which they share many common interests and within which most have to work to be successful. The primary goal is still obvious, to shift units, but the conception of the markets into which these units are inserted and are intended to exploit has been dramatically transformed in recent years.

In the 1990s, there was a paradigm shift in the ability of producers and marketers to gather information on consumers and markets. It is now possible to continually gather a massive range of data on patterns of consumer behavior, data that is consistently plotted and constantly recalibrated both geographically and chronologically. These new systems allow unprecedented flexibility and scope in data gathering and use by providing desktop access to real-time information on geographic information, including region, climate, population density, market area, post code, census area, and address; demographic information, including age, sex, family status, income, occupation, education, religion, race, nationality, and housing status; "psychographic" information, including social class, values and lifestyles, and personality; and consumer attitudes and behavior, including benefits sought, loyalty, knowledge, and attitudes towards specific products (Goss, 1995). As a result, the entertainment industry has become better at understanding how to construct and interpret its markets because of the new kinds of knowledge it is able to produce about them. These systems of information aspire, not to flatten out the chaos of consumption, but "to make space simultaneous with the irrationalities and vicissitudes of the market." This range of data collection tools is primarily designed literally to map all of the variables in the consumer–producer relationship. Far from envisioning some magical solution to what I have been calling the problem of freedom, these new regimes of market research try to bypass it, desiring instead "a type of stability assured by mechanisms that enable immediate retaliation or response to sudden change" (Harvard Project on the City, 2002:773).

Instead of trying to predict what people want, producers and retailers are trying to craft logistical and informational systems that can react almost instantaneously to even the smallest changes in the market. Inevitably, this has a transformational effect on producers. As understandings of markets change, so do the institutional goals of those serving those markets and so do the products created to appeal to those markets.[3] The

---

2   Toynbee (2000) offers a contrasting argument, arguing that the music industry gives musicians a kind of institutional autonomy which allows them to make whatever music they wish. This forms the basis of their social authorship in a market in which the music industry is distant from its own consumers. This gap gives musicians a determining role in the industry–audience relationship. As noted, this argument is based on a misunderstanding of what constitutes the institutional basis of the music industry. It isn't just the music that defines the institutional role and location of any potential autonomy, but the series of communication channels through which that music travels and becomes meaningful.

3   It is important to note that this evolution of market knowledge can have contradictory effects. For example, the demise of *Smash Hits* has been attributed to the gradual narrowing

music produced within such markets is implicitly and explicitly understood to exist within an expanding range of constantly changing relationships. These relationships are not merely reflective of the market, they are the market. The market is literally embodied in the acts of consumption which in turn constitute the spaces of consumption in which they occur. The relationships between acts and spaces of consumption have consequences which are so wide-ranging and address so many variables that any claims to "consumer agency" and "institutional autonomy" are virtually irrelevant if they are not understood within the context in which they actually exist. We can look at one such context to understand this dynamic more clearly.

Buying a CD in Sydney's CBD

Nearly every Friday and Saturday night, large numbers of young middle- and working-class men and women from the suburbs of Sydney spend a fair amount of time and money in the CBD. A significant number glide down the relatively crowded "main street" of Sydney, George Street, in gleaming, powerful and very loud cars. They drive through to the roundabout at the bottom of the tourist-friendly "Rocks" neighborhood and back up George Street or up Elizabeth Street which flows past Hyde Park. They sport tinted windows, shiny chrome rims, "mufflers" that actually amplify exhaust sounds, and compressors that make each shift of the gears sound like the labored exhale of some lumbering animal. "Hoon" culture, as it is often dismissively called, spawns many myths. It is often presumed that most participants are white men from the Western suburbs, derisively called "westies." But the words "hoon" and "westie" imply a presumed uniformity that defies the obvious reality. The presence of such "inappropriate" people symbolically commandeering spaces ideally intended and created for the local representatives of the rootless multinational financial services industry or the burgeoning local branches of the now truly global insurance and entertainment industries, might be easily viewed in standard cultural studies parlance as a "symbolic inversion" or perhaps even a democratic practice of cultural resistance. This form of analysis would frame this sonic and physical expansion into space as a kind of material and symbolic reclamation of the city. But this would be telling only part of the story.

The use of city space by these people may not always be pleasing to those who claim to speak for the city, but their presence has certainly been expected. The presence of members of many burgeoning youth cultures is symbolic of the ways in which Sydney's CBD has been transformed in the last two decades, away from the industrial uses of the harbor and the city to a focus on tourism and consumption. Sydney has now been shoehorned into the familiar mould of the "fantasy city" (Hannigan, 1998; Davis, 1999). It has been redesigned to be a fun, safe, and clean place for shopping, eating, and participation in the growing spectacles of the "edutainment" industry. These middle-class or working-class "aspirationals," as they are called, rolling through the city in their emblematic manifestations of their power as consumers,

---

of its demographic targets. The magazine's target audience eventually became so specific that it could no longer sustain the publication (Hepworth, 2006).

are constituted as simply one more group of consumers expected to use Sydney as a symbolic resource whether that resource takes the form of a nightclub, restaurant, cafe, entertainment center, theme park, or cocktail bar.

Sydney's CBD is a comparatively small piece of the region's increasing sprawl, but it is easily the most distinct and overarching symbol of Sydney's image as a global city. This small scrap of central New South Wales has accrued a noteworthy level of "social centrality," or the reputed status as a gathering place that Shields summarizes as "a willful concentration which creates a node in a wider landscape of continual dispersion" (Shields, 1992:103). As Shields notes, such central gathering places have inhered within them varied forms of sociality, some publicly valued, some not, that help constitute these places with particularly meaningful resonances. Sydney's CBD is primarily designed to facilitate a commercially definable range of consumption activities. Given this, the multinational entertainment industry knows very well where to put its stores. The CBD is a reliable economic resource pitched to the world, country, and region alike. Tourists, business travelers, cruise ship passengers, and locals are all constituted as distinct, but related markets for the glitzy Darling Harbour, the functional Circular Quay, the familiar Opera House, and the numerous arcades and shopping complexes such as Queen Victoria Building, Skygarden, Centrepoint, and the Pitt Street Pedestrian Mall. The CBD is crowded with hotels, cafes, nightclubs, and restaurants. The publicly-subsidized marketing campaigns serving the city are pitched to a national market as well as to the highly competitive global tourism market, ranging from hedonistic backpackers to those who temporarily inhabit the finest berths in the massive cruise ships which make well-publicized stopovers at Circular Quay. The increasing numbers of entertainment retailers in Sydney's CBD act as symbolic levers, central outposts of familiarity set within an urban context intended to be conducive to all manner of consumption.

Buying a CD in Central Sydney connects consumers to much larger systems of production and consumption that stretch around the world. But this reach is not uniformly connecting or universally experienced. It is experienced quite specifically depending on which target group you inhabit and the ways in which members of various demographic groups act within a consumption environment intended to facilitate the kinds of tasks they are expected to perform. While it is obvious not all such behaviors are in line with commercial expectations, it is clear that these spaces of consumption do have a shaping effect on what goes on within them. What is more clear, and more important, is that the CBD has been painstakingly designed to foster all manner of "sociality" centered on sundry related acts of consumption. Thus, the particular "connecting tissues of everyday interaction and cooperation" (ibid.:106) constituting this sociality are less important than their concentration in spaces that can accommodate a huge variety of such relations, in this case, relations that are relative to one's ability and disposition to buy things. The "social centrality" of the many specific places in which consumption is supposed to take place is constructed with expected and attendant forms of "sociality" firmly in mind, constituted by the specific kinds of relationships such spaces are intended to foster.

Sydney's entertainment retail stores are set within urban spaces which have been redesigned to channel particularly beneficial forms of sociality into their cash registers. The entertainment industry not only accepts the varied and contrasting forms of sociality found in Sydney's CBD, often valorizing "transgression" or "subversion" in their regimes of publicity, but they actively try to participate in facilitating or capitalizing on such various forms of social interaction in the hopes of benefiting from as many of them as possible. Once it was possible to posit urban sociality as a salutary, even resistant form of social solidarity. Now it is a central, well-understood, and projected aspect of marketing and consumer culture and a carefully-constructed and valuable piece of the overall planning regime which has seen city centers like Sydney's reformed for the needs of consumers, producers, and service providers, but only rarely for citizens.

The motivation to place large splashy retail stores in the relatively small and contained CBD is reflective of larger changes in the structure and function of entertainment retail, visible in the reconstitution of Sydney as a fantasy city. The Virgin Megastore, JB Hi-Fi, HMV, Target, and Border's Books and Music are all fairly specific funnels for a particular range of media forms. They are also symbolic reflections of the function of the spaces in which they are set. Each of these places is constructed according to specific criteria for an equally specific goal, not just selling, but selling enough to reach set targets by drawing business from a well-defined collection of demographic groups. Just as each store is established in a larger space designed to be conducive to their mission, the form and content of these stores is also intended to mesh with the form and content of the spaces that surround them. The goal of redesigning cities to suit specific kinds of consumption means that planners must create a suitable and productive environment to facilitate that consumption. In a fantasy city like Sydney, it is hard to imagine the redesign proceeding without high profile entertainment retail centers to anchor the material, experiential, and "educational" ends of consumption. We can consume the many products of industrial synergy in one contained space. Synergy has material forms as well as symbolic ones.[4]

They ways in which Sydney has been re-planned around the axes of shopping, eating, and entertainment are discernible from the intentions of planners and developers made visible by the division of space in the CBD. The most obvious come-on to tourists and locals alike is Darling Harbour, a series of formal and familiar options for enjoyment. Built on "reclaimed" industrial land, Darling Harbour is a centerpiece of Sydney's tourist and entertainment economy. It is also a symbolic marker of the changing structure of the economy as a whole. Darling Harbour was once a major working port. While there are still several sizable "working" areas there, their planned obsolescence has provoked much tortured comment on what exactly the harbor is for, work or play (Farrelly, 2003; New South Wales Government, 2000; Botting, 2006). The Sydney economy is relying more and more on service

---

4   In the not too distant past, one could see *Finding Nemo* at a few well-placed Cineplexes around town, buy related merchandise from nearby clothing shops or multimedia stores, and learn about the "real thing" at the Sydney Aquarium which sported a display of fish from the Great Barrier Reef that were recently featured in animated versions just up the street. The obvious irony of capturing and displaying clownfish as a tie-in to a film whose central plot device was to save one such fish from that dreary fate received little public comment (Peterson, 2003).

work, such as the tourism and hospitality industry as well as professional services in multinational industries, especially insurance, banking, and telecommunications, the latter more well remunerated than the former, but services just the same. Darling Harbour is designed to serve tourism, but also local entertainment markets as well. Set just to the west of the CBD, Darling Harbour is crowded with options including the Star City Casino, the privately-owned Northern Territory and Outback Centre, the Sydney Aquarium, the Powerhouse Museum, the Maritime Museum, the LG IMAX Theatre, and the sizable Sydney Entertainment and Convention Centres. A number of hotels sell weekend getaway packages to a variety of markets around the region, with "local" markets stretching as far as Canberra and Melbourne, and profit from the overseas traffic of holiday-makers and convention attendees (Sydney Harbour Foreshore Authority, 2004).

The CBD is studded with several massive shopping arcades. According to the Australian Retailers' Association, the 712 stores in the seven biggest arcades see over 102 million sets of feet trundling by their doors annually and do well over $800 million dollars (AUD) in business each year (Goodsir, 2004). Importantly, this mecca of consumption is dominated by only a few developers. Given the vertical integration of commercial real estate development in Sydney, the shops in the CBD are often symbolically central to the regional shopping infrastructure. Suburban versions of David Jones or other big retailers act as satellites to the main store downtown. Westfield, the biggest retail developer in Australia, has established a dominant presence in Sydney shopping, from its impressive new mall in the affluent eastern suburb of Bondi Junction as well as its more traditional and more established malls in the more suburban fringes in each of the remaining cardinal directions (ibid.). Westfield's control of about 70 per cent of Sydney's regional shopping centers allows for an integrated plan in marketing and development throughout the region, an integration in which most other major developers and retailers have little choice but to participate (Nixon, 2006). Within the social centrality of the CBD, these thriving arcades are the main drivers for the regional shopping economy.

Surrounding the CBD is an enclosed ring of mid-range, mixed-use development. In areas such as Haymarket, Ultimo, Pyrmont, Wooloomooloo, Pott's Point, and the still somewhat seedy King's Cross, a thick and dense band of high-rise apartment buildings and mid-price hotels acts as a buffer for tourists, temporary residents, and young professionals before the residential suburbs of the inner west and east begin. This complex and often unworkable grid of mixed-use inner city areas defined by distinct zoning rules and specific uses is sliced up by a lattice-work of "traffic sewers" (Duany, et al., 2000:64–72). These tunnels, raised expressways, and multi-lane boulevards are plainly designed to move large numbers of cars and container trucks ferrying the guts of the consumer economy to and from various ports of entry on the south side of the working ports in Sydney Harbour and Botany Bay, further to the south along many of the same traffic corridors. The point of this introductory geography lesson is to note how particular the infrastructure that surrounds even the most mundane act of consumption is and through this to establish the analogous sense of specificity our participation in "globalization" possesses, by definition. From this vantage point, that is at the mid-point of a sales cycle, the act of buying a CD displays an intimate, personal connection to a prodigious infrastructure that stretches from the moment your foot hits the municipally supplied footpath until you reach the register with your purchase. It includes the many integrated and competing modes of private and public transport, related "amenities" such as roads and bridges which help determine both residential and traffic patterns, and thus store locations, as well as the eventual structure of the electronic information system which ties such locations together.

But it goes much deeper even than this, encompassing what we might call the rhetoric of the streets and buildings in which multimedia shops are located, their layout, the economy of shelf space, range of merchandise, the tenor and function of other multimedia and CD stores nearby, and the expected number and range of demographically-defined human beings who are expected to walk through their doors (Garrity, 2003). We need to look briefly into the economy of value of the entertainment retail trade in order to understand its larger implications. There are larger forces of symbolic power nestled here. I don't want to provide a semiotic reading of music retailing, but an understanding of its material existence as read through the social forces that it makes tangible and visible. The goal here is not to explain their deepest and most dramatic cultural roles in exhaustive empirical detail, but to bring out the issues surrounding the cultures of consumption that frame the arguments about globalization and the music industry explored in the remainder of this book.

There are two stores which can help us frame these issues, the shiny Virgin Megastore at Martin Place and Dirt Cheap CDs, just north of the Pitt Street Mall. Given that the footpaths and streets of the CBD are often packed to the rafters any day of the week, the locations of the Virgin Megastore and Dirt Cheap are important to understand. Each is as close as possible to officially "important" places both in terms of the tourist economy and the local one; each is placed along corridors which experience high foot and transport traffic. Martin Place is a kind of semi-official town square, home to an ANZAC memorial, and the site of the old main post office. The Virgin Megastore is set in the old Commercial Banking Company of Sydney building, which remains little changed structurally since it was built between 1923 and 1925. This site is clearly deliberate, set on George Street. It suggests a kind of instant permanence to this new venture (Eliezer, 2002). Dirt Cheap is set in a small store front on Pitt Street a half block north of the pedestrian mall. It is surrounded by similar low rent, high volume ventures, most of which sell trinkets and souvenirs for tourists or cheap staple goods to locals. Dirt Cheap clearly serves a thriving local market as most days one can rub shoulders with office workers, bike couriers, and vaguely dazzled tourists. The monorail, designed to run in a continuous circuit around the main tourist destinations, runs close to each store, as do the buses which rumble down George Street and back up Castlereagh; both streets sidle up to Martin Place and the Pitt Street corridor. Given Sydney's mild climate, stores can count on reasonably consistent levels of customers throughout the year. Further, given the hemispheric contrast of seasons, tourist traffic is also reasonably consistent facing a truncated off-season with many tourists escaping both the northern and southern summers and winters at different times of the year.

The setting of each store is consistent with its products. Virgin sells the latest and most desirable products while Dirt Cheap sells remainders, slapdash compilations of recent hits, and a massive array of compiled music that has entered the public domain, including an impressive range of "oldies" from the 1950s through to the early 1990s. Pretty much everything in the store costs ten dollars. It is a repository for music that has previously been of some significance, whether it be by the Joy Division or Bob Dylan, or Wilco back catalogues, as well as classics from nearly every musical movement from the postwar era. Dirt Cheap sells music which never succeeded, succeeded once, and while no longer lighting up the charts, still holds its own aesthetically and historically. In some ways Dirt Cheap is cleverly placed, able to quickly capitalize on trends that may surprise or confound, such as the ways in which so many artists have had careers resurrected through the simple fact that one of their songs appeared in a commercial or a film. One can almost track the careers of pop stars simply by noticing how long it takes underperforming music to move from Virgin to Dirt Cheap or for suddenly popular music to travel back again. For example, not long after Madonna's American Life and Oasis's Don't Believe the Truth began to stiff, large numbers of the apparently hard-to-move CDs showed up at Dirt Cheap, dropping dramatically in price and status. Failures such as these are no longer safely contained within the articulated and glitzy womb of Virgin, but in a messy shop-front up the street with hundreds of other also-rans or past successes.

It makes a difference where and when you buy such CDs. The settings in which they are purchased have implications for the social and aesthetic status of the music as well its evolving meanings. These two shops are complex markers of the effects the literal and material existence of the actual CD have on its broader symbolic meanings. Implied within each store is an economy of aesthetic value. Dirt Cheap is a container for recent failure and legendary success, each resting in an uneasy partnership that keeps the store going. What once cost $30 at Virgin, slides easily into the bargain basement bin that is Dirt Cheap, moving easily through a channel that runs from the major producers to the major retailers and then through the subterranean sluices of secondary distributors who buy and sell such lesser goods in bulk. These two stores highlight an important aspect of the circulation of musical commodities within and through different spaces of consumption. The value and meaning of each commodity is in part determined not only by its placement within specific spaces, but on its trajectory through these spaces and the moment at which it are consumed (see Straw, 2000). We can see demonstrated here what Appadurai has so thoroughly theorized as the biographical trajectory of the social lives of commodities (Appadurai, 1988:11–15).

Each store is set up in a way that places its contents in an environment consistent with the store's intent. As the name implies, the Virgin Megastore is big. It is intended to be a sensuously overwhelming experience. Dirt Cheap is intended to be neither. Virgin can use its generous space to make itself a center for promotional events and in-store appearances of favored artists. Dirt Cheap can barely fit a decent number of customers in its close and confined space. Both spaces are consistent with their function and are ideally suited for what they do. Each store also has a way of using its respective space in ways that are perfectly suited to accomplish its respective goal. Virgin's layout is simple and well planned. The most obvious feature is the Top 20 listening stations, offering customers a free listen to the entire current chart. The selling floor still bears the bank's original fixtures, including huge marble columns supporting the beautifully restored soaring ceilings. Dirt Cheap displays new releases, classics, and a notable array of "party mixes" and nostalgia collections from recent decades in one great mass. The store excites the senses primarily by not dividing most of the collection into genres. The place is simply overcrowded with selections, exciting the mind with what other bargains might be lurking in the bins. There are huge numbers of multidisc collections of "Irish" music, "jazz" classics, and "blues" favorites which appear as immediately appealing bargains.

There are plenty of places to buy CDs and the much valorized growth of online shopping begs the question, are such stores even necessary anymore? Part of the answer is that there is a structure of feeling attached to the music industry through the megastore and bargain retailer alike. The seemingly obvious fact that entire .urban spaces have been redesigned to suit them shows us how the acts and spaces of consumption are linked, deeply and inevitably. Another part of the answer is that acts and spaces of consumption are tied together through complex relationships of coercion, consent, seduction, and pleasure (Beilharz, 2001:314–15). These relationships structure, but do not determine, how you get there, why you go there, and what you get there. It is in that moment when we reach for a CD or click to place our order that we participate most directly in the massive infrastructure of power that stretches around us and the world, not in some "global" sense of being all pervasive, but in nodes, spots, spaces, places, and moments, connected by specific streams of communication through which information and power move. Power doesn't just touch us, we touch it; we participate in its literal constitution. When we do, our acts of consumption, which are always set within overlapping systems of transport, trade, information, and the particular tools of data gathering, shape and reshape the spaces in which they happen. It is this irreducible set of relationships that constitutes the foundations of cultural power. Power is not only negotiated through some grand semiotic leveling project in which we are all fed the same information and contest the meanings of things in roughly analogous circumstances. It is embodied in our agency, our markedly aesthetic and social agency expressed when we complete an act that is both personal and predicted, sought after, and yet not quite foreseen in its precise intent and consequence. Meaning is posited as the mechanism in which power imprints itself literally on our bodies and in our minds, but we have to act to complete the transaction. When we do, our acts are noted and recorded, established as discrete and often anonymous markers of commercial effectiveness, inscribing our agency within the "constitutive field of knowledge" upon which consumer culture relies to continually reinvent itself and fine tune its ever more particular mechanisms of circulation.

Chapter 2

The Medium and Materials
of Popular Music

We seem collectively unable to recognize the theoretical basis of our work … and to move beyond our own individual agendas and unreflective, unacknowledged theoretical assumptions (Lawrence Grossberg).[1]

One of the problems with studying anything as controversial as music piracy or as reviled as the "Idol" phenomenon, is to allow the tendency towards moral condemnation of the music industry or consumers to displace more consequential forms of analysis. To resist this temptation, I am going to take both the "Idol" phenomenon and the music industry's war on the pirates seriously throughout this book by analyzing both as models of ways of consuming music in order to see how the music industry ideally intends to link producers to consumers. As noted, two of the underlying assumptions of this book are that the music industry's primary goal is to bridge the gap between production and consumption and that music bridges this gap in materially-specific ways. Whereas the last chapter provided the analytic tools to deal with the first assumption, this chapter will provide the tools to deal with the second. Chapter 1 presented the core concepts of "acts and spaces of consumption" and "the imperial condition in popular culture" to deal with the overwhelming materiality of global consumerism. This chapter will be developing tools to deal with the materiality of music and the contexts through which it becomes meaningful.

As noted throughout this book, both the piracy wars and "Idol" are primarily defined by the desires to eradicate "improper" ways of consuming music and to re-establish "proper" ways. The primary places in which these struggles are happening are in those contexts and moments in which the relationships between fans and the music industry are made tangible. I am going to focus on several foundational issues in the aesthetics of popular music that can provide a window onto the ways in which music piracy and "Idol" represent distinct models for the circulation and consumption of popular music. Primary among these issues are those aspects of music that scholars such as Theodore Gracyk argue do the bulk of the work of transporting aesthetic meaning: the medium and materials of popular music (Gracyk, 1996). I will analyze and specify how the actual sounds of music relate to the ways in which those sounds are produced, the ways in which they circulate, and the ways in which they are consumed in particular contexts. The tools presented in this chapter will help us understand "Idol," the conflicts underlying the contests over music piracy, and the evolving promotional cultures of popular music as well.

---

1   Grossberg (2002:41).

I have a fairly modest goal for this chapter, not to identify the object of analysis, but instead to establish the analytical basis from which I will be able to make clear what it is I am actually talking about when I talk about "Idol," piracy, or the cultures of consumption surrounding popular music. I am asking what the ontological status of "the music itself" is, what counts as part of a musical work, and how these ideas relate to the ways in which that work is made meaningful as it moves through the world. I am asking if the ontological status and social value of popular music is somehow permanently etched in the melodies, harmonies, or performative gestures of a particular song, or if something more complicated is at work. In order to analyze piracy and "Idol" without limiting myself to using only preconceived notions of what constitutes "popular music," I will make a series of distinctions between the varied ways in which music is produced, distributed, and mediated that can help to explain how our object of analysis is not ontologically stable enough to inhabit many of our reliably pre-existing concepts that we have so thoroughly worn thin, such as "authenticity," "genre," or "subculture." Given the range of invention involved in the creation and realization of popular music it is important to acknowledge what happens when the sounds we experience are produced and what happens when they are made public, rather than apply a priori social categories to make distinctions between this style or that genre and their presumed meanings, affects, and affiliations. The crucial analytical dynamic on which my arguments turn is between ontological distinctions and social processes. These two modes of analysis are used here as a way of distinguishing between different parts of a larger whole in specific relation to one another. The most important difference between the two is that the ontological distinctions I am making are geared towards determining what exactly the irreducible and unavoidable elements of a particular piece of music are and understanding the relationship those elements have to the social categories which surround, contextualize, and shape our perceptions of their meanings.

Ontological Distinctions and Social Categories

According to Lawrence Grossberg, the field of popular music studies has failed to craft a coherent and cohesive body of theories and methods. As he noted in a scathing essay in which he registered his disappointment with the entire field, we have a lot of theoretical problems, but not a lot of theories to solve them. Worse for Grossberg, few of the explanations we do have are specific to a discipline that lacks a common analytical language. Grossberg rightly criticizes a familiar array of transhistorical, decontextualized, apparently universal concerns of a field he suspects may not actually exist (Grossberg, 2002:41–2). While Grossberg's existential angst might be well placed, it is ultimately misleading. The distinction "popular music" upon which so many of his careful ruminations are based is itself a neutral analytic category. By that I mean, there are no material properties that all forms of what we call popular music have in common, nor can we point to any general or universal set of criteria that can tell us what constitutes aesthetically successful popular music. Further, there are no unifying processes, principles, or materials that anyone can point to that all versions or iterations of what we call popular music share. Significant exceptions to the standard array of definitions can always be found within music which is nevertheless recognized to be firmly within the family. What we collectively deem to be popular music has been and continues to be the product of a very broad range of knowledge and practice from supreme literacy to sublime ignorance, wild improvisation to strictly-notated control, or from joyously unkempt public performances to acts of private, precise compositional acumen. Our analytical methods should acknowledge this.

Part of the problem Grossberg diagnoses rests on presumed categories such as "popular music" which are simply not valid as criteria for making the kinds of ontological distinctions we need in order to understand the sounds with which we often find ourselves confronted. Social categories that masquerade as aesthetic facts simply inscribe essentialist notions of music that precede analysis. Analysis should be grounded in the material and social facts at hand, not in idealist categories which have only a slight hold on the material weight of sound, other than as tacit social agreements to call a spade a spade. This is not to say such social agreements are unimportant. Social categories are central to the discourses which constitute the cultural mediation of music. Categories such as genre and style represent a kind of collective set of agreements about how to talk about music. While they are unavoidable, they should not be reproduced uncritically as the basis upon which analysis proceeds. The social inscription of the designation "popular music" has to be understood as implicitly present within the sounds produced, shaping, and organizing productive intent, aesthetic assessment, and social reception. The processes of production and reception surely shape each other, working together in a kind of see-saw relationship, balanced over the fulcrum of mediation which, despite several decades of academic fumigation, still produces or at least informs myriad agendas intending to conflate taste and power with truth and beauty; there remain many such hegemonic concepts comfortably ensconced in the everyday lives of a great deal of music.

To get around these analytic roadblocks, I want to think about music in a more literal way. Through Nattiez, Allan Moore has provided us with three important analytic critiques to help us do this: immanent, poietic, and aesthetic (Moore, 2001:5–6). These critiques give us some of the tools we need to be able to analyze what we tend to call popular music. The "immanent" critique is a critique of the sounds themselves considered as music. What is in the music? How can we describe it? What makes a piece of music what it is? What makes it work on its own terms? The "poietic" critique is supposed to divine the intent and purpose of those creating music. Why does this music exist? What is its ideal artistic purpose? The "aesthetic" critique is a critique of the lived, situated experience of sound. What meanings do people produce from it? What musical affects does it produce? What associations do particular kinds of music have at different points in their historical and social lives? In short, what is the music actually doing out there in the world? Unfortunately, these critiques, crucial as they are, still don't actually tell what it is we are analyzing, in large part because they make only generic distinctions between the parts of a general aesthetic process. They could be easily applied to divine the intent, content, or experience of a painting, a building, or a pop song without much in the way of fundamental alteration.

Trying to discern the object of analysis from such a generic critique is fairly difficult, mostly because music is so deeply social and subjective. It always means slightly different things to different people at different times in different places. Meanings change and can even invert as circumstances change. The processes of making meaning from popular music aren't ever complete because meaning is shaped through contexts of consumption which never stop evolving. But this analytic schema does a great service in one respect. It helps us to think about music simultaneously as actual sounds, as a kind of record of the consequences of a set of aesthetic intentions, and as socially inscribed, interpretable, and evolving sets of affects and meanings. We can analyze music for what it is, what its creators supposed it to be, and what people generally think about it after it has been produced using these overlapping and interrelated categories of analysis. These critiques can help us recognize the ways in which organizing terms through which we both construct and receive meaning are not autonomous pre-existing forms. They are evolving, communal, cultural practices which are inherently related to the specific material forms in which they reach us. Popular music is constructed through series of creative and interpretive traditions and practices, not from simply static templates which exist outside any particular piece of music.

With this in mind, the major questions for analysis are not how do we define "popular music" or "popular music studies" as distinct and bounded entities or enterprises? Instead, I will ask two closely related, but distinct questions: how do we create a mode of analysis that is appropriate to how our chosen objects of study actually exist in the world, and how do we take into account the collection of material and social facts we have unavoidably at hand? To put it another way: what social and material facts do we have at hand and what analytic tools might best acknowledge their shape and character? It is important to note that the ideas I am pushing here are not coterminous with those forms of common sense analysis underlying the field of popular music studies which mostly assert the primary need to analyze the collective social interpretation of texts, but whose material grounding in sound is often left largely underdetermined. I am arguing that the actual material contours of musical texts and the particularities of their mediation and circulation inevitably focus, constrain, frame, shape, and organize our interpretations of them. Every piece of music arranges producers and consumers in specific but dynamically evolving social relationships which are always pegged to the originating text, not necessarily to any particular set of meanings drawn from that text, but to the literal thing itself. The cultural contests between producers and consumers so many have examined are not only about differences of textual interpretation, but about the very structures which scaffold our subjectivity. Therefore, it is crucial to understand the processes through which the often stormy relationships between producers and consumers are constructed. Understanding the medium and materials of popular music can help us do that.

A Network of Social Conventions

Generically, the term "artistic medium" describes the means an artist uses to express themselves using a specific and discrete set of tools. Their obvious intent is to create something that is recognized by others as a work of art. With popular music, the artistic medium would probably be most recognizable as a song or an album. Most descriptive analyses rely on concepts such as genre or style to specify and frame the content of the aesthetic analysis of such an art object, taking the material means of expression for granted. Ideas like style or genre are often used as presumptions, implicitly thought to possess a collection of generic attributes which are, by definition, tautologically demonstrative of their own descriptive validity. But "Idol" and piracy are not genres or subcultures, they are both idealized and actual modes of consumption. Aesthetically speaking, they are means, not ends. So the traditional use of the term "medium" can't help us understand much of what is important about either phenomenon. In order to craft analytic tools which are appropriate to my chosen objects of study, I want to draw on another definition of "medium," one that is not defined by the art artists make, but what they do to make it. In this sense, an artistic medium is shaped and specified by the context through which the art produced within it is made public, and thus made meaningful. Following on from Gracyk (1996), an artist's medium is not simply a set of materials, but rather a network of historically situated social and cultural conventions which define the realm over which those physical materials and the aesthetic qualities ascribed to them are mediated (Gracyk, 1996:70–71). Instead of thinking about a medium as an immutable set of characteristics or expressive tools, this conception of an artist's medium arises from a set of human practices exerted on some recognized or recognizable range of materials.

For popular music, a central part of the medium is how the range of what Gracyk calls "allowable sounds" taken together with principles for structuring those sounds are recognized and used by artists and audiences to make meaning (ibid.). An audience's reception of a work of art requires a general understanding of how aesthetic qualities and meanings emerge from the artist's particular use of their materials. The medium of popular music is the range of sounds as these sounds are recognized in relation to the conventions of the particular traditions of practice from which they arise taken together with the principles used to structure those sounds in a particular way. When we listen to music, we listen to sounds against a "horizon of potentialities and limitations" explored by artists with their materials in relation to a set of social conventions that can help tell us what sounds matter to a given tradition of practice and how they matter. An audience's reception of a work of art requires a general understanding of how aesthetic qualities and meanings emerge from the artist's particular use of their materials. The materials of popular music are not only musical instruments and the notes played on them, but also the many layers of sound production that stand between the audience and the artist through which sounds are manipulated and shaped to produce a mutually recognizable object of meaning (ibid.:72–4). The particular ways in which each layer of material is used to produce sound through specific media of presentation constitutes an historically situated paradigm of practice, each part of which has to be taken into account if we want understand exactly what the object of meaning we are analyzing actually is.

The meanings of particular songs grow and evolve through the contexts in which these sounds become public, through the activities used to create them, and the social circumstances of the experienced meaning of those sounds as music. Their meanings are altered constantly by use. Every time we experience the situated utterance or iteration of a piece of music we change its meaning in ways that can eventually become visible and knowable over time. In order to comprehend the relationships between ontological distinctions and social processes, I will argue that we have to understand how the material consequences of aesthetic practice shape the ways in which the meanings of an artist's work grow through their use of materials publicly recognized to be idiomatic and situated expressions of familiar musical conventions. This conception of an artistic medium is based around the character and type of social relationships created through the long string of actions which link the production, distribution, mediation, and consumption of popular music. Even in the abstract, generic form I am describing here, this set of relationships is extraordinarily complex.

When a work of popular music begins its travels through a medium, it already has inhered within it a series of social relationships the existence of which we can sometimes hear, sometimes not. The tangible consequences of these relationships are the collection of material and social facts whose shape and form I am trying to specify. These material and social facts include the compositional processes through which the music itself is created and the realization of that music through particular performances using specific instrumentation and arrangements (Zak, 2001:24–5). We can add to this those evanescent qualities of sound which most often go unmentioned such as ambience, timbre, or texture. The interpretable aural facts of most recorded music are often subject to intense aesthetic debate during their creation. When musicians create a recording, the final sound of that recording is shaped by creative arguments which take place within a culture of creativity often too complex to map out completely.[2] Paradoxically, the results of these debates are by definition clearly audible, but since we are not often privy to these debates, they remain curiously hard to hear (ibid.: 49–50). Further, the aural contours of public versions of most popular music are dependent on particular configurations of technological filters and mechanisms of circulation which are both historically and economically contingent. That is to say, the state of the art is constantly changing and not everybody can gain access to it. This collection of facts includes numerous acts of musical performance of composed musical materials which are captured and then shaped and reshaped repeatedly into a form acceptable to the performers, composers, and producers, a process which continues long after all of the musical performances themselves are complete. The collection of fixed sounds we hear have been mixed and remixed together in a potentially infinite number of iterations until the one final version is agreed upon by those involved. The final version is itself dependent on the varied involvement of all manner of people and institutions which have an interest in the outcome of this often long and complicated process. This includes musicians, managers, producers, and record label representatives, all of whom are enmeshed in particular kinds of power relationships with each other which ultimately shape the literal form of the final product.

---

2   Toynbee (2000) presents an interesting attempt to map the culture surrounding acts of musical creativity through a concept he calls "the radius of creativity."

And yet, the "final" product is further transformed when it is made public and moves through the purview of various cultural intermediaries eventually consumed by audiences in contexts too diverse to imagine, much less predict and quantify. What we are faced with in the analysis of the music we call popular is a bewildering series of distinct, overlapping contexts and practices of creative and compositional knowledge and activity, technological tools, aesthetic judgments, and consumption activities which shape the use and experience of music, as well as the historical, economic, and cultural contexts which shape and direct production, distribution, and reception. But we still need to find ways to identify what it is we are actually talking about in order to fight our way through this thicket of circumstance to discover our elusive analytic object, made tangible as the socially recognizable materials we call popular music.

Recorded Sounds and the History of Their Production

In order to understand how the context of production and the socially inscribed meanings attributed to that production are linked, we have to ask if there are any elements that are common and irreducible to our experience of popular music. Gracyk argues that the rock object, in particular, is constituted as the recorded sounds themselves. For Gracyk, the primary unavoidable form of rock is its material existence as a specifically constructed collection of recorded sounds. These sounds are not the performance of a work. These sounds are the work itself. They are carefully put together piece by piece and crafted with the tools at hand for a particular purpose within a specific series of contexts to form an irreducible material fact. The meanings we ascribe to rock grow primarily from how sounds are arranged in recordings. Different versions of the same song can have drastically different meanings because of the ways some of the same musical materials, whether these be instruments, harmonic patterns, or melodic contours, are arranged sonically. The associations we make with music are based in large part on the way these very particular sounds are fixed and then made public (Gracyk, 1996:18–19).

Given that the recording is most often the primary link between the producer and the consumer, it is the recording that shapes our perceptions of a work's distinctiveness and identity. We identify a work as the unique and identifiable sounds of particular recordings. We recognize the genuineness of it, its exactness and its irreducibility specifically by making fundamental distinctions between the sounds of one recording and another. Each recording, each work, can have only one history of production. It is only possible for one set of events to have resulted in that particular work and it is this connection between the context in which a work was produced and the act of discriminating recognition inherent in the act of consumption that most directly connects the producer with the consumer. While the recorded sounds we hear might be subject to misunderstanding or reinterpretation, they are unchangeable regardless of the meanings that might be ascribed to them. The material aspects of a piece of music I am trying to identify are those that are not based on the competencies of a consumer or listener for their existence nor are they dependent on some requisite level of knowledge for their identification. Put simply, regardless of what we might think of a piece of music or a particular recording, once it is produced we can't really do much to alter the history of its production or the aural contours of that production itself. Every work we consume was created by a specific series of activities which are complete by the time we consume them, by definition.

This holds true even if a work is a derivation of an original; regardless of any similarities between the two, we have two distinct works. Any remix, re-mastering, or reinterpretation of an original is itself a new work because each new derivation or version has resulted from a new history of production. To paraphrase my own argument regarding acts of consumption from Chapter 1, every new work, no matter how derivative, already has a different and unique trajectory through the world. It has been produced by a new set of actions, inserted into a new context of consumption and will have new destinations which it will reach in new ways. It is inserted into a context that has changed because of its existence, however slight or nearly invisible this change might appear to be. This new work is not a new work simply because it sounds different: it is a new and distinct work because there was a unique series of actions which produced it; a new history of production and a new work results from that new history. There may seem to be only trivial distinctions to be made in many cases, but this is not necessarily true. These distinctions, no matter how small, make it possible for us to deepen our descriptive analyses of popular music in order to understand the ways in which an ontologically distinct work shapes and produces the meanings which are later ascribed to it. This is the key point: the actions which constitute the history of production are the irreducible and unavoidable elements of a recorded piece of popular music. Basing our analysis on what happens to shape and determine the social and technical processes of music and the trajectories of meaning that trail behind and eventually overtake completed works would seem to sidestep at least some of the dilemmas of disciplinary incoherence Grossberg noted with such despondency. Further, taking as our analytic objects, those contextualized material facts of music we hear as they are made meaningful through social processes of production, mediation, and consumption, can further help us out of his bind.

The Contrasting Mediums of "Hound Dog"

> I never heard screams like that in my life. I showed them sons of bitches (Elvis Presley).[3]

I'll follow Gracyk's example and present a few "thought experiments" to make my use of these concepts clearer. I'll do so first by analyzing the familiar musical materials of two versions of "Hound Dog," those recorded by Big Mama Thornton and Elvis Presley, around which there is a detailed documentary record. Part of my motivation for doing so comes from an odd fact about "Hound Dog" that isn't always recognized as an important analytical fact. Between the time Thornton recorded the song in 1953 and Elvis recorded it in 1956 there were six other commercial recordings of the song (The R&B Box: 30 Years of Rhythm and Blues, 1994:29).

---

3   This quote is from Peter Guralnick's *Last Train to Memphis*, evidently offered to Elvis's girlfriend at the time (Fink 2002:99).

There is little doubt that Elvis's version is by far the most commercially successful and historically definitive version. Why? Is it because Elvis was an organic, if instinctive, genius who understood the needs and desires of the greatest number of music consumers from 1956 to the present? If we accept the paltry equation of consumer choice and cultural democracy mentioned in the Introduction of this book we can draw no other conclusion. Alternatively, we could argue that Elvis's unique melding of country and R&B was instantly appealing to white southern teenagers who were ripe for corruption and rebellion. His charismatic hip grinding stage presence was simply the first crack in the wall of mid-1950s repression through which a torrent of pent-up youthful energy could burst forth with all its subversive, revolutionary power to change forever the heart and soul of US popular culture. If we adhere to the "consumer resistance" school of cultural studies, we must accept this argument. However, instead of providing one more transhistorical, decontextualized explanation based on some alleged set of universal cultural constants, I want to apply another layer of explanatory tools to a phenomenon whose complexity is rich enough to warrant it.

Elvis's Sun sessions are widely regarded as representing a fundamental shift in the way in which the recording studio was used (Gracyk, 1996:13). According to those involved, the sounds produced during these sessions were recordings first and musical performances second. No longer a medium for capturing and smoothing live performances delivered into microphones and cut into grooves on discs, with the Sun sessions the recordings are the primary text. Instead of a one-take-fits-all paradigm, the advent of reusable magnetic tape allowed Presley et al. to use the recording studio to capture the favored recorded performance exhibiting the "right" set of sounds for release to the public by listening to each take and re-recording songs in reaction to them. According to a series of commentators, magnetic tape freed Elvis and his collaborators from both audience approval of new material through live performance and the "tyrannies" of the songwriters who provided them, instead allowing them to place their own aesthetic judgments at the center of the creative process. Those judgments, however, were by no means autonomous. They were clearly made with both the experience of past performances and the demands of future performances firmly in mind (ibid.:13–15). In this case, the social milieu in which the recording session occurred had a defining effect on the sounds of "Hound Dog" and its meanings.

The contrasting promotional cultures surrounding R&B and Rock 'n' Roll, embedded as they were in deepening social crises over race and sexuality in 1950s America, definitively shaped both recordings. The central difference between R&B and Rock 'n' Roll was in the ways each form was distributed and presented publicly. These contrasts had identifiable material affects on these two famous recorded versions of "Hound Dog." By the time Elvis went to record "Hound Dog," released as a B-side to "Don't Be Cruel" in 1956, he would already have been considered an accomplished recording artist. Given the success of his Sun sessions, it seems clear that he didn't change his process all that much, not surprising given the size of the investment RCA had made to buy out his Sun contract (Starr and Waterman, 2003:221–2). According to most sources, he recorded "Hound Dog" with the same general set of aesthetic intentions and practices as the Sun sessions. The fact that it took 31 attempts to record the version (Elvis chose take 28) most fans finally heard on record is hardly irrelevant to the meaning of his version of the song (The R&B Box: 30 Years of Rhythm and Blues, 1994:29; Elvis in the 50s). According to the uncredited liner notes of 1958s Elvis' Golden Records, Elvis didn't particularly like "Hound Dog" as material for recording, "but Steve Sholes decided it should be on wax since it had always caused such a sensation in his theater act" (Elvis' Golden Records, 1958). If it seems unclear why Elvis would spend so much energy recording a song he didn't really like, Robert Fink convincingly argues that this particular recording session was part of a "short, bitter struggle over the performance of sexuality in America's mass media" (Fink, 2002:97). The day before the recording sessions started, Elvis appeared on the Steve Allen Show to give what he later called "the most ridiculous performance of my entire career" (Elvis in the 50s). He performed "Hound Dog" in white tie and tails, clothes which were intentionally designed to be so tight he couldn't move freely. Worse, he was compelled to perform the song to an actual hound dog wearing a top hat who seemed unimpressed by the proceedings. It was a clear attempt to neuter after the hysteria created by his appearance on the Milton Berle Show the previous month. For Fink, the sound of this particular "Hound Dog" was an angry response to the "carnival of sexual panic" (Fink, 2002:98) then enveloping Presley. The result was a "menacing, rough-trade version of the song quite different from the one they had been performing on stage" (ibid.:97).

Consider the similarities and differences between Elvis's "Hound Dog" and Big Mama Thornton's original production of Lieber and Stoller's "imitation blues" opus released in 1953. Thornton recorded "Hound Dog" for Houston's Peacock label while on tour in California in 1952 with Johnny Otis's band. They more than likely rehearsed until they got it right, recording the final version in a single live performance, the sonic contours of which were honed and specified by the same kind of musical practices as Elvis and his band used. As they could not afford 31 takes while on tour, recording for a small independent label, most of the aesthetic judgments made by Thornton and her band were probably worked out and resolved before the final cut was made (Big Mama Thornton ..., 1992). Her single was written and produced by the songwriters themselves especially for her vocal style, a fact which Thornton capitalized on during the sessions, as she later explained. In referring to Lieber and Stoller she says "they had this song written out on the back of a brown paper bag. So I started to sing the words and I put in some of my own. All that talkin' and hollerin', that's my own" (Big Mama Thornton ..., 1992). The resulting record went to the top of the R&B charts in 1953 becoming the third best selling R&B single of the year (Edwards, 1981:58). What is certain is that, given the technology available to Thornton, she and Otis's band produced "Hound Dog" in one live take, perhaps relying on the luxury afforded by multiple takes, perhaps not.[4]

---

4   On the Peacock compilation of her work (*Big Mama Thornton* ..., 1992), the song "I've Searched the World Over" includes a false start with the band regrouping on tape. This recording, from the same session as "Hound Dog," suggests that the songs from this session were done in one take.

It seems clear that the production process was more important to the meaning of Elvis's work than it was to Thornton's. The distinctions between each work, as speculative as some of them are, are legion and most are actually audible. Thornton's more languorous version is centered on the sexual innuendo of lines such as "You can wag your tail but I ain't gonna feed you no more" and "You made me weep and moan. You ain't lookin' for a woman, you just lookin' for a home." Elvis seemingly sings to a dog whose efforts have failed to satisfy. The "witty multiracial piece of signifyin' humor" which defined his live performances of the song clearly didn't make it through the recording process (Fink, 2002:97). Big Mama's voice is intimate, improvisatory and unadorned by heavy effects. It sits front and center in the mix. As Fink succinctly notes, "Elvis just shouts," repeating each line in virtually identical fashion (ibid.:97). The guitarist in Otis's band uses a clean, smooth sound representative of the subdued guitar playing on many postwar R&B recordings (see The Chess Story ..., 1992). Otis's guitarist uses a series of restrained "fill-in" lines relying on bent "bluesy" notes in a call and response pattern trading measures with Thornton's full and throaty singing. These guitar sounds are a clear contrast to the heavy strumming and crunching, jagged, distorted guitar sounds in Elvis's version which seem to back up, but not interact with the singer.

Just as important, in Thornton's version, drummer Johnny Otis accentuates off beats on the toms and rims, completely avoiding the heavy use of the snare drum on two and four as well as what Fink calls the "tommy-gun burlesque lick" which anchors the end of each section in Elvis's record (Fink, 2002:101). In fact, the rhythm section of Otis's band, which includes hand claps distinctly accenting two and four, grooves in a remarkably understated and rhythmically complex way. Thornton both pushes and pulls the beat, cleverly singing around the downbeats by anticipating or following the first beat of a measure and hitting the downbeat at different points of the verse each time, creating a subtle and constant tension between the vocal lines and the band so often characteristic of interwar and late-1940s blues.[5] Finally, the Thornton version has all the conscious earmarks of a specific live performance, such as a vamping Big Mama slyly encouraging her guitarist to "play boy play," during his solo, telling him how it "makes me feel good," not to mention the barking finale in which the whole band joins. Thornton's very medium, that network of meanings that grows from a particular range of materials, was different than Elvis's, realized through a distinct collection of sounds made public in a dramatically different context. Thornton's band uses the markers of early-1950s R&B, the necessary and distinct ancestor of Rock 'n' Roll. Elvis and his band are clearly more concerned with thrashing out something else entirely, and for entirely different reasons.

Both recordings were commercially validated, albeit in very different ways. Thornton's recordings went on to the R&B charts, R&B being code for "black music" growing as it did out of the old "race records" category. As Alan Govenar notes, the

---

5   See Fink's provocative and eloquent reading of each version (Fink, 2002:95–102). See also the four disc retrospective compilation of Blackbird Records, *When the Sun Goes Down*. While Blackbird's white producers clearly laid down an explicitly formulaic approach to interwar blues (see Kenney, 1999:134), many of the stylistic traits exhibited by Thornton and Johnny Otis's band are apparent in these recordings as well.

record was popular, but limited in distribution because of its "low" and "degrading" status as an R&B song (Govenar, 1990:8; see also Kenney, 1999:110–13). Elvis's version was eligible for both the R&B and Rock 'n' Roll charts, doing so well on both that RCA was forced to use the pressing plants of other record companies to meet demand (Edwards, 1981:95–102; Elvis in the 50s). Nevertheless, both recordings have been historically validated as well, despite the fact that one is still regarded as far more important to the history of popular music than the other. The point here is not to make the case that Thornton's version is more real than Presley's or vice versa, but simply to note the array of factors that go into any assessment of the evolving meanings of each work. They reflect different paradigms of musical practice despite the fact that they were recorded in markedly similar ways. This is evident in the ways in which the song was chosen for or by the artists who recorded them, the ways in which the musicians worked each version of the song into shape, how this process shaped the eventual outcome, and the specific contexts through which the sounds of each recording were fixed and shaped in reaction to the expectations of those for whom those sounds were intended. For Elvis, the song was shaped by the expectations of those for whom the sounds were specifically not intended. The meaning of each version of "Hound Dog" has evolved over the years since their production. The debts owed by those who created Rock 'n' Roll to their R&B forebears have been more widely acknowledged since the early 1950s, no doubt affecting the ways in which some new listeners approach these sounds. These "same" materials have been travelling through contrasting, but increasingly overlapping mediums for decades and they have been producing distinct sets of meanings which continue to evolve in specific relation to the originating texts.

If we take into account the broad range of factors which go into understanding the technical, aesthetic, and social processes that inform our foundational assumptions of what exactly constitutes the medium and materials of a particular recording, we find that even with clear cut cases such as this, matters become fiendishly complicated. I do not harbor any illusions that this brief exegesis of these two particular versions of "Hound Dog" has in any way exhausted all possible analytical avenues. I am simply trying to demonstrate the kinds of questions this analytic framework can help us ask. For example, what material affects do social factors have on the sound of a recording? To what extent is the realization of a piece of music dependent on performance practices, those conventions and innovations that mediate between aesthetic ideals and actual sounds, shaping the particular structure of the sounds most of us will eventually hear? What material affects do different regimes of aesthetic and commercial validation have on the sound of recordings? The promotional cultures surrounding each version of "Hound Dog" and their performative histories, both in the studio and out, had notable material effects. The social and technological contexts in which each was recorded had a great deal to do with each performer's status. At the time Thornton and Elvis recorded their versions of "Hound Dog," both were working musicians. Thornton toured mostly small clubs in the southwest and west and no doubt had a different relationship with her audiences than did Elvis as he played set after set on the Las Vegas strip. Finally, Thornton was never enveloped by a "carnival of sexual panic" despite her far more blatant vocal stylings. This was not because her recording died an obscure death. In contrast, Elvis clearly noted that his live and recorded versions of "Hound Dog" were fundamentally shaped by "them sons of bitches" who seemed intent on containing him through variously contrived comic humiliations. In both cases, there are clear and mostly specific relationships between actual sounds of each recording and the social processes from which we continue to produce meaning. The public meanings that "race" music and Rock 'n' Roll had in the 1950s had a defining effect on where and how music moved and how it was received.

Turntablism as Ontologically Unstable Sound Practices

> The turntable is a musical instrument as long as you can see it being a musical instrument. You're dealing with notes, you're dealing with measures, you're dealing with timing, you're dealing with rhythm. It's ... different tools, but the outcome is the same, music (Rob Swift).[6]

It sounds odd to say it at this point, but an overly intense focus on "the music itself" can actually obscure the kinds of ontological instability that define some forms of popular music. The dynamic relationship between ontological distinctions and social processes can often extend to the most foundational elements of music, such as determining what counts as a genuine instantiation of a particular work and what elements count as part of that work. "Turntablism" is a form of popular music in which various kinds of extremely context specific compositional and performative gestures can be just as integral to the music as the actual sounds produced by these gestures. Ontological analysis of this form of music cannot distinguish a work simply by identifying the status of the fixed collection of sounds we hear. Instead, works by turntablists can exist without any clear lines between their constitutive elements some of which are compositional, performative, theatrical and, in this case, almost bureaucratic. A key theoretical insight, again made by Gracyk, can help us understand the processes through which particular iterations of this kind of music can be recognized as genuine and through which their constituent parts can be recognized as part of a larger aesthetic whole. Gracyk argues that different iterations of a piece of music can be understood as ontologically thicker or thinner depending on what is required to reproduce them. By this he means, the extent to which the recognizable particularities of a piece of music are embodied in sounds fixed by recording or in a score realized through performance practice makes a difference in how we understand what constitutes that piece of music, a distinction he draws using Nelson Goodman's terms "allographic" and "autographic." For a piece of music to be autographic, notation can play no part in its material constitution and reproduction. Instead, the history of production is central to its definition (Gracyk, 1996:31–4).

For example, a muzak version of "Smells Like Teen Spirit" will be recognized as a completely different version of that song never to be mistaken for the original; the muzak version is simply not Nirvana, it is a derivation. It references, but does not reproduce, the original. Nearly all of the elements of the original that carry much of the meaning of the song, such as the discordant mixing of heavy metal and punk, the

---

6   *Scratch* (2001).

scratch of Kurt Cobain's voice, his varied guitar sounds as well as the alternatively thundering and thudding rhythm section, are gone. However, if a performer wants to reproduce the Goldberg Variations on a piano, no one can think back to Bach's original performance and listen to others in relation to it. They may not like the performer's interpretation, but only a few will say the performer is not "playing Bach." In such cases, Gracyk argues, the performance is the end product. The standards for what counts as an "accurate" reproduction of each piece of music are simply very different (ibid.:18–20). According to Gracyk, rock is more often than not, an autographic form which is "ontologically thick." It cannot be reproduced from its source because its source is so specific. There is only one autographed version, the master recording from which copies are made for us to hear. For Gracyk, the recording is, ontologically speaking, "thick" because it is the primary form of the work itself. To put it another way, it is a heavy thing that carries most of the weight of the music's intentional, or poietic, meaning which then shapes all that is immanent in the music as well as the subsequent aesthetic experience of that music precisely because the genuine version cannot be reproduced in any form other than itself (ibid.:31–6).

While the distinction between allographic and autographic is helpful for some forms of analysis, rarely does it impinge on the real world ("My! This new Beck CD is ontologically thick! And so autographic.") We can rely on the distinction between allographic and autographic to help us understand an artist's practice and intent, but it cannot define a work's meanings any more than the distinction between medium and materials can. This is because recordings and scores are not just fixed and interpretable records of artistic intent, but acts of communication which have unpredictable consequences over a long period of time. While a particular recording might be an important thing, it is not necessarily the thing forever. It is one thing embedded in a trajectory of events and circumstances all of which have the power to alter the meanings of a piece of music. For turntablists, it is not simply the sounds created using historically situated and socially recognized performance practices that carry the weight of musical meaning, it is the specific timbres, textures, and arrangements of the sounds themselves that do the heavy lifting. In this case, the categories are not always fixed, but can have considerable overlap and interplay. A work created by a turntablist is not just a fixed record of artistic intent, but an act of communication, one that may not be the defining fact in the aesthetic life of a piece of music whose meanings, subsequent to their recorded form, exist within a much broader context. This context may include performances, reactions to those performances, and subsequent alterations of practice that may entirely reshape the way an artist works as well as public perceptions of that artist's work.

Several telling examples of the ways in which improvisational forms of composition, subsequent forms of notation, and a distinct paradigm of performance practice can intertwine over time appear in the film Scratch. The film, which documents the birth and growth of turntablism and the DJ culture, has several sequences which show how the modes of composition, notation, and aesthetic assessment within this culture are anything but clear cut. Scratch tracks the development of turntablism as a distinct form of DJing with its own cultures of composition, performance, and aesthetic judgment. In several revealing scenes filmmaker Doug Pray shows turntablists working in a variety of contexts, including one scene with the four members of the Xecutioners jamming in a room together like a garage band, as well as several long shots of dozens of well known practitioners performing at contests and house parties; these are the kinds of performances that establish DJs in their field. In one remarkable scene, John Carluccio, director of the film series Battle Sounds, explains a transcription system he helped develop to score specific pieces for other turntablists to use to analyze and learn from the work of their peers. These transcriptions work within this network of aesthetic practice to facilitate the trading of skills and moves in ways distinct from both recordings and performances (Carluccio et al., 2000).

The development of techniques such as beat juggling and body tricks, which cannot be demonstrated through recordings or transcriptions, as well as the mastery of established skills such as scratching, flaring, or breaking, are shown circulating through local, national, and international competitions. They evolve through uniquely interwoven cultures of live performance, recording, and notation, each of which is a crucial component of the overall aesthetic culture. Turntablists shape their work by composing through improvised performances for peers and one another, in public contests and through video and audio recordings which are often distributed both formally and informally through networks of contacts and aficionados. These networks are paths to employment, peer assessment, and fan pleasure all at the same time in ways that seem impossible to untangle. The networks of aesthetic judgment used by turntablists seem no less rigorous than similar networks that exist amongst jazz fans and rock guitarists, all of whom trade sounds, charts, and transcriptions in similar ways. According to many practitioners, DJs appear as singular figures who work almost as early country blues guitarists once did, that is as musicians working to display their own technical abilities, improvising within a clear but flexible set of aesthetic criteria and performance practices, who then lay their work open to the aesthetic judgment of their peers in socially approved forums, both formally and informally (Haslam, 1997:169; Poschardt, 1995:172).

The questions we can ask about turntablism in relation to the concepts of medium and materials might then take into account the various interrelated parts of the process through which their works are created and how they circulate. For example, was a particular piece of music scored or created improvisationally? Was there some opaque combination of compositional techniques involved, such as a DJ carefully notating a series of moves produced while working at home? For turntablists there is no one primary medium, no one network of social conventions through which aesthetic credibility is conferred and artistic success confirmed. Nor are there any clear demarcations between the types of materials, sounds, and performative gestures allowed into a composition. In fact, while the distinction between allographic and autographic forms might lend some idealist clarity to ontological debates, it seems to falter at describing exactly what constitutes the works that turntablists create, partly because of the improvised nature of the compositions themselves, but also because of the explicitly competitive culture of tricks and moves that act as core markers of innovation and distinction. This competitive culture even extends to "digging," or searching out the best breaks from old vinyl records from second-hand record stores which specialize in selling these primary materials. The ontological instability of this form of music is rooted in the ways in which materials are recognized within the medium as part of the form while the compositional form itself is not clearly set, but is instead heavily context dependent. Some techniques are compositional and performative simultaneously, evoking a sense of the theatrical in the context of battle for example, or oddly bureaucratic when a DJ demonstrates his digging skills live in performance by playing a sample from an obscure piece of vinyl that no one else owns; the recognition from peers and the audience is multilayered, respecting how the DJ works both in the performance context and elsewhere.[7]

DJs work within a collection of distinct, overlapping mediums, both professional and personal, the value of which grows or ebbs depending on the context in which they are employed and experienced. Recordings are not necessarily created to stand in for performances nor are performances necessarily expected to be recreations of particular recordings. Performances work as public showcases for the demonstration of new techniques or they can be more intimate and personal, relying on the feedback of friends to shape and reshape subsequent work. These three mediums, compositions distributed amongst friends, works that are transcribed and made available as published works, and performances in public contexts, are aural, visual, and written evidence of the mastery of a set of skills and particular kinds of compositional and performance techniques which are not fixed, technologically, socially, or ontologically.

Conclusion

The "problem" of disciplinary coherence cited by Grossberg highlights the diversity of approaches within the field of popular music studies which for some constitutes a crisis, and for others embodies a defining strength of the field (see also McRobbie, 1995; Frith, 2004). I would go further, arguing that the broad set of musical practices that we tend to call popular music exhibits such a range of ontological diversity, that it is hard to imagine any theoretical coherence growing organically out of the mediums and materials organized under this rubric. "Idol" and piracy are two sets of musical practices whose main features stretch well beyond the familiar analytical concepts that have come to dominate popular music studies. Piracy and "Idol" are best understood as forms of material circulation which produce specific kinds of meaning. Their meanings rest on a material base of specifically produced sounds and the contexts in which they are consumed. To close this section of this book, I want briefly to frame my arguments about how the core aesthetic ideas of the medium and materials of popular music apply broadly to piracy and "Idol" in large part so we can move beyond many of the traditionally dominant kinds of analysis found in most studies of popular music. My use of these concepts in relation to piracy and "Idol" points to the simultaneous flexibility and specificity often needed when applying

---

7 *Scratch* shows how "digging" can be as competitive as actual battles, with several DJs recalling the tricks they used to prevent their peers from finding and exploiting sources of vinyl raw material. Many DJs have even taken to pressing their own vinyl copies of primary materials, such as full albums of guitar sounds.

these terms analytically. I will apply these concepts at greater length and in greater specificity throughout the remainder of this book.

When considering piracy, the factors central to understanding the many contests over the unofficial consumption of music are the ways in which various forms of aesthetic assessment are shaped by the channels through which the sounds we desire reach us. When we download a file from someone else's computer without any of the accompanying validating materials, such as liner notes, lyrics, and information on the production, we experience the music in a distinct way. The aesthetic experience of that music is shaped by the ways in which we come across it. While some in the music industry might suggest we are coming at that music in a kind of cultural vacuum, this is never the case. Instead, the contextual forces shaping such unofficial forms of consumption simply rely less on officially sanctioned modes of understanding. As I will argue in the next chapter, the contests over piracy are in large part over the contours of spaces of consumption and only partly about protecting the property of record labels. As I argue in Chapter 4, these fights are also about maintaining a defining measure of control and influence over the contexts in which the relationships between the fan and the music are consummated. As I noted above in my analysis of "Hound Dog," and in the previous chapter, the promotional cultures of popular music are central to our experience of it. Without that context, we might not play our "proper" role in maintaining that context. This is in large part an aesthetic issue, although it has yet to be analyzed as such. The terms of aesthetic analysis used here can go a long way to helping us understand what is really at stake in the piracy debates. Regardless of the outcomes of these battles, the core arguments made by the music industry are primarily about validating some networks of practice and meaning and not others. In order to comprehend these battles, we have to understand which regimes of thought governing the consumption of popular music count as genuine and which ones do not.

Similarly, I will argue in Chapter 7 that the average "Idol's" endless string of uneven cover versions is another response to the intellectual property crisis facing the music industry. It is not an explicit response, but if we analyze the ways in which the contestants use and transform familiar music in the terms used above, we can see more clearly how and why the links forged between complete unknowns and some of the world's most popular music can occasionally become surprisingly strong. The use of a broad range of familiar music in Australian Idol is an explicit attempt to place unfamiliar contestants in a familiar musical medium, a shaping context established and maintained by the overarching narrative of the contest itself. The medium and materials of Australian Idol are strategically managed in conjunction within the intensely dramatic narrative of the contest itself in order to construct a bridge between the generic "ordinary" contestant and an "Idol" through the pop star persona that is gradually formed around each contestant to greater or lesser degrees depending on their longevity in the contest. In the process, the producers of Australian Idol showcase one set of intellectual properties (songs) through their use and interpretation by another set of such properties (contestants). Textual and semiotic analysis of the songs used is not sufficient for understanding how musical meaning is constructed through the contest. Instead, I show how Australian Idol's medium and materials are carefully shaped through the overarching strategic requirements of establishing and re-establishing fairly traditional relationships between the music industry and consumers through fairly unconventional means.

None of the prescriptions and arguments I have made in this chapter can ultimately prove capable of carving out some vaguely distinct thing called "popular music," a social category that displays a remarkable breadth of ontological diversity. Instead, understanding popular music as a collection of material and social facts whose direct consequence is an ontologically thick, material thing from which we draw, receive, and make meaning within particular contexts and larger historical trajectories is a reasonable starting point for analysis. Instead of a solution for our "problem," I have presented "Hound Dog" and turntablism as distinct examples of sound practices in which the aesthetic meanings of an artist's work grow through their use of specific materials that are recognizable as part of a particular tradition of musical practice through the contexts in which they are made public, through the modes of production used to create them, and through the particular circumstances of the experienced meaning of those sounds. Sometimes one of these factors might matter more than the others; they certainly can't all matter the same way, all the time. The ways in which musical sounds are used within "Idol" can show us how specific contexts of consumption often matter as much as the ways in which these sounds are produced and performed. As noted above, the cultural moment that defined the context of production might matter a lot more for "Hound Dog" than for an obscure mixtape made by a turntablist exclusively for friends. While mediation is crucially important in creating a structured experience of musical meaning, some meanings are more formally structured and more thoroughly mediated than others. The carefully structured "Idol" relationship, as analyzed in Chapter 6, is not only a contrast to the uncontrollable consumption of music exhibited by piracy, but a tool towards the practical inscription of traditional consumer relationships often at the expense of unofficial ones. As demonstrated here, there is an unavoidable and often unbearable density and diversity of musical practices that are routinely subsumed under the label "popular music." It is foolhardy to think we can claim them all as our exclusive domain, or imagine them all to be uniquely pliant to one or another disciplinary language or mode of understanding.

PART II
Bridging the Distance between Production and Consumption

Chapter 3

Power and Property:
CDs, MP3s, and SoundScan

The consumer has to evolve (Ken Cassar, Retail Analyst, Jupiter Communications).[1]

It is rare that any seismic shift in popular culture can be traced to the specific acts of a limited collection of identifiable individuals. But in the case of the escape from the bottle of the bedeviling genie known as the MP3, we can get about as close to a date of birth as we are likely to get. As Charles Mann described in his comprehensive study in The Atlantic Monthly, the birth of the MP3 was a historical accident and irony on a grand scale, born from the most mundane of intentions. The MP3 was created by a working group put together by the International Organization for Standardization, the body charged with determining "conventions for everything from the dimensions of letter paper to the size of screw threads" (Mann, 2000:44). The working group, called the Motion Picture Experts Group (MPEG), first met in 1988 to establish standards for the compression of digital and audio files. One existing compression and decompression program, or codec, that proved useful had already been under development by a research team acting under the auspices of an umbrella organization called the Institute for Integrated Circuits, an institute whose primary function was to develop commercial products based on research undertaken at a consortium of German universities. One of the file formats that resulted from this codec was originally intended to send high quality audio files over ordinary telephones lines. One piece of what Mann called its "buffed-up version," was intended for use on machines that could only deal with data slowly; it was called MPEG-1, Layer 3. The MPEG-1 codec was the first to make digital audio files small enough to be usefully circulated over the communications infrastructure that existed at the time. Layer 3 made large audio files up to 12 times smaller by stripping away frequencies most people can't hear in most circumstances, but retaining key aural identifying features. The research group created a free sample program to help its industry clients learn how to use the codec. The source code, however, was stored on a less than secure computer at the University of Erlangen from which it was downloaded by a hacker called SoloH. SoloH and several hacker colleagues developed the code into software that could be used to convert tracks from ordinary CDs into MP3 files. After they circulated these original efforts within a larger network of apparently highly motivated hackers, Mann reports that "an active digital-music subculture was shoehorning MP3 sites into obscure corners of the Net" only a few years later (ibid.; Cooper and Harrison, 2001; Alderman, 2001:26–7).

---

1   Jeffery (2000).

The initially quiet revolution of the MP3 seemed at first to be just one more skirmish in the rich history of struggle between the entertainment industry and its consumers. These struggles are fought out through the social lives of various audiovisual technologies in order for the music industry to maintain a medium amenable to its primary goal: making money by accumulating and rationing intellectual property. These are precisely the kinds of battles the music industry had become quite used to fighting and winning. But the battle over the MP3 was the first to be fought on the substantially new and unfamiliar terrain of the internet whose guardian is the large, wealthy, and increasingly influential computer industry whose adherents, participants, and beneficiaries extolled and embodied exactly the kind of bloody-minded autonomy in technical development that SoloH and his compatriots exhibited in letting loose this seemingly innocent technical standard on the world (Clark, 2005:B4).

In the years since the emergence of widespread file sharing, it has become very clear that the music industry hasn't been fighting a technology, or the distribution of a technology, or even the existence of particular kinds of file formats. They are combating particular uses of technology. More to the point, they are fighting particular users of technology. As has been widely noted, the MP3 was specifically designed for ease of use, universal compatibility, and freedom of transport. It is a "container technology" whose shape and function are skewed towards free circulation, not defiantly, but by design (Sterne, 2006). This is largely a technical question, asked and answered through the confluence of the technical products of involuntary industrial benefaction and what Mann refers to as the "burbling, self-organizing spontaneity" of the informal social and technical networks responsible for their perfection and distribution (Mann, 2000). The question awaiting resolution is more complicated: who gets to use it and how? That is a political question. It will only be answered when and if those with a particular interest in providing the answer can either impose their will on anyone who might have similar or competing interests, or come to an accommodation with them. While the music industry has been mightily disingenuous about the public expression of where their interests lay in these fights, they have rarely been shy about demonstrating what those interests actually are. Given the breadth and complexity of these issues, the rest of this chapter can do little more than explain what I mean by that.

Inventing Markets

Within the tide of recent writing on the changing nature of the music industry, a wide range of commentators has crafted a largely unproductive binary. On one side we have agile, populist networks of autonomous entrepreneurs, musicians, and fans dedicated to the free expression and propagation of ideas. On the other, we have the lumbering sloth of the music industry intent on smothering those ideas as well as the means of their dissemination. Many writers simply assume that the music industry's primary interest in digital culture consists of doing little more than obstructing the efforts of musicians and fans to exert greater control over the production, distribution, and consumption of music in order to maintain some vaguely defined status quo

(Alderman, 2001; Haring, 2000; McLeod, 2005; Bishop, 2005). But the major institutions of the entertainment industry, within which the dominant actors of the music industry are comfortably ensconced, have long been proactive in their efforts to shape the cultural economy of music regardless of the technological forms in which that economy exists.[2] They have been doing so since well before the familiar contemporary contours of the digital economy in music were even visible. The music industry has been dealing with the contingencies of the recent wave of technological change mostly as an unusually complex manifestation of a familiar set of problems (Kretschmer et al., 2001). This is not an industry unfamiliar with rapid change on a vast scale nor has it ever proved itself to be incapable of asserting its will within the most salient and consequential spheres of technological, economic, and political power in order to shape that change to suit its interests (Garofalo, 1999).

The music industry's recent efforts in adapting to digital distribution and consumption display a logic at odds with the binary described above. They are, however, consistent with demonstrated industry practice. Instead of a sticky resistance to change, the music and entertainment industries have been involved in a long-term campaign to harness the latest technologies for the same quotidian aims that most corporations have pursued for quite a long time: lower costs, higher profits, decreased risk, and increased predictability (Greider, 1997; McCourt and Rothenbuhler, 1997; Winseck, 2002). The literature on the perpetual approach of "frictionless capitalism" in which producers would be able to drastically cut "overheads and eliminate traditional elements of the distribution chain" allowing consumers to benefit from "unlimited choice and ever cheaper prices" is vast and has been widely influential (Kretschmer, et al., 2001:420). The music industry was hardly immune from these ideas. A familiar set of dictums has governed the music industry's response to digitalization: control content legally and technologically, co-opt new distributors and content providers, use new technologies for "old" purposes, and make branding central to the construction of relationships with consumers (ibid.: 426). With these none-too-subtle strategic goals in mind, the response of the music industry to new forms of consumption and distribution has been a gradual, if occasionally involuntary, transformation of the institutional basis on which it rests in order not simply to blunt the threats presented by the new technologies, but also to take advantage of the vast opportunities they offer.

The institutional basis of the music industry is embodied in its markets. Its markets exist as the literal relationships it has with consumers. These relationships only actually exist in reality when people buy things; without these actual, material connections with individual consumers, the music market is simply a series of very complex speculative abstractions. If we understand the market this way, we can analyze the music industry's uneven attempts at shaping both acts of consumption and the spaces in which those acts happen in ways that can help us comprehend more

---

2 Several scholars have raised important questions about the type and quality of integration the main elements of the music industry have with larger entertainment conglomerates. Burkart (2005) uses the term "loose integration" while Bishop (2005) argues that more tightly integrated "empires of sound" are the dominant institutions in the production of recorded music.

clearly the ways in which these acts and spaces of consumption form the foundations of the music industry's market and its basis in reality. The in-between contexts and the means through which most music produced by most record labels is distributed and consumed have changed significantly since the mid 1990s. The ways in which the music industry defines its market have changed commensurately. These changes have been a central driver of the larger transformations they also reflect. If we can understand how acts of music consumption are shaped by the contexts in which they happen, then we can understand how extensive the music industry's efforts to reshape and re-imagine their markets have been. In what follows, I examine how the music industry makes its markets tangible and how this tangibility evolves using the key concepts from the previous chapter: the medium and materials of popular music.

Controlling the Materials

One of the more durable demonstrations of the entertainment industry's power is the ability of its representatives to set boundaries for the use and distribution of various audiovisual technologies. Contests over the use and distribution of audio technologies in particular stretch back as far back as piano rolls and helped definitively shape the early decades of both sound recording and radio broadcasting (Coleman, 2005; Chanan, 1995). Of particular importance here are the political and economic efforts to shape the reach and use of audio technologies since the early 1980s, when the compact disc was created. There are two key aspects of the development of the CD that are crucial to understanding the political struggles over audio technology that have followed. First, the shape and character of the music industry changed markedly in the 1970s. Record labels became part of larger transnational corporations and were incorporated into much larger spheres of economic and technical development than they had been involved in previously. Second, the political reach and influence of these transnational media and entertainment corporations had become a defining aspect, not only of national politics, but global economic development, as the range of products requiring intellectual property protection grew to become a substantial share of exports from the United States, the UK, and many Western European countries (Alderman, 2001:23–5; Garofalo, 1999; Schiller, 1971; 1986; Sanjek, 1996; USDOS, 2004c). This was an epochal shift in global economics and culture that is hard to underestimate.[3] One key consequence of this shift was that record labels which often acted in conflict with consumer electronics firms as well as one another, now acted in concert more often, in large part because they had been incorporated

---

3   Clearly the literature on this subject is massive in scope and volume. Key sources include Parks and Kumar (2003), Tomlinson (1991; 2003) and Herman and McChesney (1997). As Doug Henwood has valuably pointed out, the entertainment industry's economic importance is often wildly overstated (Henwood, 2003:28). It is the intellectual property sector's political importance that is of primary interest here. This story is incisively summarized in Drahos (2002:60–65).

into larger corporate entities which found it far more profitable to act more like a cartel, rather than as part of a nominally competitive market[4] (see Dannen, 1991).

An important material consequence of these seismic shifts in the landscape of the music industry was the development of the CD. As Fantel (2001) has noted, the CD was the first real foundational evolution in audio technology since Edison. It was not an analog or mechanical model of audio reproduction, but a digital one. Also, the CD was the product of cooperation and collusion within the music industry, not competition.[5] Philips and Sony agreed to cross-license their patents on the technology used to develop and manufacture CDs to ease its development. Unusually, they agreed to formally recognize a common set of global standards on consumer audio through collusive rather than coercive means. To "encourage" the adoption of the CD, most major record labels worked to kill the cassette format in order to save production costs by obliterating the production of dual inventories and parallel manufacturing capabilities ("Memorex Moment," 2002). They also tried to gradually kill off the single format when CDs were first introduced, despite the fact that singles have long been a favored consumer choice. The major labels were afraid of "cannibalizing album sales" (Garrity and Mayfield, 2003:50). They also hobbled the development of digital audio tape (DAT) long enough to prevent it from becoming a fully integrated consumer technology by fighting a series of rearguard legislative battles to enforce anti-copying measures on manufacturers of DAT machines. Despite all of this, the adoption of the CD was still a long-term proposition. It took nearly a decade for the CD merely to carve out general parity with other formats and much longer to dominate the market. Suggestions that market forces were responsible for this format "preference" are simply wrong (see Warren, 1998; Horner, 1991; Selsky, 1990; Haring, 2000:29–32).

The political savvy of the entertainment industry grew dramatically during this same period. Lobby groups representing the film, television, radio, and music industries were increasingly able to translate their presumed economic importance to both domestic and international trade into the kind of political influence on which the US political system currently runs: extraordinary amounts of money "donated" to political campaigns.[6] As a result, lawyers and lobbyists for the entertainment industry's biggest players were able, not only to influence key pieces of national legislation, but to draft, proudly and publicly, key sections of that legislation and author the principles governing the intellectual property provisions of a series of acronymic international treaties and organizations, including those adopted by the World Intellectual Property Organization in the TRIPS agreement, as well as trade agreements such as the AUSFTA, NAFTA, CAFTA, and a rolling series of bilateral trade agreements with a continuing queue of supplicant economies (Imfeld and

---

4   In 2005, the European Commission formally accused the major labels of behaving like a cartel in their carve up of the online music market in Europe (Bolin, 2005).

5   This relationship was so collusive that it provoked a Federal antitrust investigation in 1994, an investigation instigated by a Justice Department which had been out of practice in enforcing antitrust law (Haring, 2000:28).

6   See www.publiccampaign.org and www.opensecrets.org for an incredible amount of detail on this issue.

Ekstrand, 2005; Bach, 2004; Given, 2003; 2004). The cornerstone organizations impressing the influence of the music industry on legislators to shape national and international legal codes to suit their interests are the International Federation of the Phonographic Industry (IFPI) and the Recording Industry Association of America (RIAA). As their actions, not their rhetoric, suggest, the IFPI and the RIAA have no interest in pursuing the interests of recording artists. Each exists to serve the interests of those who created and pay for their highly effective lobbying efforts, major record labels and their parent corporations. Their efforts serve as an instructive display of the ways in which the music industry's attempts to control the manner in which its materials are constructed, distributed, and used have most often met with untrammeled success, at least until recently.

In the mid 1990s, the IFPI and the RIAA began a series of targeted prosecutions of file sharers, offering a five year stint in prison to first time offenders, using the legal club of lawsuits and the economic clout their members wielded to run a series of legal file-sharing websites into bankruptcy or irrelevance (Fitzpatrick, 2000:9; Alderman, 2001). Their representatives solemnly insisted with impressive constancy and discipline that they were doing it all for their artists (USDOS, 2004a; Bishop, 2004; IFPI News: Quotes; IFPI, 2005a). The claims of the industry's humble servitude to musicians were so numerous and similar they exuded the obvious stink of a coordinated public relations campaign. Hilary Rosen, head of the RIAA at the time, told the US House of Representatives that piracy "hurts everyone by diminishing the incentive to invest in the creation of music" ("Paying the cost ...," 2002). Not only were they selflessly serving artists, they were also serving global cultural diversity. In a webchat sponsored by the US Department of State, Neil Turkewitz, the executive vice-president of the RIAA, patiently explained why the US Government's aggressive pursuit of copyright compliance around the world was important enough to make it central to American unwillingness to support the recently adopted UNESCO Convention on Cultural Diversity, not to mention attaching intellectual property agreements to more practical pacts such as trade deals, food aid, and favorable terms on import tariffs (USDOS, 2004b; 2006b; Moore, 2005:A14). He warned scofflaws, "if people want to see the creation of music remain as a professional rather than an amateur pursuit, then they will come to recognize the important of ensuring that creators are compensated for their work" (USDOS, 2006a; 2006b).

It should not surprise us that Turkewitz's employers have a very specific idea of how music can "remain" a "professional" pursuit. They have very inventive interpretations of what they mean when they say "creators" should be "compensated" for their work. It is precisely in the arena of compensation that the music industry has been particularly ruthless in securing a significant measure of control over their materials. As many others have noted, major record labels have enough clout and resources to enforce that control and comfortably ruin the careers of any troublesome artists they may represent; anecdotal evidence abounds and requires little comment (see McLeod, 2005; "Sony and the poor boys," 1999; "Fall, mountains, fall," 1996).[7]

---

7   One area in which less visible control is exerted over musicians is in the labor market. As one author noted, the major labels and one major musicians' union, AFTRA, have been the subject of a racketeering lawsuit in the United States for their control over who gets

What is of interest here are the ways in which the music created by songwriters and performers is managed as intellectual property by record labels after the contracts are signed. As innumerable sources inside and outside the music industry have confirmed, musicians simply do not benefit much, if at all from the enforcement of copyright law (Mann, 2000:50–52; Alderman, 2001:51–2; Haring, 2000:7–9). The RIAAs claims that they are merely protecting the rights of artists when fighting piracy are at best insincere, at worst fraudulent. The more clever public faces of the industry only claim that "copyright holders" are the ones whose rights are at stake, allowing the waft of strategic ambiguity as to who these "holders" might be to linger in the air. In nearly every case, the copyright holders are the major record labels. This simple fact is part of the DNA of the industry, embedded in the boilerplate language present in their standard contracts.

In one of the few detailed analyses of the actual language used in standard music industry contracts, the Future of Music Coalition has examined the measures used to construct and control music as intellectual property, generously rendering these measures in plain English. As the authors note, the structure of the music industry's labor market makes these extraordinary contractual conditions, while often an "affront to basic logic," deal breakers "for all but the most powerful artists." And, while the standard industry riposte follows the "no one had a gun to their head" logic, the authors note that the "majority of artists regularly sign contracts that seem to go against their best interests as a concession for gaining access to the means of production, distribution, and promotion that is increasingly controlled by five labels and their parent corporations" (FMC, 2001:1).[8] Not surprisingly, the most consequential clauses deal with the management of intellectual property. A primary paragraph goes as follows:

> You grant and convey to Label, and confirm that Label shall be the exclusive, perpetual owner of all Masters throughout the universe, including without limitation, all copyrights therein as a "work made for hire." Label and all parties authorized by Label shall have the exclusive right to exploit the Masters, and to use your name, voice and likeness in connection with such exploitation. The right to use your name, voice and likeness shall be exclusive during the term and nonexclusive thereafter (ibid.:2).

When translated into a more familiar argot, the FMC analysts note that "unless Congress and/or the courts speak up and say otherwise, you have no ownership or control whatsoever in the sound recording copyright created under the contract." As has been noted by the numerous sources cited above, if musicians don't recoup the costs necessary to produce, market, and distribute the record, they will not make any money from the recording, nor will they be able to sell copies of their CDs outside of their label's preferential distribution channels, nor can they let anyone else sell or use the sound recording in any movie, advertisement, or TV show, nor can they "simply jump in the studio and re-record the songs on a new CD because a separate part of

---

session work ("Paying the cost …," 2002). Some sectors of the industry have been structured specifically to exclude musicians from existing labor agreements which govern pay and working conditions for session players ("Sony and the poor boys," 1999).

8   See also Avalon, 2006; chapter eight.

the contract will prevent it" (ibid.:2–3). That "separate part of the contract" contains the "grant of rights clause" which gives the label the option to continue the terms of the contract as long as they like. However, the standard contract language doesn't merely concern itself with the terms of ownership. It is also very specific about the character of the content the label will own. Terms requiring artists to deliver "radio ready," "commercially satisfactory," or more ambiguously, "technically satisfactory" master recordings allow a label to decide what counts as legally acceptable music as it sees fit (ibid.:5).

The area of interest most relevant to the extensive public arguments over piracy is the payment of royalties. While many sources describe how record labels avoid paying royalties (Mann, 2000:50–51; Albini, 1999; Avalon, 2006), the FMCs explanation of the foundational "Controlled Composition" clause is admirably clear:

> The Copyright Office sets the statutory rate for mechanical royalties, increasing every two years according to changes in cost of living as determined by the Consumer Price Index. The rate increases are by authority of the 1976 amendment to the Copyright Act. The first rate increase was in 1981. It was at about this time that the Controlled Composition clause became commonplace in record contracts. The main purpose of the controlled composition clause is to NOT pay artists the statutory rate and to NOT increase royalties as costs of living increases; basically, to thwart copyright law (FMC, 2001:6).

A rather lengthy and convoluted series of strictures tells musicians that their music is licensed to the label at the "applicable rate," not the "statutory rate." That is, even though copyright law specifies one rate, the standard contract language specifies that the musician's rate will be three-quarters of what the law requires. Also, the label will only pay this reduced rate for a CD with a maximum of ten songs on it and the artist will have to pay the label for any "excess" production costs, a cost applicable at a standard rate for each CD produced. The label also stipulates that they will only pay royalties on 85 per cent of all CDs produced; the rest are called "free goods." Any unsold goods returned to the label from retailers are also exempted from any eligibility for royalty payments, further reducing the number of CDs from which the artist can make any money. Thus, all of the financial risk is shifted onto an artist who does not own the final product, has no control over what counts as acceptable content, no necessary control over who will record that content, how it will be recorded, or how it will be packaged and sold. The full range of contractually defined "excess" costs and "standard deductions" charged to musicians for the costs of producing and publishing "their" music can actually exceed the royalty rates due the artist, meaning the artist can actually lose money for each unit sold (ibid.:7–9).[9]

---

9   Here is the crucial paragraph in the FMC analysis:

The following example illustrates the devastating effect this clause has on royalties: Artist has agreed to be responsible for any costs of mechanicals over $0.56 (75% of statutory times 10 songs). Artist has no say over what is recorded. She records 15 songs written by the record label's "affiliated publisher" who charges the full statutory rate of $.075 per song, or $1.13 for the album. The Artist now OWES the record label $0.57 per record. In

While the boilerplate of contract language might seem too abstract to apply to the "real world," the world in which no one has a gun to their head, the consequences of the full range of legal maneuvers undertaken by the music industry have been amply demonstrated. An "impressively thorough" economic study of what real live musicians actually earn from royalties found an average annual payment of slightly over $100 (USD) in Britain and slightly less in Sweden and Denmark. Given the fact that the big labels themselves have effective control over auditing procedures and literal control over the royalty collection system, which the RIAA designed, such results should not be surprising ("Just exactly ...," 2002a; Holland, 2000g). The level of standardization of industrial practice required by the treaties and agreements that make the global economic system run suggests it is hardly unreasonable to extrapolate these results to other countries (Mann, 2000). However, the above descriptions only apply to formal contracts "freely" signed by artists. Another front in the music industry's war against paying their own contractors is the legislative front on which the very terms of these often onerous contracts can be legally redefined, stealthily shifting the ground beneath musicians' feet.

At the same time as the RIAA claimed to be recouping artists' money during its endless justifications of its legal actions against individual consumers, they were taking the money collected from their piracy prosecutions and giving it back to their benefactors. They worked assiduously to ensure that the monies collected from the copyright laws they were so desperate to enforce never made it to artists in the first place. For example, under the industry-sponsored Digital Millennium Copyright Act (DMCA) half of all internet "licensing fees" were supposed to go to musicians, so the major labels simply redefined the fees out of existence. Universal Records argued that these fees were already covered under "blanket licenses." These were the same licenses that applied to existing mail-order record clubs. Therefore the nine figure proceeds from Universal's successful lawsuit against MP3.com would not go to artists. When asked about the case, an RIAA spokesperson demurred, saying the organization was "not in the business of telling its members what to do" ("Pop Life," 2000; "Just exactly ...," 2000:3–4). For its own part, the RIAA said it would be plowing all of the monies it extracted from its file-sharing prosecutions back into anti-piracy efforts ("Greed is bad," 2003). Even US Senator Orrin Hatch, a drafter of the DMCA and one of the more rigid thinkers on the subject of copyright, saw the light, suggesting that "it comes as no surprise that the recording industry has used litigation to scare off venture capitalists." Hatch, who once threatened to publicly blow up the computers of convicted pirates, was nevertheless quite sophisticated in his assessment of the music industry's legal strategy. "They are targeting small, underfunded companies ... to establish a strong case law in this area" (quoted in Alderman, 2001:156). It should be noted that Hatch is a well-known legislative advocate for the entertainment industry, whose political action committees have contributed generously to his various campaigns ("Orrin G. Hatch, Top Contributors").

---

five years, when the statutory rate increases to $.0.91 per song, but the artist's rate stays the same, the artist will OWE $0.85 per album! Each record sold puts her deeper in the hole, and farther away from ever recouping (FMC, 2001: 8).

One conflict between musicians and the industry can help us see how the RIAA works its legislative prowess with great finesse and subtlety. In 1999, the RIAAs chief lobbyist inserted three sentences into the "Satellite Home Viewer Improvement Act" that redefined all audio works subject to copyright as "works for hire." The measure was inserted with such impeccable timing that it was rendered immune from congressional debate or public analysis. As one legislator used to dealing with the organization said, "nobody goes behind the scenes as much as the RIAA does and I think it does a disservice to the legislative process" (Holland, 2001a:7). While there was some speculative disagreement within the legal profession on the status of the term "works for hire," there was less confusion in the actual law. As noted by Billboard, "the new provision ... amends the Copyright Act to include sound recordings as ... works for hire for the first time under law" (Holland, 2000a:122). As is often the case with copyright law, this was a lonely spot of clarity. Even though a US District Court ruling only a few months earlier found that sound recordings were not works for hire, the RIAA was still aggressively pushing its "interpretation" of the law to have all sound recordings placed in this distinct and unambiguous legal category (ibid.). The legal dispute centered on the long-term ownership of sound recordings. As noted above, standard industry contracts define sound recordings as works for hire, which means they were created by employees or contractors who had no immediately recognizable ownership rights after they signed a contract. However, the ownership rights were often recoverable after 35 years. Given that the first US Copyright Act in which the issue of these "termination rights" were recognized was passed in 1978, the first round of potential recoveries was slated to begin in 2013. The new legislation gave record labels ownership for 95 years from publication or 120 years from creation; it was a considerable alteration (Gorder, 2000:78).

The RIAAs position was clear, even if its tactics were not: sound recordings have always been works for hire. Hilary Rosen said that the insertion of the new categorization of sound recordings was merely "a confirmation of the understanding that has always existed" (Holland, 2000c:9). The RIAAs chief legal counsel at the time, Cary Sherman, argued that since all collaborative works are defined under law as works for hire and, since individual sound recordings "typically constitute a contribution to a collective work," then the addition of all sound recordings to this category of work "does not substantially change current work for hire law or allocation of rights" (Sherman, 2000:77). To be clear, Sherman was arguing that even though sound recordings were not legally defined as works for hire, they should be because they are. He cited the opinions and arguments of a few friendly legal scholars, he cited congressional hearings at which record labels were casually referred to as "authors," and he noted that many artists have copyrighted their own works in this category. The one thing he did not do was cite any legal precedent or court decision confirming his argument, nor did he ever explain why special legislation was required to acknowledge something that he said already existed. Instead, he warned of the coming chaos when all recordings were bogged down in "endless disputes and negotiations over copyright ownership" should the provision be repealed (ibid.).

Not surprisingly, many lawyers and copyright experts disagreed with him. They argued that the legal reclassification of a sound recording as a work for hire was null and void because sound recordings do not fit into any of the nine categories of "commissionable works" as defined by existing legislation. They argued that ownership over recordings could only be governed by the contracts under which those recordings were made. Artists should retain their termination rights and should be legally recognized as the "creators" of the sound recordings in question (Gorder, 2000:76–8). When faced with a steady parade of well-known recording artists marching up to Capitol Hill to denounce these provisions, the RIAA and its allies scrambled to spin the issue more deftly, in the process putting forward their real concerns in the congressional hearings which followed a few months after the law had passed (Holland, 2000b; 2000d; 2000f:89). Rosen argued that this legal "clarification" benefited everyone because it "was essential to preserve the marketability of highly collaborative works like sound recordings." Industry ally Prof. Paul Goldstein of Stanford University argued that the law "does not confer benefits on one class of sound recording proprietor over another. There is no reason to believe," he speculated, "that record companies, as opposed to recording artists, will be the exclusive beneficiaries of work for hire status" ("Excerpted ...," 2000:97). Like most free-market theorists, his conception of the freedoms inherent in the market was based on a fancifully imagined "level playing field" which, far from existing on this plane of reality, has routinely been demonstrated to be a glowing ideological chimera, useful in political campaigns, less useful in contract negotiations.

True to form the RIAAs case was mired in clever rhetoric that belied the intent of its actions. At first, Rosen claimed that this legal "clarification" was needed to stop the practice of "cybersquatting," in which people registered the internet domain names of celebrities in order to auction them back to them. She also claimed that the RIAA had never tied to push this issue into law before. But as Bill Holland of Billboard sardonically pointed out, "the facts appear to present a different picture." The RIAA first tried to include sound recordings in the work for hire category in 1990. The RIAAs legal counsel at the time made the same argument as did his latter day compatriots. Sound recordings were already works for hire and the RIAA was simply asking for the inclusion of a "clarifying" amendment to the Copyright Act of 1978. By 1994, notes Holland, "the RIAA had established its own policy that sound recordings are works for hire and its legislative plan emerged" (Holland, 2000e). Holland cited a legal scholar whose legal history of the issue demonstrated that that the RIAA was trying to find a way of using a "clarifying amendment maneuver" to confirm their position in order "to circumvent the dreaded possibility of litigation when artists began to terminate their assignment of rights to record companies" (Holland, 2000e). Even after congressional hearings on the issue in 2000 and after the RIAA and industry lawyers had agreed to meet with artists' representatives to hash out the issue, the RIAA was still lobbying behind the scenes to prevent repeal of their "clarification." The only printed comment Holland could extract from any industry executive on the subject was that the entire industry was supportive of the negotiation process and that they were "committed to putting this behind us" (ibid.). And yet, 13 months later, a group called the Recording Artists' Coalition (RAC) was forced to continue the fight. Created in the wake of the work for hire controversy, the RAC had to file a friend of court brief in the Napster case to ask the judge to reject the RIAAs argument that the files in question, those downloaded off Napster's server, were works for hire and were therefore "created" by the record labels who had filed the lawsuit. An RIAA spokesperson said, "it's baffling because artists have as much at stake in protecting copyrights online as record companies" (Holland, 2001b:87).

Policing the Medium

The piracy debates have shown that even more foundational issues are at stake than questions of ownership, royalty rates, or the comparatively straightforward ethics of illegal downloading. In addition to maintaining control over their materials by vigorously exercising its economic, legal, and political power, the music industry has used similar means to exert a significant measure of control over the mediums through which their materials circulate. A 1998 research report from the SPRC, a science research program at the University of Sussex, dryly noted the underlying stakes of the piracy contests:

> For many years the music business has had very little to do with music. It essentially consists of fastmoving, unit-led production, marketing, licensing and distribution functions. How much product will sell in which territories, how quickly can they ship, how fast can they re-stock and so on. With the World Wide Web as a potential high-speed digital distribution channel, record companies will no longer be in a position to control the distribution chain (Janson and Mansell, 1998:2).

As this and other studies have shown, the music industry has been fighting the threat of what is called "disintermediation," or the dissolution of the means it uses to create the relationships with consumers on which it depends for survival (Jones 2000; 2002; Fox, 2004). While control over the distribution chain can hardly be viewed as a new concern for the music industry, it was clearly perceived as a dramatically intensified one.

The music industry has long exerted a definitive influence over the shape and character of the mediums through which its materials travel. The main consequence of these efforts has been a cartel-like hold over CD prices and the range of product availability. While lawsuits against individual downloaders have received the lion's share of media coverage, the details of the major labels' own extralegal distribution activities have been made public through a series of antitrust actions taken against the music industry in several countries. For example, in September 2002 the music industry settled a class-action price-fixing lawsuit brought against it in the United States by 42 state attorneys-general. The major labels were found to have colluded to set minimum retail prices for CDs. They agreed to pay about $67 million in cash and give 7 million CDs valued at $75.5 million to the states for distribution to libraries, schools, and other not-for-profit entities. In response to media inquiries, the attorney general for New York state admitted that the CDs would come under the "free goods" clause on standard industry contracts and thus could be written off ("Just exactly ...," 2002b:3–4). In March 2003, the Australian Competition and

Consumer Commission (ACCC) fined Warner Music and Universal Music Australia for imposing unfair practices on retailers who strayed outside the industry's preferred distribution network to buy lower priced import CDs. The retailers were found to have been economically punished for engaging in a perfectly legal competitive market activity: buying CDs from distributors of their choice. The government had removed oligopolistic importation restrictions in 1998 making such choices legal (Holmes, 2003; Homan, 1999). The irony was that the Australian music industry was enjoying record growth at exactly the same time (Chalmers, 2004a).

Similarly, the United States witnessed a seemingly archaic payola scandal in the late 1990s. After an unprecedented spate of consolidation in the radio broadcasting industry, sparked by the passage of the Telecommunications Act of 1996, the use of "consultancy fees" became one of the most high-profile issues on the Federal legislative calendar in the late 1990s. Various radio airplay consultants were found to have been routinely paying large sums for airplay. Given the dominance of a very small number of corporations over very large numbers of radio stations, the practice of "pay for play" was more efficient and lucrative than ever ("Pay to play," 1996; DiCola and Thomson, 2002). Many in the industry were either resigned to the practice or wholly supportive, with several calling it a "win–win" for radio station owners and record labels. One station director called it "a more efficient use of money for the record companies" (Taylor, 1998:82). Well after the formal outrage had passed, Sony-BMG was again found to be buying radio airplay and was forced to pay $10 million to the Attorney General of New York to settle a civil suit brought against the company to stop the practice (AP, 2005; Schlosberg, 2005).

In addition to these more colorful techniques, major record labels exert more prosaic types of control over distributors and retailers simply as the cost of doing business. While the RIAA and their major label benefactors consistently blamed file sharing for the shrinking retail base in music, many retailers cited the overwhelming pressure that is often brought to bear on them through take-it-or-leave-it pricing strategies (the ones found to be illegal in the United States), the use of "exclusives," through which big retailers can buy the exclusive rights to sell specific titles for set periods of time, and preferential supply patterns which allow favored retailers such as Target and Wal-Mart to capture market share and squeeze out independent retailers (Currier, 2003; Marsh, 2002; Christman, 2002:86–7; 2001a:67). The oligopolies of major labels, big retailers, and broadcasting corporations have produced a level of market "efficiency" which allows nearly all competitive risk to be offloaded onto other entities as needed. Staff can then be drastically cut back as the need to develop new talent can be left to "independent" labels which are nevertheless wholly dependent on distribution deals with the major labels and whose successes are then cherry-picked as required (Sams, 2004a; Fox, 2005; Zuel, 2004:16). Until recently, everything that went wrong for the major labels could comfortably be blamed on the pirates, few of whom could have imagined what would come to be laid at their doors over the years. Despite its rhetoric, few within the music industry seriously argued that file sharing could be stopped, especially when industry codes aimed at protecting file formats and preventing copying were routinely hacked within days of their release and the number of file sharers was supposedly increasing despite increased litigation. The drama surrounding file sharing and piracy is actually about managing an acceptable level of risk that will allow the major labels to maintain control over the supply chain (Hiatt and Serpick, 2006; Mann, 2000:44; "Cyber-pirate," 2003; "Just exactly …," 2002c:7).

Even if we set aside the music industry's low-cost, low-risk, high return, occasionally illegal business models, we can still see how its own hyperbole about piracy reveals deep anxiety about controlling the distribution chain. One of the music industry's main arguments in the piracy debates is that unauthorized downloads of digital song files is theft and that it costs the music industry money. These assertions are most certainly true, at least in literal terms. However, the music market is a complicated beast exhibiting many contradictions and paradoxes. For example, the RIAA and the IFPI have spent years creating, commissioning, and releasing a steady stream of reports to the business and trade press blaming file sharing for a precipitous drop in music sales all around the world. Yet their own numbers actually complicate the picture. For example, during the darkest days of the piracy crisis, CD sales experienced "a year of incredible growth in 1998 that was topped off by one of the biggest fourth quarters in history." By mid 1999 sales were still up (Holland, 1999:100). Yet the IFPI claimed that, in the five years to 2003, global music sales had dropped 22 per cent and that piracy was the primary source of the problem (IFPI, 2005b). However, when the IFPI uses the word "piracy" they are including every type of illegal operation one can imagine, many of which are run by extremely well organized criminal syndicates producing a stunning array of wares of widely varying quality. According to the IFPI's rather hysterical reports, the scale of these operations is said to rival the industry's own manufacturing capabilities (IFPI, 2004). Worse, the IFPI's numbers are far from reliable. They were called "self-serving hyperbole" in a draft report prepared for the Australian government by the Australian Institute of Criminology. The report advised the Federal Attorney General against the use of the IFPI's piracy figures in court due to their lack of reliability and painted an unflattering portrait of music and software industries more concerned with competing for the government's favor than producing sound research. When it was leaked to the press, senior AIC researchers stressed the "draft" nature of the report (Greene, 2006; Hayes, 2006).

While the music industry has been at pains to emphasize their losses at the hands of illegal downloads, the real world consequences of file-sharing networks are ambiguous at best (Jones and Lenhart, 2004). The RIAA and IFPI routinely cite studies that show an unsurprisingly direct correlation between file sharing and declines in sales figures. The IFPI has claimed that "the bulk of all respectable third party research" confirms the correlation, but they choose their sources very carefully. Numerous research reports by "respectable" third parties have shown that file sharing does not have the effects that the IFPI and the RIAA say it does (IFPI, 2005b:18–19; "Downloading 'myths' challenged," 2005; "Memorex Moment," 2002; von Seggern, 2002). An apparently less than respectable study undertaken by the Harvard Business School examined 1.7 million downloads and found that the effect of file sharing on music sales was statistically nonexistent (Oberholzer-Gee and Strumpf, 2004). The study was rejected because it undertook "a mathematical analysis of sales rather than just going and asking people about their file sharing habits" (Shedden, 2004:12). When researchers did go and ask people about their file-sharing habits, many came up with similar results. So industry representatives said respondents were probably lying about the extent to which they were breaking the law, except when the results confirmed industry fears, of course ("Music Piracy ...," 2004; Boland, 2002; Weaver, 2006).

In 2003, the RIAA decided to content itself by claiming a "total" market drop of between 10 per cent and 11 per cent. In particular, they made a great deal of noise about the drop in album sales which the RIAAs ubiquitous legal counsel Cary Sherman blamed on peer-to-peer networks. He neglected to mention the four years of uninterrupted growth the music industry had enjoyed before posting the 2003 figures, nor did he mention the remarkable positive sales growth curve which stretched from 1982 to 1995 (Christman, 2001a; 2003:7, 67; Needham, 2003:32). Even in the worst case scenarios pushed by the music industry, the losses they claimed at the hands of file sharers still cost them less than the 15 per cent of units accounted for in the "free goods" clauses they force into every standard recording contract. The RIAA even went out of their way to discount its own figures which showed that sales of CD singles rose by 162 per cent and DVD sales rose by 20 per cent during 2003, preferring to focus on the more politically convenient album sales numbers (Christman, 2003: 7, 67). Further, the RIAA rarely mentioned the fact that entertainment spending as a whole had risen steadily during the period in which it claimed piracy was killing music, with its own numbers showing that music was the largest percentage of total entertainment sales and acted as a catalyst for the industry as a whole (Christman, 2005b).[10]

Explanations for these far less dramatic figures come readily from the music industry itself. Singles have long been proven sellers, but fears of "cannibalizing" album sales prompted the market leaders to repeatedly try to kill off the format. The digital download market has brought it back with a vengeance (Hiatt, 2006:14; Garrity and Mayfield, 2003:1). The major labels have also been diversifying their offerings by pushing content rich DVDs and offering the commercial equivalent of mixtapes which consumers can buy ready-made, download themselves, or make using CD burning kiosks which have spread well beyond the confines of music or multimedia stores (Wright, 2004; Timson, 2006; Drew, 2005; Kipnis, 2004:3; 75).[11] While album sales continued to slide in 2005, the music industry made tidy profits from increasing sales of legal digital downloads, ringtones, merchandizing, and myriad other categories of commerce that were merely tallied as "nontraditional" sales. While it is hard to miss the paradox of "nontraditional" sales rapidly becoming the mainstays of an evolving industry, the RIAA and IFPI did their best (Bruno, 2006c; Garrity, 2003; Hiatt and Serpick, 2006:9–10).[12] These figures highlight

---

10 SoundScan figures for 2006 show a 5 per cent decline in album sales while "a huge increase in digital downloads had driven total music sales up" (AFP/AP, 2007).

11 The music industry has known about the popularity of mixtapes since at least the late 1980s. High Fidelity reported on the commercial reality and potential of custom mixtapes in 1987 (Esse, 1987).

12 It should be clearly noted that the vast majority of consumers are continuing to buy all of their music on CD and, at the end of 2004, only 6 per cent of Americans owned an MP3 player. The music industry's worries are plainly over the future of music consumption rather than the present (Teitelman, 2005).

the fact that some of the biggest problems the entertainment and music industries have faced have been of their own making. As has been widely acknowledged, the competition for the "entertainment dollar" has become fiercely competitive with a wider range of products available through a larger range of channels than ever before. As a result, the longstanding focus on big hits has given way to what many analysts have started to describe as markets defined by their "long tails." The changing nature of the music market, as seen in the shift from a small number of high-volume sellers to a broad range of solid performers has not gone unnoticed by the entertainment or music industries. In fact, they've known about it all along.

From Big Hits to Long Tails

The music industry has been working for a long time to gain greater control over their markets, not only through the measures described above, but also by producing new kinds of knowledge about them as well. Their efforts at using the new kinds of market information systems described in Chapter 1 improved significantly with the introduction of SoundScan in 1991. SoundScan was the first point-of-purchase tabulation system said to measure objectively actual sales specifically by not relying only on retailer sales reports. As shown by McCourt and Rothenbuler, SoundScan was created to reduce market uncertainty and increase the efficiency of retail transactions by automating the checkout process and rationalizing the distribution system. The data generated by checkout scanners was then available "for inventory control, warehousing, delivery scheduling and market analysis" (McCourt and Rothenbuler 1997:203). SoundScan was hailed as the first objective accounting of actual sales numbers free from the hype and manipulation of previous regimes of market knowledge (ibid.:205). There were, of course, hidden biases to the data produced by this new system, not to mention methods of circumvention and abuse (Strauss, 1996). Given that retailers had to subscribe to the system, it never measured all sales. Instead, there was a heavy bias towards large retail chains and larger distributors who could afford the hardware and software to participate in the system, much like the UPC system. Also, SoundScan attributed sales to distributors, not labels. Smaller independent retailers and distributors tended to be left out or marginalized. As one commentator noted, "a fact of retail life is that albums included in a major distributor's catalog have a distinct advantage over indie-distributed titles in terms of gaining shelf space and advertising programs from large chains" ("What is fair market share?," 2006). In this sense, SoundScan could only exacerbate the existing biases of the primary systems of distribution. SoundScan's operators even acknowledged that they virtually ignored some markets altogether ("Pop Life," 1997).[13]

---

13 In 1997, *Rock and Rap Confidential* reported on a sales tabulation controversy between WEA Latina and SoundScan. SoundScan reported that the Mexican rock band Mana had sold 17,000 copies of their Suenos Liquidos release in the first week while WEA Latina counted 178,000 copies sold in the same period. The label's numbers would have made the album the best selling album in the United States. As *Rock and Rap Confidential* sarcastically noted, SoundScan disputed the label's figure "on the sound statistical basis that [the] company does

SoundScan was supposed to deal with the problem of an increasingly fragmented market for the distribution and consumption of music by allowing producers to target ever more specific market segments and respond immediately to any "breakout hits" or surprises (McCourt and Rothenbuler, 1997: 202). Given that, historically, tiny percentages of total releases have often accounted for the bulk of major label album sales, the development and early use of the SoundScan system was colored by the need to quickly capitalize on trends that might otherwise remain invisible in order to manufacture the overwhelmingly big hit (Christman, 2001b; Garofalo, 1999). While SoundScan has proven to be an adaptable measurement standard, these early particularities of use show how ostensibly objective measurement standards cannot necessarily circumvent the assumptions of those using it. SoundScan is a descriptive technology, not a predictive one, dealing with consumers more or less generically the way the UPC system does. (The next chapter deals with predictive systems.) SoundScan has proved its continuing utility as the market for music fragments further, competition for entertainment spending increases, and avenues for music consumption continue to proliferate. As online resources are increasingly brought to bear in constructing an understanding of music markets, SoundScan has become a de facto scorecard in an economic environment in which long term consumer relationships are increasingly difficult to maintain (Banerjee, 2004; Fitzpatrick and Reece, 1998; Jeffery, 1999; 2000). The combination of carefully tabulated sales figures invested with an aura of objectivity and increasingly specific, available, and voluminous demographic data have changed some foundational assumptions about what constitutes success in the music industry. Given the volume of data now available through a multiplicity of sources, combined with the ability to react extremely quickly to emerging trends, the so-called "long tail" is beginning to redefine what music markets actually are.

The term "long tail" was popularized in a Chris Anderson article in Wired magazine from 2004. It refers to a statistical curve on which there is a precipitous drop off on the horizontal axis from a small number of high-selling releases bunched up towards the top of one end of the scale to a large number of low-selling releases forming a long, low "tail" stretching across the rest of the graph. Taken cumulatively, the many low-selling releases sell more than the few high-sellers over time (Anderson, 2004). The term proved so useful for describing what was actually happening in the music market that Billboard made use of it almost immediately to reinterpret sales figures on which it had already passed judgment. An article from July 2005 searched in vain for an explanation for a significant drop in the cumulative sales of the top ten albums for that year. The author noted that many in the industry could only speculate that album sales were no longer a reliable guide to the overall health of the industry. Ten months later, this view had broadened considerably. The sales numbers for 2005 were re-examined in relation to the total number of new releases as well as the number of reissues and "digital bundles" of repackaged songs from different albums. The hits were down to record lows, but the number of releases set a record high (Christman, 2005a:27–8; 2006b:9–10; 2006a:22).

---

not cover much of the Spanish-language market" ("Pop Life," 1997). See also Negus (1999) for a similar story about the Latin music markets in New York and Puerto Rico.

Given that consumers of "tail" titles are now more "targetable" than ever before, it is becoming clear that the very idea of what constitutes "success" in the music industry is changing. Until recently, it simply wasn't profitable for "bricks and mortar" retailers to allow large numbers of slow-sellers to take up shelf space that could be used more profitably for faster selling hits. Given the gradual expansion of online retailing and sales of digital downloads, the economic constraints of physical shelf space are no longer as important. Since the range of titles made more or less immediately available to consumers can now expand, virtually, without practical limit, the very definition of "successful" music has changed. The ways in which markets are currently being re-imagined is already having a direct influence over what music gets produced, what music is made available, for how long, what it will take for that music to be regarded as successful, and how the relationships between producers and consumers will be constructed and managed to produce these new kinds of success. For example, in 2000 the RIAA released a "Consumer Profile" which gave voice to their fears of an entire generation weaned on "free music" (cited in Fox, 2004). The organization cited figures that showed 18 to 24 year-olds were less likely to buy music, blaming the availability of illegal downloads for the decline. In 2006, the RIAA found that consumers over the age of 45 were responsible for buying twice as much music as any other age group and were responsible for 24 per cent of all online purchases. Similarly, an Australian advertising agency study found that those aged over 55 were consuming youth oriented brands like iPod to a greater degree than ever before (Glaister, 2006; Lee, 2006). Easy assumptions correlating relative youth, technology use, and music sales, assumptions thoroughly embedded in music industry planning for years, have been proven false, inverting a tried, but tired formula for success.

It is important to note that the music industry could only imagine "long tail" markets after it was possible to collect data that made existing forms of consumption visible and tangible to producers. They are a direct consequence of the ability to construct markets, not as a mass of generally like-minded people, but as a collection of individual consumers and retail transactions separated into increasingly specific target demographics with whom it is easier to create and maintain more specific kinds of relationships. These goals have long been the standard for the music industry, despite the varied ways in which they have pursued them. Far from sitting obstructively in the path of commerce, digital or otherwise, the music and entertainment industries have been intimately involved with creating greater flexibility and efficiency in their markets specifically by trying to exert increasing control over them. They have pursued these goals by working to shape the ways in which acts of consumption are contextualized and realized, not only to combat unofficial and illegal forms of consumption, but to more accurately measure legal consumption as well. They have been doing so since at least the early 1990s. In a retrospective article on the introduction of SoundScan, the author remarked on how the new sales figures compiled using the novel point-of-sale tabulating system produced "a long list of success stories" that showed how "a number of new acts thrived in the light of reality-based charts" (Mayfield, 2001:8). Even with all of its limitations, SoundScan was already displaying a tail of some sort, but no one seemed willing or able to find out how long it was.

More to the point, the music industry was excitedly exploring the possibilities of a digital economy in music even during the worst days of the piracy crisis. Even as the RIAA's representatives made their sober, scolding recitations of doom, several of the music industry's preferred providers of prognostication were reporting a future at odds with the one invented by Cary Sherman and Hilary Rosen. In 1997, Jupiter Communications predicted that online music sales would reach $1.6 billion by 2002. In 1999, Forrester Research predicted that digital downloads would haul in an estimated $1.1 billion in a few short years. They also predicted that digital "web packs" would become standard, offering fewer songs for lower prices than full albums, while in-store kiosks would facilitate the process of making custom mixes (Atwood 1997; 1999). Faced with the declining effectiveness of radio and television to sell music, researchers and industry analysts routinely pointed to the necessity of offering flexible consumption formats and more tightly targeted marketing based on increased use of a broader range of data to match increasingly well defined consumers with the titles they were looking for as they wrestled with a much wider range of available options (Jeffery, 1999:43–8; Fitzpatrick and Reece, 1998:88). As one industry insider succinctly put it, "more than ever you'll need a good catalog" (Jeffery, 1999:78). It should come as no surprise that these industry forecasts appear to be so prescient. There is often only a hair's breadth between description and prescription in this field.

Many of the conflicts and contradictions within the music industry that have arisen in relation to the development of digital distribution and consumption highlight what many have called the "productivity paradox," a confounding circumstance in which extensive investment in new technologies does not necessarily pay off with economic growth. As Winseck argues, many of the utopian visions surrounding the new technology "ignore the fact that uncertainty and risk are the corollary to information abundance" (Winseck, 2002:97). The communications industries have responded to the inherently increased measure of risk they face by using "monopolization strategies, surveillance and technological design as methods to reduce uncertainty, manage risk and influence the evolution of new media and the information society" (ibid.). Winseck convincingly demonstrates that the pursuit of monopolization strategies reflects "an obsession with reducing perceived inefficiencies in organizational control through surveillance" and are "basically attempts to internalize markets and new technologies as a means of anticipating and exerting influence over the evolution of new media" (ibid.:108). Does this sound familiar?

Clearly, the music industry has pursued these strategies most aggressively in the one area in which they have historically been the most active, and vulnerable: consumption. Consumption is the reality of the music market. Each time we consume music we are a central participant in the material expression of a system of power. The information produced on consumers and their acts of consumption shapes the ways in which the many struggles between consumers and producers inform the strategies and practices used by the music industry to combat less favorable forms of consumption. There is certainly no unanimity with the music industry on how to turn their recent struggles to their advantage, but if we want to understand what those in the music industry see when they look at their markets, we could do worse than to look at those myriad instances when these markets become momentarily real, legally or otherwise.

Chapter 4

Mediating and Manufacturing the Investment in Desire

Consumption became a matter of psychology when the commodity was stripped of the burden of being useful (Hiromi Hosoya and Marus Schaffer).[1]

The picture in the newspaper is striking and odd. A young man with a clipboard and various electronic devices draped over his body stands in the aisle of a City Train winding its way to Sydney's CBD. His mouth is open, his head is tilted back, and his right hand extends slightly out, up and in front of his body, reaching to find the note he is about to sing. This is not an aspiring performer on his way to a master class at the Conservatorium, but a contracted employee of an advertising firm, singing along to the tunes he has stored on the MP3 player he is hawking to the visibly bemused, annoyed, and confused commuters (Lee, 2004e:3). This young man is representative of a paradigm shift in the ways in which advertisers address their imagined publics. According to many of those paid to think seriously about advertising, markets which once consisted of a physical economy of products now consist of an attention economy of brands. The young man on the train was engaged in what professionals call a viral marketing campaign, inserting knowledge of a product into what one presumes was an otherwise healthy social body. For many in the world of advertising, marketing, and public relations, getting attention for a brand by successfully injecting knowledge of it into consumers' everyday lives is the obvious keystone of success. This knowledge comes with a price tag and the costs can be steep. Knowledge of products can't be thrown around randomly. It has to be presented within those compelling, complex, distinct packages we call brands. Brands are not distinguished from one another only by their use value, practicality, or quality. They are distinguished from one another based on the relative value of the public's perception of them, perceptions which shape their asset values as measured by their "brand equity" (Henwood, 2003:18; Solomon, 2003:23). The asset value of a brand is determined independently of such mundane concerns as productivity, infrastructure, or pensions. These conceptual coat racks have achieved the status of tangible commodities and they are becoming very valuable (Antony, 2003).

There are several principles of the relationship between branding and the attention economy of particular interest to the consumption of music. First, a successful brand must have a belief system attached to it. It must possess what experts call a "spiritual" dimension to produce the added value needed to transcend mere monetary calculations of profitability. Second, this belief system is a necessary facilitator of

---

1 Harvard Project on the City (2002: 560).

the kinds of long-term relationships that cement customer loyalty. Third, and more practically, the value of a brand lies in the ability of its producers and managers to exert the market power invested in it to impose on consumers what economists call a "monopoly rent," or a substantial gain over the normal profit rate (Henwood, 2003:18–19). It is this kind of progressive economic thinking that allowed Elvis Presley to earn $51.5 million (US) in 2005, even without the possibility of a live show or new material. Elvis's continuing success is a product of his brand power, which has only been increasing since his alleged death. Given the possibilities for reviving dead people offered by digital media, one practitioner in the field suggests that "dead celebrities could be worth more than live ones" (Coultan, 2006:28). The Elvis brand, a strong performer since the early 1950s, demonstrates that otherwise vague notions like familiarity and comfort have a sharper edge. For some, cases such as Elvis's prove the inherent value of brands. If they can reanimate corpses, what else can they do?

The music industry has long been in the happy position of being in the business of owning and producing assets to which people demonstrate implicit and intense kinds of loyalty. How many of us buy an artist's new CD without listening to it simply because the last one was really good? Or because we have all of the other ones by the same artist? How many of us spend absurd amounts of money for concert tickets with their attendant service charges and ancillary costs simply to stand in a concrete bunker filled with massive numbers of people only to be bombarded with painful levels of sound for 90 minutes, leaving with our ears ringing and our hearts palpitating? There are reams of studies, memoirs, and exegeses showing the extraordinary kinds of belief and meaning people can place in music and musicians (DeNora, 2001; Shakur, 1999; Doss, 1999). The lengths to which many will go in order to pay "monopoly rents" to consume music is one of the form's more distinguishing features. I will not be arguing here that ideas like "brands," the "attention economy," and "viral" marketing represent particularly new phenomena. Instead, I am trying to pinpoint what many within the music and entertainment industries imagine their industries to be by analyzing the strategic actions they take to construct markets and reach consumers. There is little question that a new lexicon of ideas has entered the music industry's marketing and production vernacular. These concepts are often used as just one more set of tools to bridge the gap between production and consumption. In some cases, the new tools are old ones that have been redesigned. In others, marketing professionals have generated genuinely novel ideas on how to reach people. The point of this chapter, much like the last one, is to examine the ways in which the music and entertainment industries are changing their practices to meet the challenges they face and to demonstrate the means by which the music industry is trying to exert specific types of control over the environments in which music is consumed in order to connect with consumers more profitably. As Moore (2003) has presciently argued, there is a "materiality" to brands that is rarely accounted for in the scholarly literature. Moore asks a key question about our understanding of the cultural work of brands: "How can the concrete sensuous reality of such tokens-in-use act as a relay for the more abstract associations that branding professionals try to 'encode' in the consumer experience?" (Moore, 2003:332.)

It is an article of faith in popular music studies that the meaning of music is socially constructed. Meanings accrue to a piece of music from the moment of its creation. The material contests over the means and methods that shape the ways in which music moves and becomes meaningful are central to the music industry's ability to reproduce its often ambiguous and inchoate methods of success. The primary lesson I want to draw from the following analysis is that the meaning of music is not just a measure of artistic accomplishment, sensual pleasure, or social connection. It is also a measure of economic value and social power. Many of the problems the music industry faces increasingly lie in the level and types of influence and control it has over channels through which music circulates and becomes meaningful. These problems have been enumerated previously, but can bear reiteration particular to the concerns of this chapter. First, the global consumerist economy has grown wildly in scope, scale, and complexity since the mid 1970s and often seems out of control to those trying to carve out some measure of product visibility. Recent studies indicate a massive, exponential increase in the amount of information available to most people and a concomitant difficulty in sifting through that information to find those bits that are relevant and useful (Paulson, 2003; Cochrane, 2003). Furthermore, media uses and practices on the part of consumers have steadily grown more flexible, inventive, and thus problematic for those trying to persuade people to use media the "right" way. Technology has allowed not only material access to information but more complicated and contingent ways of using and experiencing that information. This is especially true of films, music, and television programs (Hills, 2006; O'Grady, 2007). Finally, the exponentially increased demands made on people's time and attention produced by increasingly pervasive forms of media have changed the dynamics of the economics of advertising, now commonly referred to as the "attention economy."

To deal with obstacles to the predictability of their markets, the music and entertainment industries have been stumbling and lurching towards new economies of meaning. Brands are central to these new economies. They act as conceptual containers designed to provide the necessary distinctions that allow new products to stand out amongst an ever larger range of increasingly available products. This is especially true of the music and entertainment industries whose products have become far too easily available for those industries' taste. A crucial corollary to brands is the concept of "ambient media." Ambient media are media forms which are mobile, pervasive, and severed from traditional forms of broadcasting and media consumption. Those using such media forms to create awareness for their brands must implicitly recognize the type, character, and quality of media use by consumers as well as the kinds of experiences consumers have of products through different kinds of media. While the means and methods of manufacturing and mediating desire for music often evolve rapidly and unpredictably, the goal rarely changes. The goal is to profit from the circulation of musical materials through credible networks of meaning. The music industry profits best by making musical materials course through those mediums most amenable to the efficient and profitable conferral of specific types of meaning on those very materials. This can best be accomplished by creating and controlling effective networks of social, economic, and cultural power.

There is a paradox between the means increasingly used to reach consumers and the principles which structure the industry's preferred range of allowable uses of the information and intellectual property on offer. As I argued in the previous chapter, the piracy wars were primarily about controlling the circulation of specific types of information legally recognized as intellectual property, especially in relation to the ways in which these forms of property exist within specific technological containers. The goal of the music and entertainment industries in fighting piracy was not only to ration material property, but to ration intellectual property to which value had been added. Value added products are, it seems silly to say, more valuable than similar non-value added products. This fact underpins the concept of a "monopoly rent." But where does that "extra" rent come from? Value is added through the conferral of specific types of meaning on those products, meanings predicated on specific channels of communication which help to authorize and confer those meanings. These "extra" meanings accrue as materials travel through specific channels of distribution and consumption. This is where the music and entertainment industries try to add the kinds of value they find most obliging to their commercial aspirations. Many of the most important, used, and valuable channels through which music moves and acquires these special kinds of meaning are growing outside of the music and entertainment industry's direct or indirect control. As the actions of the RIAA and the IFPI have demonstrated, there are two ways to deal with such channels: destroy them or monopolize them.

In order to break into the new channels through which popular music travels and acquires its variously constructed meanings, the music and entertainment industries have found it necessary to violate the supposedly iron law of property rationing that governed their campaigns against the pirates. Between roughly 2001 and 2005, the marketing arms of the big labels began to throw their products around quite indiscreetly. Music marketers seeded peer-to-peer networks with specially chosen tracks, supplied club DJs and "mixtape" producers with special versions of new music, and started mimicking the pirates and hackers against whom they had been fighting so nobly (Werde, 2004; Shapiro, 2007; Crosley, 2007; Strauss, 2000; Hay, 2003c). In this period, the crux of the piracy problem had become clear. There were so many disobedient consumers and producers who thrived on the promiscuity of file-sharing networks that the industry found it had no way to beat them without also joining them. There is a great deal of truth to the idea that the exponentially increasing amount of easily available information was harming the music and entertainment industries. But potential loss of money wasn't the only threat presented by these new networks of consumption. Another very real threat was the dissipation of the kinds of social and economic credibility conferred through carefully designed and controlled networks of power through which music was supposed to move. The trick for the music and entertainment industries was to codify the material and conceptual shape of the many informal channels of music consumption into a shape more suited to the addition of value and the extraction of profit. The ideas which the music and entertainment industries are more and more reliant on to accomplish this goal are the very ideas once purported to be their undoing.

An Economy of Whose Ideas?

The music industry doesn't only need to make technical connections with consumers, it needs to make emotional ones, too. However, with the advent of widespread file sharing, the music industry was having an increasingly difficult time asserting that there was any implicit or necessary connection between these two tasks. This fact has been amply demonstrated by fans expressing their love for their favorite artists by downloading and trading their work without any money changing hands. While the real economic costs associated with illegal downloading are ambiguous at best, the cost to the music industry's credibility amongst fans has been significant as fans and critics have repeatedly and publicly questioned the very need for a music industry. Indeed, as Cavicchi (1998) has shown, fans often craft clear distinctions between their affection for artists and their lack of emotional investment in the system that produces them (Cavicchi, 1998:60–85). Given that the economic relationships fans have with the music industry often contrast starkly with the emotional investment most fans have with artists, it should not be surprising that there are two discrete tasks required to bridge these two distinct gaps between production and consumption. The character of these two types of relationships is so different that the broad sets of principles and ideas that govern the music industry's ability to manufacture an investment in desire flatly contradict those which govern the construction and operation of its legal and technical infrastructure. Yet in both cases the goal is the same, as Campbell and Carlson concisely note, "the primary function of marketing is to reduce uncertainty in the marketplace" (Campbell and Carlson, 2002:588).

The ideas that are increasingly shaping the consumption environment for music are of an odd vintage, part anarcho-libertarian political theory, part postmodern theories of consumption expressed with a healthy dose of marketing jargon. While a wide range of authors clothe their preferred versions of these ideas in the dubious garb of cultural radicalism, the underlying premises which conjoin them are somewhat less than revolutionary. Probably the most widely distributed expression of these ideas is John Perry Barlow's variously titled manifesto on the nature of the information.[2] Barlow's admirably clear arguments were intended as a riposte to those corporate and political actors working to rid cyberspace of copyright infringement by locking up content through various proprietary technologies. Barlow argued that the internet hasn't so much changed the essence of information, as it has exposed that essence. For Barlow, cyberspace demonstrates that information is not a thing to be possessed, but an activity to be experienced. It is spread through propagation, not distribution, endlessly and relentlessly replicating itself, allowing both producers and consumers to benefit without loss to either party; in short, information is an endlessly renewable resource. The mutual benefit created by this resource creates special kinds of relationships, collectively shaped to be of maximum value to all parties. Instead of profiting directly from individually-costed transactions, producers can derive benefit by creating as many relationships as possible by spreading knowledge and information in a different kind of cultural economy. In this new

---

2   The version I am using is called "The Economy of Ideas" published in *Wired* magazine in 1994 (Barlow, 1994).

world, familiarity and authority trump scarcity and anonymity. Power is distributed and negotiated between producers and consumers; it is not wielded by anyone. Like many libertarians, Barlow imagines a world in which all the mess and disorder of politics and culture eventually dissipates in the face of unfettered expressions of mutual self-interest (Barlow, 1994).

If we set Barlow's libertarian idealism aside, we can see that his model of the ways in which information facilitates relationships between producers and consumers is widely accepted. Academic studies of consumption as realized through varied examinations of active audiences and empowered consumers, as well as the rhetorical manifestos and weightier tomes produced by corporate marketing gurus all align quite neatly with Barlow's central arguments, often pushing past them in an undifferentiated celebration of the swaggering agency of consumers. Shorn of their tinge of radical libertarian politics, these ideas are much more mundane than many of their more dramatic iterations make them appear. The key argument is that, contrary to the obsolete assumptions of the past, consumers are not the "passive recipients" or "unwitting dupes" of the culture industry as posited by the collectivist-minded sponsors of the mass culture theory and the Frankfurt school (Solomon, 2003:10, 37). They are agents who exist in communities defined by candor and passion. They trust those within their circle and distrust those outside of it, especially corporations and advertisers. Consumption is an activity in which inherently skeptical consumers eagerly and excitedly participate by expressing a dominant if not dominating form of power over producers and marketers. The industrial age metaphor for marketing, hunting the consumer as prey, has been replaced with metaphors such as this breathless trope: "mirrored fractal nets within nets, the collective intelligence of the human race unfolding in real time" (Locke, 2001:21, 67). Producers should no longer consider themselves at war with consumers, but in league with them. Consumers, both as individuals and as members of groups, must be seen to have their own consuming "repertories" and "logics of practice" which, when deciphered and understood, can lead to very profitable forms of "mutual" advantage (Locke, 2001; Solomon, 2003; see also Frank, 2000:282–3, 303; Poster, 2004).[3]

From Barlow's cyber-libertarianism to varied expressions of academic and populist postmodernism, a few key conceits mark this odd body of work. The first is a radical anti-modernism which uniformly mistrusts and misconstrues the oppositional scholarship of critical mass communications studies as pessimistic and elitist. It does so by deftly sidestepping the question of power, merely asserting that technology and the market have made the distribution of power equitable or has even tilted power over the consumer economy in favor of consumers (Solomon, 2003; Neisser, 2006). The main evidence cited is usually the difficulty advertisers have in reaching consumers. Second, consumer markets have fragmented into more lifestyles, demographics rings, and fractured identities than can be adequately served by any overarching entity. This dramatically dilutes the power of corporations, forcing "them" to chase "us," not vice versa. Rarely do any commentators connect the fragmentation of markets with the ability of producers to construct increasingly

---

3   Frank (2000) and Poster (2004) present intellectually engaging critiques of these ideas.

finely tuned bodies of knowledge about those markets. Third, this ideologically-laden body of speculative hyperbole considers the experience of consumption as virtually coterminous with subjectivity. If we do have any experiences that transcend the experience of consumption these only seem to serve as idealized models of consumption, that is, the kinds of experiences to which the facilitators of consumerism should aspire. Finally, technology has given marketers the opportunity to insert themselves into people's everyday lives in a seamless and almost invisible way. This allows marketers and cultural producers to craft deeply intimate relationships with consumers through new, more effective modes of surveillance in order to track their movements, actions, moods, and attitudes minute-by-minute, hour-by-hour (Lee, 2004b; 2004c; 2004d). This form of exploitative data gathering is often referred to as "inclusive" or "collaborative marketing" (Sawhney, n.d.). As Thomas Frank has succinctly demonstrated, the "intellectual task at hand is not just legitimation, it is infiltration" (Frank, 2000:305). The question is, how is this infiltration accomplished?

Brands and the Attention Economy

It has been somewhat hysterically estimated that the average resident of a large metropolis like Sydney might be presented with 3,000 commercial messages a day (Lee, 2004e). It is this kind of communication environment that makes account planners go weak in the knees. As many have argued, the more taxed public attention becomes, the more valuable it becomes (Davenport and Beck, 2002; Brody, 2001). Regardless of its sociological vacuity or validity, this notion of the "attention economy" is an established reality for advertisers. It has inspired new thinking about how to create lasting, flexible, and evolving relationships with consumers. Many have taken to paying people to go to bars, cafes, clubs, and even private dinner parties to talk up the relative merits of a product to complete strangers and friends alike in the guise of casual conversation. The phenomena referred to as "viral," "tipping point," "word of mouth," "peer-to-peer," or "whisper" marketing are increasingly being used in an attempt to slip through the cordon of skepticism said to be surrounding a supposedly hard to reach public (Griffin, 2004; Gladwell, 2001; Goldhaber, 1997; Henry, 2003; Lanham, 2006; Rosen, 2000).[4] The problem inspiring these new promotional vistas is clear. Advertisers feel they can no longer grasp or hold our attention. The intense competition for people's attention and through it consumer action, has inspired a significant shift of emphasis away from traditional methods of reaching consumers, as advertisers acknowledge and struggle with the overwhelming complexity of consumer culture. Young people are said to be particularly hard to target with traditional advertising campaigns (Frew, 2003). The attention economy is a complicated and often contradictory response to a media environment that appears less and less reliable and to consumers whose behavior is

---

4   Some marketers hire actors to pose as tourists who ask actual tourists to take their photo. They take the opportunity to extol the virtues of particular digital cameras. Others use cars with film projectors in the boot to show promotional videos on the sides of buildings near traffic clogged roads during peak hour (Lee, 2004b and 2004e).

often poorly understood (Elliott and Jankel-Elliott, 2003). As I have noted several times in this book, these challenges have been caused partly by the increasingly sensitive measures of market construction used in market research, a story to which I will return shortly.

The primary weapon thought most effective in combating this generalized attention deficit is the brand, or more specifically brand positioning. As Marsden notes, marketers can now use various "memetic" techniques to exploit associative meanings. Techniques such as "meme mapping," or tracing the "semantic DNA" of various brands by using databases of adjectives to analyze the associative networks of subjective meanings attributed to brands by consumers, can help determine how a product is positioned in the minds of consumers. This provides, he claims, "a recipe of meaning, allowing us to imbue objects, including trademarks, with meaning" (Marsden, 2002:307). Many within the music and entertainment industries have been using these strategies to bring new life to old brands through music and vice versa. The music industry has been transforming the primary commercial applications of its intellectual property by exploiting brand associations and contiguities between music and other products. The associations between music and other brands are less about the specific meanings of the respective products on offer than about their larger social meanings. As one industry representative put it, marketers have "moved on to messaging that includes more of your life than just the product" (Anderman, 2005).

Some of the more influential brand associations have been between various artists and McDonald's. Beginning in 1994, the fast food giant started featuring custom compilations of hits by top sellers such as Garth Brooks, Tina Turner, and Elton John. The collections were offered at discounted prices in conjunction with various meal deals. The initial promotion sold more than 5.5 million CDs (Rifkin, 1994). This effort was the fast food chain's initial foray into a new domain in the pursuit of that holy grail of brand positions: cool. While McDonald's had long been comfortable with a commanding position as a "family" institution, campaigns by health and environmental activists had begun to chip away at their market dominance. Part of McDonald's "marketing revitalization" was to expand its brand by "trying to buy the cool factor." In 2003, the restaurant chain commissioned the Justin Timberlake song "I'm Lovin' It" for its first globally uniform ad campaign because "Timberlake is cool," apparently (Gotting, 2003a; 2003b). Under increased pressure for promoting childhood obesity and its ruthless targeting of children in its marketing campaigns, the fast food giant's response was to target children with even greater precision and purpose. They did so by aligning themselves more closely with specific parts of the music and entertainment industries. Denying it was a contributor to widespread childhood health problems, the firm began giving free music downloads from Sony with every sale of a Big Mac. CEO Charlie Bell suggested that "in marketing, we've said there is music, sport and fashion. Music is a key area that some of our marketing will be built around" (McIntyre, 2004a). There is little doubt that the campaign was aimed squarely at the youthful demographics sought in common by the two corporate empires. Bell continued his commentary on his company's public service ethos. "A byproduct" of the campaign, said Bell, is "teaching kids to download properly rather than do all the pirating" (ibid.).

The ways in which the music industry and advertisers are merging their brands are numerous. The goal is uncomplicated: establish a lucrative position by creating positive associations for your brand. As the music industry has moved aggressively to couple its products with other brands, both to highlight the attractiveness of new artists and revive old ones, one victim of these trends has been the humble jingle. Instead of hiring a songwriter to craft some miniscule moment of "memetic" identification through music, marketers are trying to find existing music or commission new music to slide in under their products (Anderman, 2005). Instead, the most obvious marriage of brands is to couple current or "emerging" artists with similarly "positioned" products in the standard thirty second television advertisement. Car and mobile phone companies have been credited with launching the careers of many bands by using the band's music in an ad. When the Dandy Warhols's song "Bohemian Like You" was used by Vodaphone in Europe, it sparked a spate of publicity that pushed them from being a band with average sales playing mid-size venues to the top of the pop charts in several European countries and headlining the Reading Festival in only a few months (Dig!). When Dirty Vegas's song "Days Go By" appeared in a Mitsubishi ad, resulting sales pushed them into the Top Ten in the United States while Mavi jeans performed a similar service for Maroon 5. One of the more established areas of "media synchronization" is video games (Koranteng, 1993).[5] Capitol Records saw their band Ok Go top Billboard's new artist chart after "Get Over It" made it into Madden NFL 2003 (Block, 2002).

One of the most visible forms of brand partnership is the use of "classic" songs in new ads. The use of artists such as Nick Drake for VW, Led Zeppelin for Cadillac, The Rolling Stones for Microsoft, The Cars for Circuit City, Free for Wrigley's chewing gum, or Supertramp for The Gap "is extraordinarily cost-effective," said one industry representative. Advertisers can build on "immediate consumer recognition and retention" of familiar music and thus, "much less media time is required to establish a campaign" (Lichtman, 1998; Koranteng, 1993; Anderman, 2005). The exhumation of so many songs through television ads led some marketers to bemoan the difficulties they faced in finding fresh oldies to catch the ears of young consumers (Steinberg and Smith, 2006). Many labels began getting around the obstacles of excessive familiarity by pursuing slightly more obscure "indie" artists. As one Melbourne art director noted, "with the whole blurring on genres … it's becoming less clear-cut as to what mainstream is." In yet another permutation of "buying the cool factor," Jack White began selling Coke and the "fiercely independent" Lisa Miller started selling car insurance (Blackman, 2007).

The deals between bands and brands are becoming far more complex than a simple marriage of songs and products. For example, in 1999 BMG began developing "brand-sponsored interactive games" on the internet in which their artists appeared as characters in the game and presented exclusive performances or interviews on related websites (Wilson, 1999). In a similar vein, the sponsorship of tours and other live events has become an area of intense competition and creativity largely due to

---

5   The "advergaming" phenomenon is so lucrative that some in the gaming industry worry that "games are in danger of becoming the subsidized marketing wings" of the entertainment industry (Manktelow, 2005).

the unique nature of the events themselves (Porter, 2006). In 1995, VH1 sponsored not simply a tour, but the act of buying tickets for a tour. The network's "Tickets First" promotion was designed to create interest in the 1995 tour by Tom Petty and the Heartbreakers. The promotion was centered on a one hour show hosted by Moon Zappa which featured performance clips by the band and a live interview with Petty himself. Viewers were given a number to call to vie for 400 tickets on offer for each tour venue. Nearly half a million people called in 15 minutes in pursuit of 19,200 "early release" tickets (Stanley, 1995). Some promotional agreements display a level of integration between musicians and advertisers that is near total. Robbie Williams and T-Mobile based their 18 month partnership around the associative brand concept "closer." As T-Mobile's VP for Consumer Marketing said, "our corporate philosophy is all about helping the consumer get closer and lots of people want to know more about Europe's most popular music personality." To this end, the company worked out a deal with Williams to sponsor his tour and have the singer appear in their television ads. The company also agreed to stream clips from the singer's live shows to customers via "official tour mobile phones" along with behind-the-scenes footage of the artist in the studio and on tour (Immel, 2006). Collective Soul has gone one step further eschewing any pretence of independence by going to work directly for the Leo Burnett agency as "artist-in-residence" (Steinberg, 2005). According to some analysts, there is a growing unanimity amongst ad agencies, record labels, and brands that those involved "need to take the band/brand relationship further than just sponsoring a tour or CD." The trade marketing manager for Seagram's suggested that their "promotions are designed to reward participants with experiences money can't buy" (Goddard, 1999).

The coupling of musicians and various product brands has had a significant impact on a wide range of music industry practices as efforts at brand association have grown beyond the distribution of CDs with happy meals or MP3s with mobile phones. The practice has grown more widespread and has reshaped several foundational areas of the music industry, from promotions, production, and distribution to the structure and content of recording contracts. The mania for brand partnerships has even produced several innovative business models. For example, in 2006 EMI signed a contract with the metal band Korn that gives the label not only a piece of album sales, but a percentage of everything the band earns regardless of the source. They signed Robbie Williams to a similar deal several years earlier. The company claimed that both acts recouped the initial investment quite quickly (Porter, 2006; Seabrook, 2003). Deals such as these mark a clear departure from the heavy reliance on CDs as the primary revenue stream for record labels. When such practices become part of standard industry contracts, it should be clear that it is an integral piece of the industry's conceptual DNA. One of Def Jam's VPs for marketing claimed that the music industry was on the verge of creating nothing short of "a new model for revenue sharing in branded entertainment." Instead of simple, short term partnerships between one product line and one song, deals will involve profit sharing between the record label and associated brands. For some within the music industry, such deals are simply a contractual recognition of the obvious, "a true blurring of commercial content and artistic content" (Paoletta, 2006). Far from simply tacking a clever song by a cool artist onto an existing product in order to craft an attention grabbing television moment, record labels, advertisers, and brand sponsors are collaborating to create songs, ad campaigns, live events, full tours, special appearances, and exclusive material across a wide range of media in a seamless blend of sponsored content the sources of which are not always as easy to identify as one might assume (Blackman, 2007; Wilson, 1999).[6]

The recent slump in album sales has been widely cited as the source of the ardor with which the music, entertainment, and advertising industries have wooed one other. However, the success of the McDonald's campaigns, as well the long-standing efforts of other brands such as Pepsi and Coke, demonstrated the potential revenue gains of cross-promotions at least as far back as the early 1990s, well before album sales started their decline[7] (Anderman, 2005; Gotting, 2003b; Paoletta, 2006; Koranteng, 1993; Murfett, 2006; Porter, 2006). The institutionalization of the cross-promotion of music in television ads, films, video games, and just about any other promotional media form one might care to name was the obvious offspring of the consolidation of the music, advertising, television, film, and digital media industries. The primary benefit of cross-promotion for consolidated media industries is that the risk of launching a new product, artist, or song is shared between different companies or different arms of the same company. This makes promotion less risky, more cost effective, more profitable, and easier to justify in-house. Further, the "two main pillars of promotion," radio and television, "aren't the resources they once were" (Steinberg, 2005). As one entertainment marketing professional argued, he is "using other people's real estate and other people's noise and other people's budgets" to make his artists more visible (ibid.). Whereas the contractual standard for "acceptable" music in the past was "radio friendly" music, now it is "brand friendly" or "ad-ready music." Monte Lipman, president of Universal Republic, the home of artists such as Jack Johnson and Godsmack, dryly notes one simple, guiding fact: "The music business is healthy. It's the record industry that's in crisis" (Paoletta, 2006).

"Collaborative Marketing" through "Ambient Media"

The research and implementation strategies designed to combat the scarcity of attention and infiltrate consumers' lives are instructive to examine. This is especially true of those techniques used to create and shape the actual consumer relationships upon which successful brands depend. Successful brand partnerships are not

---

6 A telling example is the provenance of Avril Lavigne's songs from her debut album. She claimed in a *Rolling Stone* interview to be able to knock out a hit in a few hours. However, when a journalist actually spoke to the songwriters also given writing credits on the album, they claimed to have written the songs on commission with the record company adding her name only because it was a stipulation of their contracts. Not surprisingly, Lavigne's record label's attribution of creative credit in order to maintain Lavigne's "anti-Britney" image has been highly nuanced (Butler, 2003:9).

7 For example, every song on Moby's 1999 album *Play* was licensed for a commercial or soundtrack. Such thorough "synergy" marks the existence of a mature phenomenon, not a nascent one (Wright, 2006; Gotting, 2003b).

random occurrences. They are based on extensive research and data gathering. Recent techniques developed by the marketing profession to gather consumer data are designed to form closer, more exacting relationships with consumers. These relationships might be termed "content rich." They act as a complement to the intensive data collections methods surveyed in Chapter 1. These techniques are designed to ferret out the mundane, everyday details which can bring meaning and life to otherwise chilly demographic data. Even a cursory examination of phenomena such as coolhunting, relationship mining, or peer-to-peer marketing shows how the cultural studies shibboleth that institutions use strategies to dominate while individuals use tactics to resist has become a blurry maxim at best (see Poster, 2004; de Certeau, 1984). Instead, the advent of so-called "ambient media" has seen advertisers and marketers move into areas such as social networks theory, diffusion research, human geography, chaos theory, and germ theory to dig up both metaphors and practical case studies to guide their understanding of the ways in which ideas and products are disseminated. The goal remains to acquire those particular kinds of social meaning for a product that can make producers larger sums of money (Gladwell, 1997). There are two key facts about ambient media that are of interest here. First, media forms such as peer-to-peer networks like LimeWire and BitTorrent, internet search engines like Google or the search tools used by online retailers such as Amazon, websites like MySpace or Facebook, chat rooms, blogs, and mobile phones, all allow users to participate in vast, constantly evolving social networks. Second, these tools are designed in such a way as to make all participants the originating agents of their own unique experience of the networks of which they are a part simply by using the technology in the expected way. The information trails produced by every action and interaction that happens within these networks provide valuable intelligence from the field (Stonehouse, 2005; Kohler, 2003).[8]

In order to collect and use this information, many within various branches of the culture industry have been utilizing market research techniques that recognize the type, character, and quality of media uses by consumers. This includes studying media such as mobile phones, blogs, and their consequent social networks, but also the kinds of experiences consumers have with different products and the ways in which knowledge about these products spreads within social networks using techniques like coolhunting and consumer ethnography. According to a few of the less timid thinkers in the field, these networks represent nothing less that "a perfect storm of consumer power" (Neisser, 2006). This power is expressed primarily through acts of consumption. The music and entertainment industries can only find

---

8   On this note, one of Microsoft's "most ambitious research projects" is called "MyLifeBits," designed to create "a digital chronicle of one man's life." A mundane description of the goals of this project from the *Sydney Morning Herald* offers no hint of trepidation: "Every phone call is recorded, as well as every program he watches on television or listens to on the radio. Every web page he visits is logged. Everything he does on his computer—including which windows are active at anytime and the amount of mouse and keyboard activity—is logged." One of the project directors hints at the purpose of the endeavor: "Digital memories will yield benefits in a wide spectrum of areas, providing treasure troves of information about how people think and feel. The opportunities are restricted only by our ability to imagine them." The keywords here are "treasure" and "trove" (McMahon, 2007:13).

success, it is said, by submitting to the new-found power of consumers as expressed through new forms of consumption. The buzz facilitated through internet-based social networks is regularly attributed with the powers of creating instant fame, or infamy, of making or breaking new films, television shows, and CDs, validating or destroying the months of planning and strategy behind new product roll-outs with a few well-placed critiques in the blogosphere (Stonehouse, 2003; Thomas, 2003a; Purcell, 2003; Dale, 2003a; Rosen, 2000). "Consumers around the world are taking charge," exuded one visionary, "transforming their relationships with brands from ordinary buyer to reviewer, inventor, designer, ad creator, champion or critic" (Neisser, 2006). Few seemed to acknowledge candidly that internet traffic and power doesn't just flow one-way. But it was clear to some that if managed properly, a whole new world of data gathering possibilities had opened up, complete with ready-to-wear theoretical models of information use and consumer management to justify their use. Oddly, the hated anti-populist metaphor of consumer-as-prey returned with a vengeance.

One set of techniques comes almost directly from academic anthropology, altered somewhat for ease of use, deliberately shorn of the ethical commitments that now mark its academic parent. It relies on what might loosely be called "ethnography" to study consumers in their natural habitats. In the faddish jargon of the marketing industry these practices are called coolhunting or trendspotting. Those adept at employing such practices are the "new rock stars" of the advertising industry. As one coolhunter suggested, "to understand how an animal behaves, you have to go to the jungle—you don't go to the zoo—so we hang out with them, we play PlayStation with them in their homes." This particular coolhunter "stalks cool people out shopping, watching what they buy and grabbing them afterwards to ask why they bought brand X over Y—a technique called shadow and grab" (Clements, 2005). One eavesdrops on consumers as they shop, surreptitiously insinuating himself into conversations. Another installs hidden cameras, noting down facial expressions and bodily nuances, approaching those caught on camera later to ask for an interview (McLaren, 1998).

The goal of coolhunting and trendspotting is to figure out who the "innovators" and "early adopters" are and how they influence the rest of us to follow their lead. The problem is that the diffusion of ideas is thought to be an inherently interpersonal phenomenon. Ideas slide down the food chain of cool from person to person as the "innovators" guide the "early adopters" who then show the "late majority," that is the mass market, what cool is; ideally, even the "laggards" might eventually participate (Gladwell, 1997). Trendspotters don't look for cool products, they look for cool people, but the search for cool people is surprising in its complexity. A prominent writer about such social trends argues that the paradoxes of cool make traditional marketing techniques virtually useless because innovators "are the last people who can be convinced by a marketing campaign." However, they are the first to exert their cool influence because "their definition of cool is doing something nobody else is doing." Industry cannot manufacture cool because cool cannot be manufactured, it can only be observed in those who are already cool. But cool can only be observed in those who are cool by those who are themselves also cool, as cool cannot really be observed by anyone else. So the tortured logic of cool is determined by the taut hermeneutics of the cool themselves. To use Gladwell's pithy phrasing, "you have to be one to know one." The result is that a prominent and influential branch of the marketing industry has based its existence on a teenage aphorism that signals "the ascendancy, in the marketplace, of high school" (ibid.).

According to many, the kinds of social networks that have long surrounded the consumption of popular music are unusually susceptible to infiltration given the passion many have for their favorite artists. The harbingers of cool are not simply followed around to have their insights harvested, they are drafted and inculcated into the culture of focus groups and strategy meetings so they can proselytize to their friends, family, and colleagues on the benefits of this or that CD, band, or artist. One widely used technique is the creation of "street teams" to push particular products (McLaren, 1998). For example, M80 was a network of Backstreet Boys fans who dedicated themselves to convincing their peers to buy the band's products. They spent a great deal of time phoning in thousands of votes to video request programs such as "Canada's Hitlist" and MTVs "Total Request Live," phoning local radio stations to push for airplay, amassing e-mail lists for their own "viral" publicity campaigns, and visiting chatrooms "to lure other fans to join in their virtual promotional wilding" (Quart, 2003:53). The street-team networks organized by record labels are often seeded through the distribution of free CDs and DVDs in magazines and newspapers or MP3s on controlled access websites. The "user" has to register on a label's website to use the product, thus facilitating the process of personal data collection and enlarging the pool of potential "team members" (Fox, 2002).

Building on recent direct marketing efforts such as the "Music Marketing Network," record labels and advertising firms have been creating their own networks of volunteer fans who are gradually formed into "a veritable army of enthused promoters" (Bessman, 1994; Strauss, 2000). Using state-of-the-art geodemographic software, a central directorate can target and mobilize regional "grassroots" networks of fan volunteers through e-mail and text messages getting them to phone and e-mail their local radio stations to convince them to feature new releases. In return, volunteers receive various "rewards" such as "exclusive" song files, stickers, and CDs to keep and distribute to friends and other fans (Strauss, 2000). Sometimes these "volunteers" are "employed" as interns and receive formal instructions from their "employer" to push the right products at the right time as a formal part of a coordinated marketing plan (Pesselnick, 2001). Some entertainment and marketing companies have taken to "asking" their employees for their personal mobile phone and e-mail lists to "mine" their relationships for potentially well-placed contacts in other parts of the entertainment industry (Bulkeley and Wong, 2003). When all else fails, marketers simply pay their own employees and contractors to blog and chat for them on commission (Armstrong, 2006; Jones, 2000). The central attribute all of these efforts at marketing must have is the incandescent glow of popular approval. This is harder to produce than it sounds. As one advertising executive found, "things can become overhyped and backfire." If too many media outlets in too many places pick up on the self-generated buzz about the next big thing circulating in the chatrooms and blogs of the world, then "everyone is being offered the same exposure ... The campaign can die early because you aren't building loyalty. The way to keep it alive is by giving unique pieces of coverage and video content to the key players" (Garrity, 2006). Surely some coolhunter out there already knows who they are.

One of the more obvious channels used to reach new recruits is that ultimate form of "ambient media," the mobile phone. Like many forms of digital media, advertisers seem cognizant of the opportunities and the perils of using traditional advertising campaigns through new media. Mobile phones are becoming a primary form of multimedia consumption, acting as a social network hub, web surfer, MP3 player, video player, camera, news gatherer, and gaming console all in one (Head, 2005; Norrie, 2007). However, unsolicited text messages are most often unwanted and ineffective when not contextualized within an existing relationship with a customer. Some of the more familiar ideas for reaching consumers through their mobiles, such as exclusive content and special offers, were often not as successful as some expected ("Marketing's ugly duckling," 2006; Aster, 2002). But the consumption of music through mobiles has exceeded all expectations. In only a few years ringtones went from a monophonic novelty crafted mostly by customers to direct samples of popular songs accounting for billions of dollars in annual sales. The formal recognition of ringtones as a music format came in 2004 when Billboard launched a ringtone chart and the American Music Awards introduced its "Ringtone of the Year" category. If any further proof were needed, number one ringtones began to routinely outsell number one singles around the same time and, perhaps inevitably, a boy band became the first to release a single exclusively to mobile phones (Sullivan, 2005; Petradis, 2004; "Continuing ...," 2004; Hanman, 2006). While many in the music industry were taken by surprise, mobile phone companies were not. Mobile phones represent all the advantages of "ambient media." Users can personalize ringtones, assigning different tones to specific callers (Emling, 2004). Users can order music on the fly without interference, hassle, or even a credit card as the cost is simply added to the user's phone bill (Barton, 2004). A music "fingerprinting" technology has even come into common use, helping users identify and buy a song they might hear while they are out (Lowe, 2003). More important, the music industry was finally able to move out in front of at least one digital technology, helping to design systems that will not allow users to transfer acquired content to other users or even to their own SIM cards. "The songs are supposed to be disposable," said one industry representative (Manktelow, 2004).

Manufacturing Desire by Managing Subjectivity

The latest tools purported to save the music industry from the problems of selling its own products have been built on the intellectual foundations of "collaborative marketing." Using processes called "collaborative filtering," websites like Amazon. com and CBS's Last.fm are designed to allow user actions and recommendations to drive the evolution of their navigation tools, shaping music categories and establishing the boundaries of groups of like-minded users. The humble notation "Other customers who bought this product also bought ..." on each Amazon page is based on a great deal of information drawn from massive, constantly evolving databases which chronicle user actions (Locke, 2001:78–9). Similarly, Last.fm makes users download software which monitors their use of media players like iTunes or WinAmp. "Each time they play a song," one report notes, the software "relays the information to the Last.fm database, where it is used to build a profile and match each user to people with similar tastes" (Jinman, 2006). One outgrowth of this model is Pandora.com which uses actual musical characteristics to guide the evolution of user navigation tools. The benefactor of this model of musical taste mediation is the Music Genome Project whose director claims that it can "capture the essence of music at its most fundamental level" (Castelluccio, 2006). Those running the project asked expert musicians, music theorists, music critics, and what they call "music programmers" to analyze songs and profile them based on large sets of "predefined attributes." According to the project founder, Tim Westergren, "we ended up assembling literally hundreds of musical attributes or 'genes' into a very large musical genome. Taken together these genes capture the unique and magical musical identity of a song" (ibid.; Bruno, 2006d). These musical attributes number over 400 and are a broad measure which includes most traditional musical elements which describe particular types of sound, but also include categories like "angry lyrics and vocal-centric aesthetic" (Jinman, 2006). The project tracks its users' actions and uses the information they provide to fine tune its understandings of which musical attributes matter to which users in which circumstances. Users can respond to the choices Pandora provides, adding songs they feel fit to their playlists. They can also tell Pandora why they made the choices they did and the process of refining the algorithm continues apace (Hipp, 2006; Castelluccio, 2006).

Using terms like "community" and "member," Pandora's designers like to appear as if they only care about the music. Westergren argues that they proceed "in the most objective way possible, without letting an artist's popularity, image, or marketing budget affect whether or not we included a particular song in a playlist." In essence, they are claiming to take no heed as to how members of their "community" make their musical choices or actually experience music in the real world. Instead, Pandora's designers want to create an "objective" system designed "to figure out what you like about music and give you more" without referring to the subjective experience of music. Their work is guided by a panel of experts who ply their trade with as little intrusion from the outside world as possible (Serpick, 2006). When that world does intrude, it is for very specific purposes. Sony recently signed a deal with Pandora to license all of its music used on the site for an undisclosed percentage of its advertising revenues. Logitech has developed a portable player capable of receiving a custom radio stream from the website. It is unclear where Pandora's owners store their "community" preference data, who might have access to it, and how much they have to pay to get it (Walsh, 2006; Bruno, 2006a).

These devices inevitably have a feedback effect on what music gets produced. Increasingly, new artists will have to fit themselves into different kinds of slots in different ways than before. Whether these new slots will be substantially different in function than existing ones is less than certain, despite the scientific protestations of the algorithm massagers. One endeavor which sums up the endless quest for market certainty is a software package designed by the Spanish company "Polyphonic Human Media Interface." It is called "Hit Song Science" (HSS). Credited with correctly predicting the success of Norah Jones's first album, HSS is now being used by all major record labels "to screen new musical acts and pick singles they hope will click with listeners" ("This software …," 2004). HSS has isolated 20 aspects of song construction and, based on a mathematical survey of 30 years' worth of Billboard chart hits, can measure the chances a song will become a hit on a scale from one to ten. Some of those charged with finding new artists claim that the technology simply reinforces decisions they would make anyway. One label employee points out that "95 per cent of hit songs in the past 50 years are high scorers," a tautology that passes without acknowledgement. HSS only exists to create "hits" as defined by songs that have already been proved "hits." The category "hits" is apparently self-evident and self-justifying. HSS is a clear reflection of the priorities of the contemporary music industry, helping its employees craft an insular method of removing doubt from their market. Many who have used HSS claim that it has already improved their ratio of hits to non-hits; given the performance of the big labels over the years, it could hardly have made things worse (Tatchell, 2005).

All of this strategic manipulation, begging, and pleading is, of course, predicated on the existence of music people might actually want to consume, at least in the estimation of those producing it. The targets of this infrastructure of persuasion are not the vagaries of subjectivity and personal taste, but the inevitable risks to predictable profitability. In the place of a foolproof system of hit prediction, there is a messy, complex, self-perpetuating system of advance self-congratulation and speculative praise heaped on artists in an effort to manage audience subjectivity and remove as much risk from the market as is practicable. The pervasive use of charts, award shows, canonization through year's-end best-of lists, decade's-end best-of lists, century's-end best-of lists, best songs of all time lists, albums you must hear before you die lists, critics' picks, listeners' polls, the proliferation of "new" genres and radio formats, are all tools geared towards differentiating products in terms of brand value, public profile, and acknowledged meaning. These tools, as well as those such as the Music Genome Project and Hit Song Science, represent the long-held dream of rationalizing music consumption, tools that embody what Adorno called "pseudo-individualization" and "pre-digestion." They are the very tools which have produced such specious "genres" as "grindcore," "metalcore," "dark ambient," "folk metal," "melodic death metal," "psychedelic trance," "nu-nrg," "stupid house," "acid house," "nu soul" and many, many others (Jinman, 2004a; Scherzinger, 2005). These devices are used by those selling music to make a very careful type of argument about the value of their product. They try to demonstrate what is "good," without wanting to define it. They want to show us what is "popular," without trying to specify exactly what it is. They want to tell us what to consume, knowing they can't, because if they do define what is good or popular they are also implicitly defining what is bad or unpopular. They will immediately chop off a large chunk of their potential market and thus increase risk. Instead, they chip diligently around the edges of market risk in as many ways as possible. They try to manage audience subjectivity by exerting a defining power and influence over the mediums through which their musical materials travel and the contexts within which it acquires meaning, aggressively trying to shape perceptions of those materials to fit into slots they themselves have created.

Part III
The Spectacle as Consumption Environment

Chapter 5

Constructing the "Idol" Empire

I'm very global in my outlook (Simon Fuller, creator of the "Idol" phenomenon).[1]

One of the more incongruous expressions of the "Idol" phenomenon took place on December 26, 2003. Eleven newly-crowned "Idols" hailing from northern Europe, the UK, North America, South Africa, Australia, as along with the awkwardly named "Pan Arabian Idol," gathered in London to perform for a television audience "estimated" to number anywhere between 100 and 200 million viewers; the size of the potential audience depended on which press release you read (Needham, 2004). One judge from each of the 11 local shows offered their evaluations. World Idol, as it was called, sought nothing less than to discover "the best singer in the world" (World Idol, 2003). The format of the show followed a familiar path. Each "Idol's" road to victory was profiled in a short video, the tone and character of which was identical to similar "Idol Journey" videos presented on local programs. Then each "Idol" walked out onto a fairly standard "Idol" stage to perform one of their signature tunes to a pre-recorded backing track after which each of the judges offered their mostly acrid commentary. The forum was decidedly unfriendly. Few of the judges offered anything other than the familiar brand of flamboyant dissatisfaction for which "Idol" is famous, often getting into arguments with judges who insisted on conspicuously praising "their Idols." The program received withering criticism from television critics and from some influential "Idol" luminaries. World Idol was a rare failure of the form that was never repeated.

World Idol failed largely because the format of the show did not allow for the production of the kinds of public knowledge borne of audience experience that forms the foundational connections between contestants and fans. Viewers were instead confronted with their local "Idols" competing against ten relative strangers whose extensive personal histories could only be noted in passing. Further, the rules of the show did not allow viewers to vote for their home "Idols" in order to prevent larger countries from outvoting smaller ones. By the time the producers had crammed the show full of ads, video diaries, the carefully edited criticisms of the judges, and the actual performances, there was very little time to establish new audience relationships or deepen old ones. But we can learn several important things from World Idol if we view it as an emblem of the specific type of globalization that produced it. The most important clues come from the performances of the "Idols" themselves. Despite their diverse geographical origins, World Idol's contestants offered a marked uniformity in their performance styles, repertoire choices, and the general impressions they were trying to convey. All of the contestants except for

---

1   Sanghera (2002a).

the "Pan Arabian Idol" sang in English. Few chose anything other than familiar international pop standards to perform. It was an odd, enlightening spectacle to see contestants barely fluent in spoken English belt out pitch perfect impersonations of Robbie Williams, Elton John, and Christina Aguilera. Each moved around the stage with confidence, smiling at the cameras, using a familiar array of standard pop star gestures known the world over. There was the bright smile with the head tilt, the sassy change of direction, and the march forward to the front of the stage to hit one's mark prior to the climactic phrase. The gestures, the songs through which they were expressed, and the vehicles for their expression were not German, Canadian, or South African in origin or form, but embodied the generic, low-risk aesthetics of the international branch of the contemporary popular music industry.

While World Idol made the uniformity of the "Idol" phenomenon plainly obvious, the show was also defined by an equally obvious, but tightly controlled form of unpredictability. This unpredictability offered audiences the opportunity to contribute to a chimerical choice, not between success and failure, but between more or less credible versions of success. As I will show in the following two chapters, it is the tension between uniformity and unpredictability that defines the kinds of relationships that form the core of the "Idol" phenomenon. As I will argue here, the success of "Idol" has been shaped from its inception by the desire of its producers to manage any potential risks almost out of existence by carefully controlling the images performers project, the mechanics of the contest, and management of the "Idol" brand. They have done so by adhering to the principles and practices of a very specific type of corporate globalization. It is not the type of globalization of popular music produced by subtle, contingent, and complicated interactions between musicians and fans who eventually help spread "their" music around the world, nor it is produced by the power politics negotiated between a tiny minority of powerful musicians and their record labels in order to produce the kinds of "global" success now expected of high-profile artists. "Idols" are explicitly developed as brands. They are acquired the way a corporation might acquire any brand. They are purchased as contracted labor and gradually fitted into a pre-existing, pre-formatted communications campaign. These new brands are tested in the marketplace, altered to fit consumer requirements, and are eventually replaced through an inevitable process of planned obsolescence. The key thing that distinguishes "Idol" is that its producers make the entire process unbearably public.

"Idol" pushes at the analytical limits of the handful of terms which dominate academic discussion of the globalization of culture, such as "glocalization," "hybridity," the "global ecumene," and "creolization" (Featherstone et al., 1995; Hannerz, 1992; Patterson, 1994). The common use of these key concepts centers on analyses of the "negotiations" undertaken between individuals and larger forces set within a largely optimistic or occasionally triumphant narrative. But if we are to take a concept like negotiation seriously, we have to consider the conditions under which such negotiations take place, the relative positions of the parties involved, and the forces which shape the outcomes. "Idol" doesn't demonstrate any of these concepts to be false, merely limited in their ability to deal with the dynamic forces which have underpinned the specific form of corporate globalization that made it possible. It takes a willful denial to view "Idol's" various consumerist expressions and entreaties as negotiations. "Idol's" producers do not require the give and take of cultural exchange and mutual influence. Their arena is not built on some delicate bargain between parties seeking some measure of mutual benefit in a risky venture whose final form is uncertain. The "Idol" relationships are commercial transactions between parties seeking guarantees of comfort and certainty. "Creolization" in some fancied "global ecumene" does not lead to familiarity, it leads to a fickle inconstancy of consequence. "Idol's" producers do not seek this kind of risk. They have chosen an altogether more plainly worn path.

The Strategic Imperatives of Global Brand Management

Many well informed business and music industry analysts once doubted that "Idol" would survive for long. Given the fates of shows like Star Search and Popstars, such concerns may have seemed warranted once. However, most such worries defined survival in terms of contestants continuing to sell albums after their "Idol" auras wore off. It should be clear by now that the distinct lack of long-term success on the part of the vast majority of high profile "Idol" contestants has not proven a hindrance to the show's longevity. It is not surprising then that many of these same industry analysts have since asked in varied tones of wonder how an inexpensive, poorly produced reality television show of complete unknowns singing second-rate versions of other people's music became a dominant global television franchise (Peers, 2003; Stanley, 2003). A large part of the explanation for "Idol's" success comes from the strategic principles which underpin the processes of global brand management. One main reason for its worldwide success has been the abilities of its producers to exert a brand power far beyond the norm. In their study of Starbucks, Thompson and Arsel (2004) demonstrate, in contrast to much argument about the globalization of consumerism, that "the interpenetrations of the global and the local do not happen in strictly symmetrical fashion." Some entities, corporations, brands, or particular individuals are simply more powerful than others. Their power is wielded specifically to assume a hegemonic brand position, thereby shaping the contexts in which consumption of related brands occurs and directing the development of both local and global markets (Thompson and Arsel, 2004:633). This is a power consumers or smaller competitors cannot have in equal measure. Brands such as Starbucks exert power well beyond themselves. They inspire imitators and force competitors to mimic their tactics in order to overcome drastic imbalances in economies of scale. The wave of "Idol" imitators that flooded the global airwaves in 2002–2003 shows how "Idol" exerted such power, forcing numerous competitors to expend substantial resources to develop music-based reality shows, resources that were, in almost every case, wasted (Hay, 2003a).[2]

"Idol" has been a success for many of the same reasons Starbucks has. Starbucks did not invent coffee, they reinvented the experience of the coffee house. "Idol" did

---

2 Industry analysts have suggested that "Idol" inspired the resurrection of *Star Search* and *Making the Band* as well as the creation of *Nashville Star, Today's Superstar, American Juniors, America's Most Talented Kid, America's Most Talented Senior,* Telemundo's *Protangonistas de la Musica* and *Born to Diva* (Hay, 2003a).

the same with televised talent quests. Neither Starbucks nor "Idol" were responding to any perceived crisis on the supply-side of their respective markets. There was no shortage of coffee or music prior to their existence. Each was reacting to a whole other set of concerns on the demand side. It has been the ability of each brand to manage the experience of consumption in novel ways that has made them hegemonic. As Thompson and Arsel show, brand hegemony is particularly important for brands whose producers can only distinguish their products through our experience of them rather than producing some practical measure of innovation or invention in the character of the product itself (Thompson and Arsel, 2004:632). In this sense at least, "Idol" is the Starbucks of the music industry. It is not some tacky omen of things to come, but a perfectly adapted expression of the economic exigencies of the present.

The central forces which have shaped "Idol's" global expansion are those which have shaped the globalization of the entertainment industry generally. As noted in previous chapters, the vertical integration of global cultural production has made managing the experience of consumption not only much more specific and exacting, but possible on a scale once unimaginable. The sea change in the technology used to produce, distribute, and experience music and a music industry now embedded in the larger structures of the entertainment industry, confront music producers with a markedly different terrain on which to work their magic. This terrain has proved very amenable to the creators of "Idol." Just as important, the debt load most media mergers dump on new corporate partnerships produces an intense pressure to make greater profits at lower costs. This is a central feature of an economically convulsive global media sphere. The oligopoly of major music labels has become practiced at finding ways to turn costs into profits in response to a corporate practice that presents extensive possibilities for cross-media promotion. The reach for greater profits at lower costs through economies of scale and intrafirm synergies made possible through vertical integration have long defined the strategic imperatives of the music and entertainment industries (Haring, 1996). These goals have predominated largely due to increased competition for finance capital in deregulated capital markets, a defining feature of the phase of economic globalization that began after the global recession of the late 1970s (Greider, 1997; Herman and McChesney, 1997:52–61).[3] When viewed through the prism of these core tenets of global business strategy, "Idol" is a remarkably clear reflection of the priorities of a music industry that has morphed into a very different beast than it was just a few decades ago. "Idol" provides an opportunity for its producers to turn the often expensive and unpredictable process of finding and cultivating new talent into a profitable promotional spectacle and "marketing juggernaut" (Maley and Davis, 2003:3).

They have done so by exploiting what was, even in the late 1990s, a comparatively unexplored market in pre-adolescent children. "Tweeners" were said to hold anywhere between $150 and $260 billion dollars in spending power in the early 2000s and were credited with being a driving force in the music industry, breaking

---

3   Greider's book is a lucid and clear introduction to the central role of deregulated finance capital in the global economy. Haring's hyperventilating critique of the music industry takes on added significance when these two unrelated books are read in tandem (see his Chapter 4: "Smoke and Music").

acts in which mainstream radio and television did not show any interest (Taylor, 2001; Ault, 2003). Tweeners were perceived to be a high-risk, if lucrative, "moving target" (Ault, 2003). "Idol's" creator, Simon Fuller, had already honed his now keen abilities to move with them (Sanghera, 2002b; Scott, 2002). His success with the Spice Girls and S Club 7 showed that this market could be safely exploited by seamlessly integrating marketing and programming content (Pendleton, 2003). As numerous studies before and since have shown, most pre-adolescent children either don't recognize or don't care about this distinction (Ebenkamp, 2003). "Idol's" dominant brand status grows from the show's integration of a variety of brands acting in service of the larger "Idol" brand. These brand partnerships are spread throughout the show's various arms providing what one economics reporter called an "impressive number of revenue streams." These include money from telephone and text message voting, exclusive deals with internet portals and service providers, exclusive sponsorships deals for touring and public appearances, extensive use of product placement, traditional spot ads on the shows themselves, and extraordinarily lucrative licensing fees from the sales of the show around the world (Sanghera, 2002a; "Pop Idol rings up …," 2003). Deals with Nestlé and Nokia in Britain, Coca-Cola and Ford in the United States, and Maybelline and Mazda in Australia resulted in such entities as the American Idol's Coca-Cola "Red Room" where the contestants nervously await their fate, or Australian Idol's "Mazda Idol Journey," short videos which recount the sorry fates of expelled candidates (Kleinman, 2003; Pendleton, 2003). One record label head summed up the bargain "Idol" had made with the music industry. "'It's a cash machine,' the unnamed executive said. 'You take away A&R research costs, you increase rights income and engage consumers in compelling TV. The artistic rub is that its junk karaoke'" (Burt, 2003).

"Idol" has proven to be anything but junk to investors. "Idol" was credited with allowing America's Fox Television network to survive several serious financial crunches and thrive as a genuine competitor to its more established rivals. "Idol's" managing company, 19 Entertainment, posted year after year of spectacular revenue growth. These high profile accomplishments attracted a rich acquisition deal by CKX Inc., a brand management firm owned by Robert Sillerman (Day, 2003; Larsen, 2003; "American Idol and Elvis …," 2005; Szalai, 2007). CKX, which stands for "content is king," also owns the rights to David Beckham, Elvis Presley, and Muhammed Ali. The deal was financed by Bear Sterns and Co., one of the most powerful private equity firms in the world. One can comfortably speculate a deal with such serious people was one of Fuller's long-term goals. The deal has apparently given Sillerman license to prognosticate at some length in public about what the music industry should be doing to improve its fortunes. He told the New York Times his earth-shattering ideas about how entertainment content will soon be something "distributed through cellphones, BlackBerries, computers, whatever" (Sisario, 2005). In 2006, he kindly lectured Billboard's "Music and Money Symposium" about how "the true muscle in music—the creators of it—will assume their logical position in the economic food chain. They create it," he opined. "They deserve the lion's share of wealth from it" (Bruno, 2006b). Given the management and financial structure of Sillerman's recent acquisition, one can only assume he has a very particular notion of what the term "creator" might mean in practice. The importance of Sillerman's pronouncements lies not so much in their content as in his increasing power to enforce them.

The Idol Aesthetic: Medium and Materials

When Simon Fuller began pushing the idea of a more ambitious global "Idol empire" to the music trade press, he said he would need three things to be successful: quality singers, viewer empowerment, and a "televisual" show "people would watch like a soap opera" (Hay, 2003b:84). Not coincidentally, Fuller has outlined here the three core relationships which must be consummated for any iteration of "Idol" to be successful: the relationships between "Idols" and the show itself, between the Idols and their fans, and between the music industry and consumers. These relationships comprise the "Idol" medium, that network of social and cultural conventions which defines the realm over which "Idol's" materials and the aesthetic qualities ascribed to them are mediated. This collection of social networks shapes and conveys the meanings of variously experienced aesthetic conventions which in turn facilitate connections between "Idols" and their fans. The Idol medium is not simply the stories the show tells us, that "special moment" of performance which captures our imagination, the carefully constructed pop star persona each contestant wraps around themselves, the songs, or even the trappings of reality television. The medium that makes "Idol" work consists of the assumptions and processes that structure the experience of recognizing what is important and meaningful about the story, the persona, the song, or that special moment. "Idol's" materials tell us what is important and meaningful about the show only when they are circulated through that larger, all-encompassing medium. For "Idol" to succeed, the show's medium and materials have to help us recognize these meanings successfully enough to engage our direct participation in the show. As the next two chapters show, this has proven to require an enormous amount of effort.

As I demonstrate in the next two chapters, the Idol medium shapes and directs the look, sound, and feel of the "Idol" materials. "Idol's" animating purposes, from which I am drawing out its larger meanings, are inextricably bound up in the most minute particularities of each version of the phenomenon. This is the genius of the format. It is a supremely flexible and adaptable concept, but it is also unchanging. Audiences always know what they are getting, but they never quite know what to expect. The producers acknowledge the agency of their audiences and seek to capitalize on this agency by offering a broad range of opportunities to participate in the program. These opportunities to participate become gradually more intimate and specific over the life of each contest and are only specified by the audience through their actions as consumers. Strategies for inciting effective participation can be discerned in all areas of the show, from the choices made by producers, judges, and contestants alike. The overall strategic environment shapes the ways in which the program produces musical celebrities through a long series of aesthetic choices. These choices extend to the conveniently ambiguous and malleable regime which shapes the success and failure of the hopefuls as well as contestants' choices of repertoire and modes of self-presentation, shaped and motivated by the practical demands of the contest itself. These systems of value are couched within forms of "art talk" which are vague, pervasive, and impossible to dislodge from the larger strategic imperatives which contextualize and produce them. Crucially, it is "Idol's" system of aesthetic order in the guise of gradually branded contestants acting within a rule-bound series of media events through which the larger values of the music industry are made comprehensible and material.

Each "Idol" franchise is a long and complicated process of establishing and maintaining what Couldry has called "media rituals," social relationships created and facilitated by symbolic means (Couldry, 2002a). "Idol's" rituals are presented through a series of familiar actions on the part of audience members, performers, and judges all placed within a formal terrain of consumption connecting the audience to "the wider transcendent patterns within which the details of social life make sense" (ibid.:3). These ritual frames and the terrain in which they do their work are informed and structured by an evolving regime of strategic thought and action designed to clarify and contextualize the very idea of what it means to be a pop star in an environment in which many of the traditional methods of producing musical celebrity have been shaken to their foundations. "Idol" claims to put things right for us. As Silverstone (1993) has noted, television often acts as a "transitional object" sustaining what he has called our "ontological security" (Silverstone 1993:590–92). Our experience of the world, our formed sense of the common and the practical everyday knowledge that sustains these implicit social connections to the larger world are given support and confirmation by a whole range of symbolic expression. "Idol" is one such semiotic security blanket.

The music industry is faced with the varied threats of global piracy, the expansion of the entertainment industry to "ambient media" such as mobile phones and MP3 players, as well as increasing amounts of money spent on competing content such as DVDs, ringtones, and video games. Selling CDs has become almost a sideline to the very profitable multimedia use and reuse of the industry's vast stores of intellectual property through all manner of media, most of which barely existed at the end of the last century. The "Idol" phenomenon shows us how the music industry can incorporate existing pieces of a rapidly changing media environment to establish and maintain connections with audiences through almost every type of media and the varied formats and inventive ways in which we consume and use them.[4] Through these, "Idol's" varied relationships gradually grow ever more intimate, active, and reciprocal over the course of the contest by encouraging increasingly specific acts by consumers to complete a continuing chain of transactions. In order to overcome the perceived attention deficit, the producers of "Idol" have created a series of texts

---

4 *Australian Idol* has used the following forms to construct its promotional culture: live and pre-recorded television in reality, magazine, music video, and documentary formats, extensive product placement, traditional spot advertising, live and prerecorded radio programming, websites, chat rooms, electronic bulletin boards, e-mail promotions, ringtones and text messaging on mobile phones, DVDs, CDs, live performances, and print media campaigns producing extensive coverage of many aspects of the contest. Of particular interest are the fan pages on the official website on which audience members can play a variety of contests and betting games.

and events that exist in parallel to a related series of continuously available sites of consumption. Producers allow for many kinds of participation while constantly offering more specific and more active levels of involvement.

"Idol" is an audacious expression of the high-profit, low-cost corporate strategies described above. Instead of the costs and risks of traditional A&R, "Idol" transforms the process of finding and nurturing new talent into a profitable spectacle. However, for each franchise to work, producers must appear to mesh local music industries and fans with global structures of production and expression. We can see in "Idol" a far more strategic regime of globalization than many accounts in cultural studies present. My analysis conforms to neither the cultural populism which places consumers at the center of popular culture, nor to political economic analysis which posits a dominant role for the culture industries. Instead, in the next two chapters I analyze how the dynamic relationships between one hegemonic music industry brand and its audiences are produced through specific materials as they circulate through an equally specific and carefully structured medium. "Idol" has given the music industry a compelling story into which the show's producers can integrate an imposing palette of products circulated through a wide range of consumption venues. The "Idol" franchise system has created a consumption environment which, for the show's producers, has become its own reward. "Idol's" creators have found novel ways to produce and reproduce the structures of feeling created by the relationships between fans and pop stars upon which their industry is dependent for survival. It can act as a public midwife to the births of new pop stars, foregrounding its assumed role as transparent, earnest, and benevolent facilitator of the best undiscovered talent it can find, and through this giving us all the drama, tears, pleasure, and pain we can stand.

Chapter 6

Building the Authentic Celebrity: The Structure of a Spectacle

He is one of the first people in artist management to treat artists as entertainment brands … He understands the big picture (Lucian Grainge, CEO of Universal Music UK, on Simon Fuller).[1]

My office is in the Seymour Centre, a theater complex just south of Sydney's CBD. The Ten Network uses this esteemed building to film the second round of Australian Idol, the "Vocal Boot Camp," in which a field of over 100 aspirants was cruelly slashed down to 40 contestants in the first series and 30 in the second. For three days in July, camera crews and technical staff crowded in and around the building, with contestants dancing and singing inside and out. As I went to and from my office, from my office to the printer, or to the kitchen, I could hear singer after singer giving it their all downstairs. When I entered the building, I had to pass by the broadcast truck and its massive transmitter. I often lingered at the door to watch the small monitor on which the raw footage was visible. In the vestibule backstage which leads to the elevator to our department, the sound was particularly clear. I often heard the demonstrations of contestants and remonstrations of judges humming through the architectural quirks of the building. Outside, I often saw more than one group of young singers huddled in small circles, intensely preparing their group auditions which they had only a few hours to prepare. Mobile camera crews hovered over them until an officious looking stage manager came to collect the singers for their audition.

This was all the more exciting and interesting because the Seymour Centre auditions are very secret, coming several weeks before the televised run of the program begins. This odd experience briefly removed the carefully constructed frame from Australian Idol, allowing me to see the extensive infrastructure that went into filming this bunch of performers who, at this point in time at least, had yet to appear on our television screens. Also, I knew from the first series that these three days of filming would result in, at most, 90 minutes of breathlessly-narrated television. These ample efforts seemed all the more strange because, if the producers really wanted secrecy, they should have simply avoided the expense of using the highly visible Seymour Centre and moved to their own studios in the comparatively removed suburb of Ryde. What later became clear to me was the extremely calculated nature of the Seymour Centre auditions. The venue was chosen to promote the illusion that the contest was only about talent, an argument that even the most avid promoters of

---

1   Sanghera (2002a).

"Idol" acknowledge simply is not true (Hay, 2003b). The time and expense of hiring the Seymour Centre was more than amply returned in the extensive use throughout the life of the program of the footage collected during those three days in July. Every time footage of those days was broadcast, I was reminded of the extensive narrative construction of Australian Idol, the architecture of which I will outline in this chapter.

The Well-Structured Spectacle

Australian Idol ostensibly lays bare the process of creating a pop star. Yet with so much made visible, much is rendered opaque. Specifically, "Idol" is defined by the construction and use of a medium which consists of many carefully tuned strategies of narration, publicity, and promotion. These strategies create, shape, and contextualize a broad collection of materials designed to help construct credible musical celebrities whose emergence is sanctified through a seemingly open process of public ratification. This medium, like any other, is designed to make some things more visible and more meaningful than others. It does so by constructing the three key relationships described in the previous chapter, the relationships between the "Idols" and the show itself, between the "Idols" and their fans, and between the music industry and consumers. The ways in which each relationship is constructed and maintained makes crucial aspects of "Idol" meaningful even as the producers constantly try to erase the imprint of their own strategic designs. They try to naturalize the success of their "Idols" by asserting the unassailable credibility of their innate talent to render transparent the mechanisms used to construct the meaning and value of that talent.

The next chapter deals with the musical and textual content of the first two series of Australian Idol, but in this chapter I track the narrative sweep of these first two series. I focus on the well crafted and finely tuned publicity strategies present at every stage of both contests. I will analyze the ways in which the structural context of the show creates a story that links the contestants to the audience, the audience to the show itself, and then to the music industry more generally through its various, celebrated mechanisms of public participation. It is through this complicated array of marketing exercises that "Idol" shows itself as a bundle of highly successful methods for making money from popular music. What I present here is a portrait of a well-structured spectacle. The producers of this spectacle use varied tactics for grabbing the attention of a significant part of the Australian viewing public. They rely on the galvanizing stories of ordinary people, a few of whom are transformed into stars by rising to the challenge of public celebrity, the more successful fitting themselves into the pre-existing mould of pop star, establishing and confirming public expectations of what exactly this fraught term actually means. The goal of "Idol's" pervasive, grandiose publicity campaigns is to craft a series of authentic celebrities who will become credible pop stars, cheerfully dealing with all of the joy, chaos, and adulation such a persona entails. It is the meticulously structured, overarching narrative of the contest itself which ties its disparate expressions together. Relating the stories of contestants rising through the ranks of pretenders is intended to shape our experience of "Idol," maintaining and heightening our interest as the drama unfolds. It is this narrative of aesthetic order, in the face of perceived industrial chaos that is intended to draw us into the spectacle. Instead of a fairly simple and potentially monotonous series of judged performances upon which we are asked to comment through statistical tabulations of our sentiments, "Idol" presents us with performers who grow into real pop stars right before our eyes, just as we expect them to. We are asked to embrace the most credible pop star personae a few form around themselves throughout the competition. The producers cast the music industry itself as a neutral carrier of the story; it is the public that writes the ending.

The "Idol" medium is emblematic of an industry that is becoming dependent on ever more elaborate and subtle regimes of publicity.[2] Selling CDs is almost financially ancillary to the "Idol" phenomenon, acting only as one profit center among many. Through a close reading of two iterations of this phenomenon, we can track the progress and deployment of the strategies used to shape what becomes a series of "authentic celebrities" (Tolson, 2001).[3] We will see how the presentation, branding, and shaping of "Idol's" attractive young charges filters through a spectacle that is primarily a vehicle for the music industry to craft intimate, active, and long-term relationships with audiences, animated by a continuous process of strategic publicity in which we are all invited to participate. Through a seamless arc of media events, Australian Idol is presented as a non-stop story of ambition and success. While there are peaks and troughs in the publicity campaigns, they never seem to stop.

In many quarters, the "Idol" phenomenon has become a byword for bullshit. The competition appears so carefully controlled as to be rigged. The contestants are not generally seen as "real" musicians by many in large part because their experience appears to be so transparently commercial. As such, the traditional mythology of authenticity in popular music on the whole is implicitly unavailable to the producers of "Idol." So the show's producers continually play on existing notions of what constitutes an authentic relationship between public and star to construct a different kind of celebrity. The credibility of the show is based on the ability of the show's producers to demonstrate that the mechanisms they are using to create pop stars are valid. It is just as important that the show be perceived as honestly rendered as it is for the winner to be seen as a legitimate musical celebrity. The two tasks are inseparable. This is because the "Idol's" main actor is the music industry itself which uses contestants as vehicles for crafting relationships with consumers. The more you watch the program the more clearly you can see the processes through which the contestants are crafted, promoted, and sold. It gradually becomes clear that these populist icons are emblematic of an industry reinventing itself in a media

---

2   This paradox has been crucial to "Idol's" success. For example, the wardrobe choices of the contestants become an increasingly important aspect of each campaign as the contest wears on. Yet, despite extensive features on the fashion designers involved in the production on *Inside Idol* and elsewhere, this aspect of the production received almost no critical comment. The appearance of each potential "Idol" was simply naturalized. Such transparency marks the ultimate success of product placement advertising.

3   I do not use this term in precisely the same way as Tolson. However, I have relied on his exploration of the idea of "being yourself" which has been transposed slightly here to "becoming yourself." This idea is explored at length in the next chapter.

environment that presents remarkable challenges and surprising opportunities. The strategies for producing and promoting Australian Idol suffuse the contest. From the cattle call auditions through to the Grand Final at the Sydney Opera House, those chosen to continue in the contest are required constantly to re-establish their credibility and develop or discover, seemingly in full public view, those mystical qualities that will inevitably lead to pop stardom. We can follow this animating dynamic from start to finish.

The Prelude

The publicity campaigns for the first series of Australian Idol began well before the program itself was broadcast. Expectations had to be stoked and curiosity encouraged. There were two key themes that producers would hammer home throughout the long months of the contests. First, they would continually explain how the technical aspects of the process of choosing an "Idol" worked, long past the point one might assume such explanations were necessary. Producers clearly wanted to promote participation and advertise their openness to all. Second, they focused on establishing the credibility of the contest by loudly and repeatedly proclaiming its apparent, glaring necessity and its perhaps less obvious honesty. The producers of Australian Idol had an advantage. Both American Idol and the UK's Pop Idol were broadcast in Australia before series one of Australian Idol began. The producers of Australian Idol were able to anticipate criticism and clarify issues right from the beginning. The introduction of the first series of Australian Idol was presented to an audience presumed to be familiar with the phenomenon in general, but perhaps a bit hazy on the specifics. A pronounced theme in the early rounds of publicity for both series was educational. It seemed that potential audience members needed to have the basic concepts of voting and the shape and structure of the competition repeatedly explained to them. This was true both for the format of the program and the auditions process as audience members and "auditionees" alike were prepared and coached on what was to be expected of them (Jinman, 2003). These instructional guides to the show continued to appear throughout the contest, suggesting a pleasingly helpful and ecumenical attitude toward latecomers and the unconvinced. It was further expected that the generic contours of the "Idol" phenomenon would be filled out as expected. At least one judge was assumed to provide the role of a harpy, modeled on the bitter and flamboyantly cruel Simon Cowell. The program would be "every bit as effective and all-encompassing" as programs such as Big Brother to "drive consumer interaction with the program on multiple levels," according to the executive producer ("Australian Idol to hit …," 2003). It is important to note that the all-encompassing "Idol" narrative is built on the foundations of exactly this kind of simultaneous production and satisfaction of public expectations.

The second key theme was existential. We were offered many answers to the much asked question, "What is this thing called Australian Idol?" The simple answer was that "Idol" was an incredible success. As the executive producer of the Australian franchise noted, Pop Idol and American Idol sold CDs and created several real live pop stars, but did so in a candid, if occasionally defensive manner.

Australian Idol is "a completely honest format," he insisted, "unashamedly looking for the best talent in the country" (Iccarino, 2003). These two pillars of support, undeniable success crafted from hard work and the discovery of "ordinary" people with extraordinary talent, would work in tandem to demonstrate the essential honesty of "Idol." The executive producer never tired of asserting the truth content of his show, especially in relation to other music-based reality shows. "I'm hoping the Australian public will see someone who has natural ability," he suggested. "Those other shows manufactured the acts" but "Idol" was different. He deftly implied that producers had no shaping role in the aesthetics of stardom, allowing contestants to dress themselves and move however they wished on stage, a point to which I will return later (Thomas, 2003b). To underscore the material point, "Idol's" producers, and rank outsiders alike, repeatedly noted that the vast majority of CDs produced by the music industry fail. As music industry analyst Phil Tripp noted, more people are killed by lightning in a given year than have successful debut CDs, a rhetorical nugget traded often by executives of the sponsoring label, BMG (Scatena, 2003/4). This stark rebuke to the music industry by its own representatives had a ring of bland candor to it. Producers could tautologically prove the value and honesty of "Idol's" transparent mediation of stardom whenever they wished, simply by pointing to its own superior success to failure ratio. Every iteration of "Idol" had been a success, they crowed, with new releases almost uniformly reaching the top of the charts in 11 countries. Of course producers could only define success this way by casually ignoring the countless "failures" upon whom their several successes were resting. It did not occur to the producers that they were faithfully reproducing the very failure rate they were criticizing. In the face of mild criticism from the independent music press, a few high-profile musicians, and other record labels, the producers of Australian Idol were bent on having this program taken seriously, installing their credibility-seeking publicity campaign well before any actual criticism was heard, and maintaining it long after most critics fell silent (Davis, 2003b; Sams, 2004b).

The Initial Auditions

The televised Australian Idol relationship begins with what has proved to be an engaging first act.[4] Thousands of ordinary Australians queued up outside venues throughout the country, many sleeping in car parks and on footpaths, practicing, singing, and performing for the mobile camera crews with a seemingly spontaneous abandon occasionally mixed with a measure of meticulous preparation. We are presented with their youthful vigor in all its varied guises. "Idol's" spectacle of the ordinary begins here (see Couldry, 2002b:287–90). The initial auditions were framed as a kind of first come, first served festival. Those in the queue who obtained entry into the massive waiting area entered an informal gladiatorial arena. The assembled

---

4   The ratings for the first two series of *Australian Idol* followed the same general pattern. The initial programs rated well, but subsequent rounds did not. Then, ratings grew during the "Final 12" through to the Grand Final. The final three programs of the first series were among the highest-rating programs in Australian television history (Maley and Davis, 2003; Dale, 2003b).

hundreds or thousands waited on their convention center chairs, many with family members, partners, and friends in tow, a gesture of intimacy and support encouraged by the producers ("Sydney Auditions …," 2004). A staging area with a conveniently placed piano and several wireless microphones provides a venue for impromptu performances ready-made for broadcast. The shoulder mounted camera and lurking boom mike, the staple instruments of reality television, collected endless hours of footage to be culled and edited for controlled distribution throughout the life of the series and insertion into the vast product range flowing in the wake of the Grand Final. The bounded chaos of the mass auditions provided plenty of shots of nervous wallflowers and demonstrative performers, all waiting for what can only be seen as a daunting or even terrifying two minute a cappella recital in front of judges whose potential for abuse or dismissal is well established.[5] The mass auditions were carefully stage-managed to highlight those with the right kind of talent, against a backdrop of the ironic, the delusional, and the downright untalented. Each edition of the program began with a summary narration of what had happened up to that point. These jump cut stories constantly reestablished and cemented the central narrative dynamic of the contest showing us how the cream eventually rose so profitably to the top. We cannot help but be convinced of the worth of those who survive such a process.

The introductory episodes of the second series of Australian Idol are perfect examples of this process of re-narration. Series two started on a Wednesday at 7:30pm, hard on the heels of yet another episode of Big Brother. There had been a fairly extensive advertising campaign to welcome the show back. The ads focused on the judges with dreamy presentations by slowly drifting cameras as each judge stood on what looked like a small "Idol" stage with their most characteristic comments from the first series gurgling in the background. They smiled ever so slightly, moving subtly in slow motion. The logo appeared in a burst of confetti, giving us a mild hint of what's to come. Then a McDonald's ad appeared with the notation "5:30am: Australian Idol 2004 auditions" on the bottom of a screen filled with hopefuls sleeping out on the footpath in front of the audition venue. One of their number was Ronald McDonald, the welcoming corporate patriarch whose eponymous employer was "proud to support Australia's young talent." When the actual program began, viewers were presented with a montage of moments from the first series ending in that singular moment when the words "And the winner, Australian Idol, 2003, Guy Sebastian" were announced. The previous year's program was tersely narrated beginning with the words "2003: the phenomenon arrived" followed by a series of quick cuts of massive queues, screaming auditionees, moaning failures, clever pranksters, and laughing judges. Then the words "Dreams were shattered" appeared along with the tears and singing of a few of the more recognizable contestants, several of whom had become momentarily famous for losing it completely on national

---

5   As noted, the first series of *Australian Idol* began after the first series of *Pop Idol* and *American Idol* had established the template for the format. It should be noted, however, that *Australian Idol* never quite sank to the depths of humiliation and abuse that *American Idol* often reached (see Dale, 2003b). For an excellent reading of the narrative structures of *American Idol*, see Stahl (2004).

television. Then, the words "Stars were discovered" appeared and we saw Shannon Noll, the runner-up who became perhaps the ultimate commercial winner of the first series. Noll's familiar image faded into quick shots of each member of the "Final 12" performing individually and then together for the song "Rise Up," co-written by one of the "Idol" judges.[6] This pleasingly short story ended with the moment for which we had all been waiting, ably concluded by fireworks and triumph, then it was straight to Melbourne and 2004 (Australian Idol: Series Two, July 13, 2004).

The immediate narrative contrast between the talented and the talentless from the mass auditions is framed by a voiceover notation describing "the torture, the tears, the tantrums" that defined the process. The judges were clear on what they expected this year. Mark Holden offered his subtle adjudicatory regime: "I'm looking for someone who's life has been to this point and will be forever, music ... I'm never going to say no to quality," he continued, "I'm going to say yes to quality." Marcia Hines said, "What I'm looking for is raw talent. Enthusiasm as well. And a willingness to learn." Ian "Dicko" Dickson was more tactical, suggesting, "I think the contestants this year will be a lot more savvy. They've all seen the show. I think they'll be pushing us a lot harder. I think they'll be asking for second songs. They'll be bringing all the begging and the pleading out. And I don't think they'll take no for an answer." The producers added another official voice to the auditions, the voices of the rejected. As co-host Andrew G. noted, "This isn't a one-sided competition. At Australian Idol we like to be fair so even though our contestants have to deal with stuff like that," meaning the flurry of rejection meted out by the judges, "this year our contestants will be able to bring out their very own frustrations and their furies and how they feel about our very own judges with their very own 'Idol Cam.'" The "Idol Cam" was a separate camera before which the failures could sit down and sound off about their treatment. Threats, name-calling, and other such outbursts abounded, establishing the outlines of a conversation that would dominate the show: the judges judging, the contestants contesting.

The explanatory element of the program is also made abundantly clear from the beginning as the path of the contest is explained in the form of a televised walk through. We are told how, over the next two weeks, the judges will carefully whittle down the multitude to the Top 100 and then to the Top 30. Those are the 30 people you will vote for, they tell us, so be ready. They dangled the payoff of the Grand Final in front of us as the reason why so many people had queued for endless hours. They bragged about how Guy Sebastian had made music history when his debut single and album became one of the highest selling records of all time for a new Australian artist. They noted that Guy is now performing for a global audience (on World Idol) and how on a recent visit to the United States he performed for "over 65 million people" (on American Idol). They showed us those in the queue who had been up for 36 hours straight, whose bums were wet, who were cold, tired, and from all appearances a little bit desperate, as an enticing contrast. Within this long explanatory and celebratory montage there was an absolutely crucial piece of reality

---

6   "Rise Up" was co-authored by *Australian Idol* judge Mark Holden. It was used to kick off the "Final 12."

television footage. The producers began to craft a particular intimacy with us as Andrew G. took us on a tour of the Melbourne auditions:

> Now for those of you who have never been to an audition before, it can be a scary place. First, there's the competition. [Shots of singers and dancers in the queue giving it their all outside.] There's hundreds in front of you. Then, you register. Then, it's down to the holding room. And there's lots of fantastic voices which makes you feel even more anxious. Finally, you hear your number called, then it's down to the audition room and there they are. [Grim faced judges greet the camera.] Will you melt down? [Shots of nervous auditionees messing up and playing for time.] Will you lose your memory? Or overstay your welcome? Well, get ready, the Melbourne auditions are about to begin as the judges dish it out: "It was like a crap Brazilian soap opera" and the contestants throw it back: "Dicko, you're a dickhead" (ibid.).

After re-narrating the first series and providing an instructional narration of what's to come in series two, we finally reached the first commercial break.

When the auditions themselves are shown, we begin to see "Idol's" aesthetic hierarchy firm up. The truly useless are dispatched with appreciated speed through such nuanced comments as "Crap," "I've got nothing to say except thank you for coming," and the all-purpose, "Next!" The taunts are leavened with a healthy supply of pithy one liners: "That wasn't so much a performance as a painful exorcism," or "That's not a voice. That's a weapon of mass destruction," and the helpful but cruel, "You've got a decent voice, but you're not cool enough. I think you should get a ball gown and go sing on a cruise ship" (ibid.). We are deeply grateful for the rare exceptions and these are marked out for us with the verbal equivalent of a huge blinking sign. Marcia Hines told one singer, "You walked in and you were so sexy, and you know who you are and it's so good to see," while Mark Holden told another, "I would like to have heard 20 per cent more power up at the top there, just to show me you've got it." Importantly, those who were clearly a cut above the rest were asked a series of leading questions such as "Where have you've been?" and "What's been going on with you to get you to this point?" The initial audition of one of the eventual finalists for series two, Anthony Callea, was prefaced with host Andrew G. whispering conspiratorially to us about the singer's bright future. Callea's audition felt scripted when of course it wasn't, and of course at the same time, it was. It was the kind of script that doesn't actually have to be written down or even acknowledged, it just goes with the territory. The simplest praise was often the most telling: "I can hear your voice recording very well and I can see you lighting up the screen" (ibid.).

There is an essential paradox in these first few weeks of televised mayhem. These auditions are some of the most tightly-controlled and well-orchestrated events on television precisely because "Idol" survives on creating a foundational level of unpredictability. This lack of predictability requires constant re-narrations of what has gone before. The first few weeks of the competition exhibit the greatest tumult and anticipation. We see the greatest number of rejections and arguably the most raw, visceral, and unscripted emotion the program will show us, all of which is compressed into the least amount of actual programming time, framed in an authoritative documentary format. You can see the rage for control coming out in the extremely careful editing; some singers get a little bit more attention, some are completely ignored until they surprise everyone later in the contest. Yet all of this blood and thunder is presented to us in the past tense. By the time the program goes to air, the first two rounds had been completed over the course of three months. When the live programs begin, the producers have already crafted for us a complicated relationship between "talent" and "determination" made visible through the manipulation of an absurd amount of candid footage. The tight scripting coupled with the unique ability of "Idol's" producers to the let go a little bit makes the whole thing work, carefully editing the improvised footage to make the chaos meaningful by highlighting a series of telling visual and aural markers. If it weren't for the horrible performances, the crying, and the anger, the inherently modest number who go through might not be recognized as potential "Idols" at all. The "Idol" relationship is easy for viewers at this point. We are asked only to watch and learn, understanding that our actions will eventually have consequences. The producers are just easing us into the shared responsibilities that lie ahead.

Behind the façade of the legions of deluded also-rans, the seemingly random good luck visited upon those apparently unaware of their "gifts," and a sense of tenacious accomplishment by a few polished performers, the mass auditions are designed primarily to craft compelling television, structured by the rules of participation which govern access to the auditions. These rules form a kind of "how to" guide for making a contemporary pop star. The "auditionee" must be between 16 and 28 years old, they may not have entered into any contractual agreement with a publisher, manager, or agent, and they must agree that any record of their presence at the auditions remain the property of the producers in perpetuity. Finally, they must "dress to impress" ("Sydney Auditions …," 2004). These rules are supplemented with two far less visible sets of "producer auditions" through which every potential participant must pass; talent is only one of many concerns in these hidden hurdles (Dennehy, 2003). While these preliminary auditions were not quite invisible, they weren't exactly a central part of the narrative.[7] The producer auditions were not televised, nor were the judges even present while they were taking place. Those camped outside the many venues waiting for their 30-second shot at stardom simply did not cycle through their respective televised auditions one by one as we were led to believe. They were edited into the audition shows to create the appearance of a tense atmosphere of hope and doubt that never actually existed in the way it was presented on television. These initial interviews are used selectively as a tool of entertainingly edited "reality" television to produce both the "freak show" element of the proceedings as well as the gradual emergence of a particular kind of talent highlighted through a shrewd mix of the sublime and the ridiculous. The auditions firmly fix a hierarchy of ability and determination from the outset. The two days of producer auditions are merely a practical necessity. "Idol" is a rule based structure. It exists to establish the lines of aesthetic authority that will be followed throughout the

---

7 The producer auditions are a kind of public secret which receive only tangential acknowledgment in the promotion regime surrounding the show. However they have been the subject of much caustic comment by rejected applicants on the extensive "Idol" message boards (Chartsong Productions, 2004a).

contest. The consequences of these early funnels are significant, but the television viewer is confronted only with the alternately elated or crushed auditionees and exhausted judges whose efforts by no means go unrecognized. Their arguments and assessments frame what will become an extended aesthetic discussion on "what it takes," "who has it," and who doesn't. It's not entirely clear at this stage what "it" is, but the judges seem to know it when they see it.

The "Vocal Boot Camp"

Round two, referred to as the "Vocal Boot Camp," raises the stakes considerably. The initial rounds of televised auditions are rendered complete through extensive commentary and occasional teeth-gnashing on the part of the panel of experts and rejected contestants. It is round two that confronts potential "Idols" with the enormity of their responsibility. In series two, the gauntlet was thrown down in the brutish presence of Ian Dickson. "A seriously suited Ian Dicko Dickson" gave the troops a stern talking to during an introductory session that appeared to be a cross between an intake interview at an employment agency and a preparatory spruiking at a Tony Robbins seminar. "In five months," he said, "someone in this room is going to be one of the most famous, one of the most successful and one of the most wealthy young people in Australia. Dig deep and show us what you've got" (Australian Idol: Series Two, July 27, 2004). Then, the assembled were separated from the herd, put into groups of ten, sent on stage, and asked to explain why they should be the next Australian Idol. It was like a meeting of a local chapter of a cult of pre-celebrity. Afterwards, numbers were called, performances were given, criticism was offered, and people began to disappear. The spectacle now gets serious.

In round two, each contestant was asked to audition again in order to weed out anyone who was already performing at the perceived limits of their ability. This is the first time people once accepted are knocked out and it begins to become clear what it is going to take to win. The hints of individual branding begin here in earnest as specific singers are singled out and highlighted, some more than once. Footage from the original auditions is presented again, allowing viewers to compare the two performances in case they tuned in late, squeezing just that little bit extra out of the extensive footage gathered at the cattle calls. Producers recapitulated many of these short "Idol Journeys," some ending as expected, some ending too soon, constantly noting that one would not be ending at all. The structure of the "Vocal Boot Camp" was designed to highlight the excitement and the "agonizing pressure" which all of the singers were now under. The hosts kept telling us just how tough this was going to be (ibid.).

The contestants chose their own songs to perform in round two and, as the specific contours of the contest being to clarify themselves, it became obvious that the judges didn't want some cookie-cutter pop star. They wanted someone "special" with "natural talent," but also with a unique profile, who can take advantage of opportunities as they appear. Several contestants were knocked out for singing the same song they performed during their original audition. The judges made it clear that they wanted flexible performers with enough raw material to shape into the appropriate form, whatever that may be. The emotional contours of the program are also dramatically specified in this round. We were presented with a few quick life histories which explicitly built on what was revealed at the original auditions. This sort of talk humanizes an ugly process, one which often ends in tears as the thudding intonation, "And as quickly as that, the Australian Idol dream ends" rings in the air during the commercial breaks (ibid.). The program produces the kind of on the spot reactions we saw during the original auditions. Many of those who made it through expressed surprise and confidence as well as kind words for other contestants that highlight the difficulties they now know they are facing. The reactions of the contestants and judges were sometimes surprisingly kind and earnest. Dicko and the other judges were presented as knowledgeable people less interested in humiliating contestants than desperately trying to get these young musicians to improve, to exceed expectations and make themselves better performers and better people. At one crucial juncture, Dicko stormed into the waiting area to inform the hopefuls that they were not making the grade. "This has been a crushingly disappointing morning," he said as he started in on them. "The one thing that is missing is personality. It doesn't matter how good you can sing, if you don't connect with the public they are not going to buy your records. It begins here with us. Knock our socks off." Dicko's rants were presented as an earnest expression of his burning desire to bring the best out of these people. He knows how hard it is to be a pop star and he wants them to know it too. He wants them to take his warnings seriously and rise to the challenge. Yet the whole project can also be incredibly good natured and constructive. The successful contestants often applauded those going home. Some were amazed at their success, one saying "I have really only just discovered I can sing," while others said "I can't believe I'm here. I'm just not that good really" (ibid.). The humility and the self-effacement are palpable. We are shown their effort and their sacrifice. They are tired, they are scared, but they are determined.

A central part of succeeding in Australian Idol is the ability to demonstrate that you can grow as a person and as a performer because of the challenges you face during the competition itself. On day two of round two, a stark challenge is presented. All of the contestants must collaborate with two or more other contestants and give yet another "performance of their lives." This harsh task demonstrates to us the earnest intent of those still involved. The performers are asked to return the next day after preparing all night. It was left to Musical Director John Foreman to explain to them how the whole thing would work. As an introductory slogan he said, "this could potentially be the most important 24 hours of your lives so far." Foreman told the contestants they would be asked to perform a particular song, leaving the particulars of the performance, such as choreography and harmonization, up to them. This is probably the most difficult requirement of the early rounds of the competition and it makes the fun and fanciful mass auditions seem very much like a thing of the past (ibid.). The 70 per cent attrition rate in round two reduces the talent pool from over one hundred to a mere thirty or forty. We are guaranteed drama and it is made clear to viewers and performers alike that being an "Idol" is not really much fun at all. It is in fact an ethical relationship with the public to whom, it is stated repeatedly, all pop stars are indebted and beholden.

At the beginning of each episode, we are shown the kinds of problems and arguments that animate the program in order to make what is happening have a broader meaning, showing us how the narrative is tied together throughout the long months of the show. The key themes that emerge in round two are hard work and determination. Round two is the one stage of the competition intended to sift out those who, while talented, are routinely described as "not ready" for the intense demands of success. It is structured around two key tropes on which producers play on during these intense few days, fairness and opportunity. It is clear from here on out, the program will force contestants to take advantage of their opportunities and the producers try to demonstrate the meritocracy they are consciously constructing. In pursuit of fairness, the "Idol" producers are unusually public about the importance of presenting "unbranded" aspirants as the contest moves forward. This contractual condition of participation has obvious benefits for the producers. It frees them to create and build a publicly credible persona for each potentate more or less from scratch. It is also a central pillar of the narrative of the enterprise itself. To appear credible, the contest must appear fair; anyone with a head start cannot fit the pre-existing container of "Idol," by definition. Several singers who had already signed management agreements before series one or had engaged in unauthorized bouts of self-promotion during the show, were not only ousted, but were forced to make public apologies to those who supported them throughout the show for these various excursions beyond the bounds of the "Idol" brand (Australian Idol: Greatest Moments, 2003).

From the "Semi-Finals" to the "Final 12"

The hopefuls who survive the rigors of the "Vocal Boot Camp" are presented as appealingly ambitious or naively optimistic individuals with varying degrees of talent. It is during "Semi-Finals" that we begin to see the crude moral economy of Australian Idol, present at the inception, work more visibly and in increasingly refined forms. Judges pointed out more than once to suspected underachievers that a decent performance was simply not good enough. When one singer objected to criticisms of his choice of repertoire during the "Semi-Finals," stating that he chose the song because he liked singing it, he was upbraided for his pretension. He was rebuked for not taking the public into account in his aesthetic choices (Australian Idol: Series Two, August 15, 2004). It is made clear through such episodes that talent is never enough. Those truly blessed are those with not only the voice or the look, but the will to work both into saleable shape. Already carefully chosen from the multitude, they are offered an opportunity to make the most of their inherent yet unformed ability; for this they should be grateful. Their aesthetic credibility is an implicit, if formless presence by this point in the contest. They require the guiding hand of industry insiders and the eventual ratification of the public to achieve stardom. Through the facilitation of the competition in the form of knowledgeable industry veterans who never tire of giving stern admonitions and warnings of misdirected charisma, contestants are asked to prove themselves through an extremely concentrated period of intense self-presentation and re-creation.

The "Semi-Finals" offers viewers their first opportunity to participate directly in the proceedings, well after contestant branding has got under way. While lazy claims of some nascent televisual "democracy" and "do-it-yourself" stardom were made by producers and commentators alike through the promotional culture surrounding the show, the "Idol" medium is specifically designed to manage the uncertainty it produces. It becomes clear, as more viewers participate, that "Idol" is nothing if not well-planned ("Australian idle …," 2003; Davis, 2003a). By the time we reach the "Semi-Finals," the central act of consumption that marks "Idol" as special, the voting, finally begins. It is very clear by then that the few remaining contestants are already established at least as potential pop stars, by design and necessity. It could hardly be otherwise. The idea of asking the television audience to vote on participants with ambiguous brand appeal is strategically risky. Semi-finalists are surrounded by all the trappings of their presumed roles and are well on their way to "becoming themselves" through public realization of their dreams. Their status as ordinary people clings to them only as a slight scent of a former life; this is, after all, the whole point. Each of the semi-finalists is introduced to us through a multi-part documentary miniseries presented on the ancillary magazine format show Inside Idol which has been specifically designed to grab our attention and inculcate in us the values that "Idol" is promulgating through its simple and clear narrative. The contestants take us home with them. We meet their friends and families. We see where it all began and we see how far they've already come. More important, we see the subtle, considered, and gradual growth of "Idol's" regime of aesthetic judgment. While the judges offer commentary intended to shape the voting process, most of the decisions that will determine the composition of the "Final 12" are not up to them. And while the surviving contestants remain on probation, singing only truncated versions of their repertoire, not yet allowed to perform on the big stage, at least we can finally begin to imagine exactly where this story might end.

It is during the "Semi-Finals," and especially the "Wild Card" round, when the aesthetic dimensions of the competition take a dramatic turn towards the high stakes presentations of the "Final 12." By this point, the contestants are not as distinct from one another in their abilities. Much finer distinctions have to be made in distinguishing between those who have the potential for stardom and those who do not. Contestants must work within the established framework of pop stardom they and the contest have crafted thus far. The full range of aesthetic choices looms large in these rounds. Unusual choices in repertoire, wardrobe, or performative gestures now have to be justified in terms of broader perceptions of appropriateness and fit. While only occasional asides are offered to acknowledge the growing infrastructure of aesthetic tutelage upholding these choices, including a vocal coach, choreographer, a movement coach, music director, wardrobe staff, not to mention the Maybelline style team, it is clear that a tremendous amount of effort is going into shaping every aspect of these high profile performances. Those chosen for the "Final 12" give a short performance after their ascent to demonstrate their gratitude, remind us of their profile, and proclaim their artistic right to move forward. This is a subtle indication that the public is not yet fully trusted to distinguish between the various unstable brands on offer. We are not quite the participants we are expected to become as the branding process proceeds.

The "Wild Card" round is an exceptional aspect of the process of choosing the "Final 12." It appears to contradict the drama of rejection by giving some contestants another chance. The Wild Card has several effects of note. First, it reasserts the authority of the judges, giving them a chance to contest decisions made by the public. This re-centralizes the public service ethos of the program, paradoxically by destabilizing decisions made by the public. The "Wild Card" asks the public to vote again for contestants they have already rejected. The judges help us out by rising above the fickle emotion of the moment, offering disinterested choices based solely on aesthetic criteria. The Wild Cards have a contradictory status. Their public validation is weak, but their aesthetic status is strong. Their success is based solely on their ability to grab what is well and truly their last chance. This opportunity is not dependent on the whims of viewer preference, but on the hard evidence of their adjudicated talent. Those who succeed acquire the direct blessings of the judges. Second, the drama of the "Semi-Finals" peaks in the "Wild Card" round. The Wild Cards perhaps understand what is at stake more than the other contestants. They have peered into the abyss and stepped back buoyed by their own abilities and internal fortitude. They are showing us that no one is safe. Each of the final three contestants who stood on the brink of performing in the Grand Final at the Opera House in both series had faced elimination in either the "Semi-Finals" or the "Final 12." In the second series, several finalists recounted how they faced their own potential final performance, clawing back their right to continue through the sheer force of their talent and determination.

And it is here that we see the relationship between "Idol" and its audience growing ever closer. The producers begin to forge broader connections. Affective investment begins to shift ever so gradually from particular contestants to the program as a whole. The lengthy rounds of the "Final 12" cement this shift. Each week, the lowest three vote-getters are separated from the dwindling herd. The one contestant receiving the lowest vote total leaves the show. A short, emotional farewell documentary, entitled "Mazda's Idol Journey," is presented chronicling the "Idol" experience of the unhappy candidate. The documentary creates an almost funereal mood. Within the narrative of the program, this weekly display of "Idol's" changing aesthetic hierarchy functions as the dramatic equivalent of a weekly "Wild Card" round, this time with permanent consequences.

Perhaps no other event in the "Idol" continuum proves the proclaimed truth of the enterprise more than the unexpected departure of a favorite contestant. The inherent instability of the acknowledged status of the comparatively few contestants subject to audience ratification is the central fact of the climactic rounds of the program. There were two events in series two that highlighted the structural importance of these events. The first was the resurrection of Anthony Callea in the Wild Card round. Callea had been viewed as a hot favorite at different points in the show, but was voted out by the public. When the judges brought him back for the "Wild Card" show, the tension surrounding his reappearance was conspicuous. Callea was confirmed as a valuable commodity only through an unprecedented and unique collaboration between the judges and the public. The second event was the shock departure during the "Final 12" of Ricky Lee Coulter. The sudden end of her "Idol" dream was greeted with an outburst from Dicko. "This is a scandal," he bellowed.

"Get off your arses and vote Australia." It was this event, perhaps more than any other of the contest, that showed just how important and consequential the relationship between the audience and the contestants is. While it is obvious that "Idol" needs viewers who eventually become voters, it is the conflation of these two roles and their social underpinnings that defines "Idol's" core relationships. The goal of the program is to encourage a gradual increase in the level and quality of participation, from interested viewing to repeated and enthusiastic voting. It is often presumed that it is the quality of the performances that inspires voters or at least forms the aesthetic baseline of the contest. But the producers seem keenly aware that people vote for any number of reasons and they avidly encourage all of them. They don't seem to care why people vote, just that they do. They only need demonstrate the consequences of not voting. It is in these crucial defining moments, when the shock of a surprise departure sets in, that "Idol" reaches its apotheosis. This act of directed consumption enriches both the quality of the contest and the bottom line.

Interestingly, during the crucial middle rounds of "Idol," and especially during the "Final 12," the branding process stretches well beyond the apparently incapable bounds of the contest itself. Perhaps the most crucial aspect of these rounds for producers is the difficult job of shaping distinct public personae for a changing roster of as many as thirty people in less than a month. Three key pieces of this process are the weekly magazine format show Inside Idol, the one-off reality format program Idol House Party, and the intimate portraits of the final five contestants presented on Australian Idol: Up Close and Personal. These programs offer what is redundantly described as "exclusive" access to the "behind-the-scenes" world of Australian Idol. We are presented with portraits of the contestants including descriptions of their family life and backgrounds as well as their thoughts and fears on the trials to come, not just on the show, but in life. All three programs appear to describe all that goes on outside of the contest itself, including live appearances in various shopping centers around the country and the inevitability of impromptu autograph sessions out in the streets of Australia's major cities. But these shows are as crucial to the ultimate success of the show as any of the performances. It is the process of crafting each contestant's public persona that will persuade the public to continue participating in the lucrative voting process. It is in these rounds of voting through which the producers hope to forge the peculiar kind of audience investment in the program itself that begins the downhill rush to the finals. Further compounding the producers' dilemma is the fact that mere affective investment in individual contestants is not a sufficient outcome for a successful show. They have to create an aura of both good faith and credibility for the program as a whole as well. As contestants inevitably fail and leave the show, those who supported failed candidates must not abandon their responsibility in choosing a singular "Idol." The producers have to facilitate the transfer of investment to the remaining candidates through trust in the program itself.

The show's credibility can only be achieved through the appearance of equity and fair play. The status of those proceeding to the higher rungs of the contest is never firmly established, but has to be continually and strategically re-established. The producers do this through a continuous, multi-format display of a gritty combination of "natural" talent, hard work, and public appeal. Each increasingly weighty choice of repertoire, wardrobe, and performance style can only break the hopefuls; each successful performance only raises the stakes higher. This tense maintenance of status as a deserving celebrity runs in tandem with the increasingly attentive and reciprocal relationship between the producers and the audience. The lucky few who were told with a flourish so long ago, "You're Going to Sydney" after round one, are then faced with what appears to be a difficult challenge in rounds two and three: establish yourself in short order as a performer with "the X factor" (Australian Idol: Series Two, July 14, 2004). A fine voice and interesting look must be supplemented with the hard work necessary to harness those intangible qualities only made available to the public and the performer because of the contest itself. When the public is eventually asked to participate directly, it is both to produce and to ratify exactly this quality. Indeed, the X factor cannot exist without this curious and complex kind of tautological validation.

"Idol's" sheen of participatory democracy grows throughout the "Final 12." The dwindling number of contestants rely more and more on our help to survive. Their celebrity is specifically produced to appear shockingly unstable, fleeting, and under constant threat from a public whose decisions are not supposed to be reliable or predictable. From the "Semi-Finals" to the "Final 12" to the "Final 2," favorites can easily become also-rans who might limp out of one round, but storm through the next. The drama can only be heightened, securing our interest by requiring our input. As any advertiser can tell you, an effective campaign must end in action on the part of the target audience. The clever branding regime established in the early rounds, the precisely timed inauguration of text message and phone voting, as well as extensive "fan management" through internet chat rooms and bulletin boards (see Stahl, 2004:228) channels our participation to help shape, produce, and complete the meanings of the contest. These active and often inventive relationships allow the eventual "Idol" to claim a credibility the means of their success otherwise renders suspect. These activities appear to consummate the relationship, but they require literally months of constant effort across a wide range of media to coax out of us. The effort that goes into it is quite simply staggering.

The Grand Final and Beyond

It might be counterintuitive to regard the finals as the least problematic strategic aspect of the competition for the producers, but in a way, the success of the finals is more or less a done deal before the big nights arrive. Certainly the publicity campaign surrounding the finals is the most traditional of the lot, conforming to familiar expectations of what a gala should be. Contestants arrive before a screaming crowd in limos which are themselves well placed products, symbols of the luxury to come for the eventual "Idol". In the first two series of Australian Idol, judge Marcia Hines performed in an outdoor concert heralding the arrival of the stars of the moment, a distinct honor given her status as both a sterling performer and earnest assessor. In Australia, only the Sydney Opera House will do as a venue. Its white sails are an instantly recognizable symbol of the nation's expressive center. The final decision confronts viewers with the clearest choice of the entire contest. Given the extensive polling (and wagering) which preceded the finals of the first series, which correctly predicted the triumph of Adelaide's "bro with the 'fro," Guy Sebastian, the entire event had an air of certainty to it that had not been felt throughout the contest. It was much more of a coronation that a completion. The second series offered a much more contested choice, giving us Casey Donovan, a "surprise Idol," with her distinctly unglamorous looks and "attitude," visually summed up in her apparently inexhaustible collection of death metal t-shirts, telling us she was doing nothing more than being who she was, gradually becoming what she eventually became, a story I will examine at length in Chapter 7.

But the Grand Final proves to be yet another strategic marker in the "Idol" story as the many firmly established "Idol" relationships continue well beyond the expected conclusion. In a fascinating re-narration of each series of Australian Idol, Australian Idol: The Winner's Journey aired on the Thursday following the final nights of each contest in the slot reserved for Inside Idol. The stories of Guy Sebastian and Casey Donovan were presented in hour-long programs that showed their home lives, Sebastian's life as a voice teacher in the Adelaide suburbs, Donovan's childhood in Sydney's western suburbs and their subsequent journeys to stardom. Viewers were given an "exclusive" peek into the recording of their debut CDs, sessions which began before the confetti had been swept from the Opera House floor. The clips depicting their lives prior to "Idol" were of ambiguous vintage. While clearly shot during the contest, producers remained cleverly silent on the exact date of production: somehow they were not quite in the past, present, or future, but floated in some eternal in-between. As each "Journey" was chronicled, we were allowed to see an intimate portrait of an anxious contestant transformed into "Your Australian Idol." There could be no doubt of the virtue of Sebastian's and Donovan's struggles, nor of their well earned victories. "New" footage showed Sebastian reluctantly commenting on the other contestants at the Adelaide cattle call at the prompting of the mobile camera crew. Donovan's original audition was shown in full to reveal remarkable praise from the judges that was not part of the original broadcast. Each story ended with teary-eyed mothers and fathers exultant at the final decision as they stood in the front rows at the Opera House. Not only is the entire run of each series dramatically recounted in documentary format on the Australian Idol's Greatest Moments DVDs, framed by each "Idol's" humble triumph, so are the stories of each member of the "Final 12" and the paths they trod through the contest. These reiterations serve to reinforce, not only "Idol's" status, but the status of the program itself, confirming the benevolence of the industry it so dutifully profiles. We are taken behind the curtain of stardom, allowed to see its elegant and obvious machinery grind inevitably to what appears to be its long-awaited conclusion.

Appropriately, there is no off-season for Australian Idol. At the end of series one, a controlled series of rollouts of the lesser "Idols" began and continued right through the second series. The grand final runner-up, Shannon Noll, mounted several tours in support of two hit singles from his debut collection. The first was a beefy remake of Moving Pictures' 1980s power ballad "What About Me?," a cleverly implicit reply to the preceding hysteria over Guy Sebastian to which Noll could only be a supportive witness. It became Noll's signature tune, cementing Noll's regular Aussie bloke status so cleverly established during the contest. Noll's second single was a pedestrian version of "Drive," a song written by Bryan Adams, confirming

Noll's power pop credentials via analogy. Another contestant, now known simply as "Paulini," widely perceived to have been treated poorly by both the judges and the public, emerged with her own debut collection. Entitled "One Determined Heart," fronted by a series of conventional R&B songs extolling the virtues of struggle and belief in oneself. It was released to coincide with the start of the second series and received a particularly visible sponsorship position. In both cases, the content of the songs explicitly played on public perceptions of their respective "Idol" experiences. The stories of these and other former contestants from series one also received extensive publicity in a crowded collection of product placement advertisements on the Inside Idol magazine program. The new lives, personal and musical, of these rising stars were chronicled and displayed alongside the profiles of the new crop of hopefuls, implicitly conferring upon them at least the potential for the success enjoyed by the veterans. The profiles of those who had benefited from the program's largesse completed a blanket of "Idols" that stretched continuously over the seven months between the end of the first series to the start of the second. Literally, not a month went by without an opportunity to consume our "Idols" in one form or another.

The Contours of a Long-Term Relationship

The story of Australian Idol moves like a mercury glacier. It always seems to be moving at breakneck pace. It is impossible to pin down at any one moment. Yet somehow it takes forever to get anywhere. The overarching story is familiar enough, but it is always moving, evolving through thousands of passing moments which are constantly being recontextualized through a process of re-narration present in every expression of the program. The producers relentlessly collected footage at every stage of the contest, deploying it every format possible throughout the life of the program in order to create, reshape, and transform each storyline in response to all manner of events, expected or not. Given the ephemeral nature of the program and the events it contains, such constant efforts at reestablishing and reshaping these events ease them into conformity with the expected narrative contour they both create and satisfy regardless of the dramatic shifts of meaning and emotion that might occur within that narrative. The stirring story produced by the contest is obviously the heart of the entire endeavor. It is what holds all of its distinct iterations and varied channels of expression together, keeping the audience interested and engaged. Given the extraordinary number of avenues for audience participation, "Idol's" success has been cleverly and carefully achieved and strategically maintained through a series of events that continuously offer us new products that never seem to stop appearing.

The eventual "Idol", and those publicly validated lesser "Idols," entered a contest explicitly framed by fairly naïve ideas of celebrity, an initial frame that was repeatedly re-established in the varied iterations that not only suffused the contest, but kept appearing in different formats after the final vote. The edited footage of the early rounds captured the contestants speaking only of their love of performing. They appeared to be seeking no more than a venue to display their talents and sentiments. As the process wound its complicated way from the initial audition within the vast throng to a series of increasingly daring and very public musical gambles, the naïve vision of imagined celebrity gave way to the much more burdensome role of pop star. The judges made it clear that being a pop star is not simply about talent or ability. These carefully crafted authentic celebrities found themselves trying to create and embrace a publicly credible persona unavoidably founded on an ethical and reciprocal relationship with the public. They were not allowed to forget that it is "we" who put them where they are; in short, they owe us. Yet within the structure of this curiously intimate spectacle is a nagging sense that "life is a constant audition" where you are only as good as your last performance (see Stahl, 2004:227). It is the music industry, embodied in the steadying hands of the judges unambiguously resting on the tiller, sometimes lightly, sometimes heavily, that guides us through the course of events to which we are all subordinate. It is made clear that the producers, sponsors, audience members, and the "Idols" themselves are all hostage to an unpredictable chain of fortune. We are reminded constantly, this is "our Idol." We created them so we should take them seriously.

"Idol" is routinely pilloried for its crass commercialism, yet it remains an unalloyed success. Viewers keep tuning in, advertisers still clamor to sponsor all aspects of the production and the merchandise keeps selling. Most important, the music industry has a rolling showcase for its own operations. The structures of feeling it exists to produce take on a kind of subtle explicitness that ensures their perpetuation. The creators of "Idol" have produced an audacious and arrogant spectacle in an industry faced with many dire threats. They have made a profitable virtue out of an economic necessity. The expensive and unpredictable process of finding and nurturing new talent has not only been made more reliable, it can actually turn a profit. The brand of celebrity produced by "Idol" possesses more than the mere sheen of populist approval, it embodies that more valuable commodity, public attention, however annoyed, obsessed, reluctant or enthusiastic it may be.

Chapter 7

Becoming Who You Are:
The Content of a Spectacle

There's nothing wrong with music for the masses and giving people what they want (Simon Fuller).[1]

There are a series of telling moments in Australian Idol: The Winner's Journey from the second series in 2004 which can tell us a great deal about how the content of Australian Idol is shaped and presented. In the first, the eventual winner, 16-year-old Casey Donovan was preparing for her group performance in the Top 100. Breathless narrator, co-host James Mathison, framed Donovan's second round appearance by noting how close the young singer had come to crashing out of the competition altogether. Donovan showed up for both her original audition and the round two "Vocal Boot Camp" in more or less the same outfit, a "death metal" t-shirt, board shorts, grungy runners, and a roomy cotton tracksuit top. The judges commented on her appearance on both occasions. Mark Holden speculated that she was hiding "behind a protective mask of death metal clothing." By round two he was certain that "there's more there with you." Dicko told her "Those clothes, they're not doing you any favors." It looked to Dicko as if she "was hiding behind that style" and he warned that her "image would become an issue" the longer she lasted in the competition. After her second dressing down, Donovan remarked that she was happy with how she looked, emphatically telling the other contestants she was "soooo comfortable." The next day, however, the narrator informed us that "a brand new Casey emerged." She arrived for the final round of performances in round two in a dark skirt, a new hairstyle, and had even "unearthed her long lost make-up bag." Donovan was given full credit for the transformation which proved to be a lasting set of "improvements" (Australian Idol: The Winner's Journey, 2004).

Surrounding this rich vignette was a series of remarks by various "Idol" luminaries intended to sum up Donovan's accomplishment and explain why she had become Australia's second "Idol". During the judges' long arguments over the final few singers to be included in the round of 30, Marcia Hines made her pitch saying, "We have made this girl come out of herself something fierce." Mark Holden pushed her as someone who "truly can communicate with a lyric and she does it straight through her spirit." Donovan herself offered a similar explanation. "I guess they just see me as Casey. I'm not putting on an act. I'm not doing anything I wouldn't usually do. I guess they seem me as the person I am," as the show slid easily into Donovan singing Vanessa Amorosi's up-tempo number "Take Me As I Am" from a "Final 12"

---

1   Hay (2002).

performance. Later in the program, Australia's first "Idol", Guy Sebastian, conferred his benediction on Donovan. "I'm a Casey favorite," the "Idol" veteran remarked. "I kind of dig her honesty. Just how real she is. I think when she sings there's nothing contrived about her. She's really just herself and that's probably why she's got so far." This was followed by scenes from a styling session which brought the soon-to-be-Idol to frustrated tears. After she had ascended to the throne, Dicko summed up Donovan's "Idol Journey" with his usual industry executive concision. "When it comes down to it, it's about communicating emotions. And week in, week out, Casey gave us love, pain, and lust and we believed her and that's why she's there." The script for The Winner's Journey dubbed her "the mistress of the slow reveal." Mathison continued the theme. "She's a young woman of many moods and contradictions. At sixteen she is just like any other teenager." His final narrative monologue worked its histrionic way from start to finish in just under a minute, its emotive contours sharpened by images of Donovan's dramatic transformation:

> Throughout the arc of the Australian Idol Journey Casey has shown a whole other side to her personality, one that few of us would have guessed way back at the first audition day in Sydney. She's shown us sweet and tender Casey. She's given us angry, defiant Casey. And she's shown us a young woman who sometimes speaks for the bruised, fragile child in all of us. She's shown us Casey Donovan and for that we're all truly grateful (ibid.).

My goal in this chapter is not to prove that these descriptions of the "ordinary" truth of an extraordinary "Idol" are somehow untrue or inauthentic, nor is it to examine novel deployments of familiar myths of authenticity in popular music. These determinations have been thoroughly explored elsewhere in relation to a variety of manufactured pop phenomena and are not unusually revelatory or illuminating of "Idol's" narrative constructions (Holmes, 2004; Leach, 2001; Stahl, 2002). Instead, I want to examine how the shaping methods of "Idol's" various storylines act as the smoothing machines of a carefully managed but unpredictable competition through which the substantial range of aesthetic materials at hand are manipulated as a tacit acknowledgement of the manufactured nature of pop stardom. There is a constant tension in Australian Idol, between the revelation of each contestants' "inner Idol" and the processes through which this apparent truth is revealed. These tensions show us the central paradox of "Idol": how does someone become who they already are? "Idol" carefully and necessarily straddles an artificially drawn line between crude manufacture and spontaneous revelation. In doing so, these inherent tensions produce an extraordinary spectacle in which unknown performers become celebrities who have earned the right to their fame by summoning inner resources which only exist because of the competition itself. As noted previously, there are three relationships that make this struggle tangible: the relationship between the "Idols" and the show, between the "Idols" and the public, as made meaningful through their love of performing and "communicating emotions" through music, and between the music industry and consumers as facilitated by the contestants through the long months of competition. These relationships are the animating core to the enterprise.

These relationships constitute the "Idol" medium through which the broad range of "Idol's" materials are made meaningful as they are made public through a complicated array of strategic promotional exercises implemented across a broad range of media forms which are designed to establish and maintain these three core relationships. It is the materials of "Idol," the songs, the performances, the visceral emotions, the moments of dramatic tension, and those ancillary revelations used to create each contestant's public persona as spread through this medium, that are the particular concern of this chapter. The narrative drama of transformation as realized through each candidate's presentation of these materials acts as the bonding agent through which a bewildering array of moments of calculated tension, triumph, and failure are organized. I will examine how this complicated and fluid set of relationships is mediated using an array of carefully framed materials through which the pop star personae of the contestants are constructed. These helped establish two sets of "Idols" from the first two series of the show: Guy Sebastian and Shannon Noll from series one, and Casey Donovan and Anthony Callea from series two. These four contestants gradually and inevitably became real pop stars by becoming themselves during the program through the use of materials distributed through a medium designed to fix "Idol's" primary relationships firmly in place.[2]

"Throughout the Universe, in Perpetuity"

Although it is difficult to distinguish between "Idol's" three core relationships while they are being simultaneously constructed and reconstructed, it is not difficult to figure out where they begin. They begin with each contestant signing over their immediate futures to the show's producers. While the specific contracts used in Australian Idol have not been made public, given the substantial financial liabilities that would result, a contract used in the first series of American Idol was published on the internet, circulated by an entertainment lawyer consulted by the parent of one potential contestant. The contract stipulates that the producers are granted "the unconditional right throughout the universe, in perpetuity" to use (or not) the contestant's "name, likeness … voice, singing voice, personality, personal identification, or personal experiences … life story, biographical data, incidents, situations, and events which heretofore occurred or hereafter to occur" in connection with the program (Olsen, 2002). The conditions of the contract make the chain of command clear. The producers have granted themselves the sole power to shape and reshape each "Idol's" story specifically through the materials they supply to the show. One particular clause seems peculiar to the nature of the show. Contestants agree not to disclose any information about the inner workings of the program or the details of the contracts they've signed or they will be liable for damages of more than $5

---

2   I am focusing on only these four contestants because they are, by definition, the only four contestants who can give us a detailed understanding of the full range of content from each series. Also, I am focusing only on a small number of contestants due in large part to the extraordinary amount of material each series of *Australian Idol* generates. I collected 12 six-hour video tapes of broadcast footage from the second series alone. This collection of material is supplemented by two DVDs each of which features a documentary nearly three hours long, profiles of each member of the "Final 12" from each series, and a "Video Jukebox" offering more than 20 performances from each series.

million (ibid.). These two key aspects of the contract establish the foundations of the relationship the contestants will have with producers during the show and beyond. They are less artists to be developed than brands to be created and exploited in the service of a more encompassing brand. Central to the business model expressed by this contract is the control over exactly how public representations of each brand will be made.

The relationships between the potential "Idols" and the public began with their appearances before the judges in what was purported to be their first hurdle, their brief a cappella auditions during the mass audition process. Yet even at this earliest of stages, the role of the producers in helping the most promising contestants emerge from the much larger morass of jokers and also-rans was clear. When the four distinct singers under examination here showed up, their obvious but inchoate talent was on clear display. Their auditions presented us with a framework for understanding what "talent" actually meant in these unusual circumstances, the ingredients of which I will draw out from a series of specific moments analyzed in the bulk of this chapter. The particular abilities of each singer were made obvious through their choice of repertoire, the reactions of judges, and the coaching each received as they were told they would be going through to the next round in Sydney. The comment and conversation on offer from the judges served to distinguish between different tiers of talent, offering advice and encouragement to those marked to continue after the producer auditions and opprobrium or abuse to those we were told were "delusional" or "kidding themselves." The four eventual finalists I am studying were given couture advice and were encouraged to adopt a more personal performance style. The public was coaxed into seeing the particular potential of each performer framed through their readily apparent "gifts."

As noted in the previous chapter, the praise of the judges was not the spontaneous embrace of innate talent as presented on television. Each singer had already performed for "Idol's" producers. They performed the same song for the judges, footage of which would be used on the first show of the season.[3] In each case, the singers were asked leading questions about their look, their lives, and their commitment to their craft, intimate and specific questions obviously prepared in advance. Through this manipulation, the public was introduced to each young singer specifically through the ways in which they were inculcated into the competitive culture of the program. The manipulations of the chronology of each singer's emergence into celebrity were legion, not limited to their initial introductions. Our "introduction" to these singers occurred not only through the seemingly straightforward audition process, but

---

3 In some cases, auditionees were told to return the next day, wearing the same clothes for their televised audition. This aspect of the original auditions was tacitly acknowledged on the summary program *Australian Idol: the Winner's Story* from series one. It was also the subject of angry comment by unsuccessful auditionees on the "Inside Australian Idol" website <http://users.tpg.com.au/libertyx/idol/>, accessed on July 27, 2004. This directorial sleight of hand was particularly obvious during the Canberra auditions in series two as the producer auditions and the televised ones took place at different venues (Chartsong Productions, 2004a).

through numerous reiterations of their success in the early rounds of the competition, after each had already emerged as contenders.

This should not be surprising. The task facing the producers in the first two rounds of the show was daunting. They had to sift through thousands of performers to find and highlight the one hundred or so who would have a legitimate chance of success. They had to capture the complete audition process for all of these performers to make certain they had a substantial record of the beginnings of those few "Idol Journeys" that would later become the pillars on which the producers would gradually place the entirety of their narrative endeavor. As each series wore on and the decreasing number of singers left in contention for the finals emerged, television audiences were re-introduced to finalists in programs such as Australian Idol: Up Close and Personal and Inside Idol in more intimate detail than ever before. Through these necessary tactical maneuvers we can see most clearly how the simultaneous construction of each core "Idol" relationship worked from the start to focus our attention on the singers, obscuring the exact nature of the machinations that brought them before us. The "original auditions" were framed from the outset by a process designed to serve the goals and values of the producers, not those of the singers. The singers were treated as malleable instruments enlisted to help shape themselves to suit the demands of the show.

Most of this chapter will focus on a series of key performances in which the contestants expressed their agency primarily by adhering to a series of formal rules and informal practices to accomplish familiar tasks through unique means which, by definition, only they possessed. It is in these moments that the dramatic narrative of the show became most clearly wedded to the materials the singers used to traverse the moments of transformation each faced. These moments demonstrate most clearly how the musical content of Australian Idol is inseparable from its mediation. Even the most obvious and dramatic live performances rested on a tremendous effort undertaken by hundreds of people to contextualize and exploit these moments of managed uncertainty. The obvious paradox of a "reality" show which creates unreal circumstances for its realization notwithstanding, the "liveness" of Australian Idol was most tangible when contestants had the most to lose, or gain, from a particular performance, the stakes of which were tautologically created and resolved by the structure of the program itself. These moments were so adroitly managed by the show's producers that they became formulaic. The contextual forces surrounding the contestants were consistently deployed to enact and maintain "Idol's" three core relationships. In order to satisfy the expectations placed on them to "express themselves" through other people's music, performers worked in a tightly controlled context, enmeshed in an enormous infrastructure of aesthetic tutelage. The moments analyzed below show how the tension between the ordinary person and the pop star they were becoming could never be resolved. They were two parts of the one whole.

The paths that led each of these four performers from their original auditions to the Grand Finals of series one and two are instructive. Each initial performance set in train a series of aesthetic and thematic associations framed through narrative devices that determined the specific course through which the contours of each singer's "Idol" persona were established. This complicated process stretched from the moment each singer met the show's producers to the Grand Final and beyond.

And it encompassed a global ambition, an ambition rooted in and making manifest the interrelationships between Australia's dominant popular music cultures and the global stage on which the "Idols" were said to be performing. While the musical and contextual coding of contestants may seem too obvious for any sustained analysis, we can learn two very important lessons from the ways in which the finalists were framed throughout the competition. First, we can see how the producers were able to create a context in which the contestants could "perfect" the particular musical abilities they brought with them to their respective auditions, abilities which are the primary materials of the "Idol" story. The trajectory of each contestant from their a cappella auditions to stardom were incorporated into the overall narrative of "Idol" specifically through the evolution of these materials. Displaying the distinctly musical trajectory from ordinary singer to extraordinary pop star is the ultimate display of the contest's credibility.

Second, we can see the ways in which a local iteration of a global phenomenon is produced. If Australian Idol were simply that, Australian, it would have little meaning, even in Australia. But for a music industry in which overseas success is a significant marker of value and credibility, not just for stars but for the industry generally, the global stage on which these singers were presumed to be performing gives the contest much of its meaning. Thus, the ways in which each set of finalists represents some notion of what it means to be both an Australian and an Australian pop star shows us the ways in which the "Idol" phenomenon is able to mobilize the cultural meanings of local or national pop stardom on an implied global stage in order to demonstrate its value and purpose. The choices made by the producers and the contestants with regard to repertoire, performative gestures, styling, and wardrobe clearly show us how the strategic coding of each singer gradually coalesced into a publicly credible pop star personality, each of which struck a chord with significant segments of the Australian public within this implied global context. The credibility of Australian Idol, still an open question for many, rested in the abilities of these determined young people to carry the weight of the show's meaning to a waiting and eager public through materials the producers used to construct the story of how they became pop stars.

The "Battler" and the Cosmopolitan

By the time of its long awaited conclusion, the first series of Australian Idol had been re-defined by the relationship between the eventual winner, Guy Sebastian, and runner-up, Shannon Noll. Despite the hundreds of performances, heartbreaks, and scandals, the producers' constant reiterations of the story of series one boiled the contest down, mostly in retrospect, to a contest between two carefully coded performers: Sebastian, an R&B singer with a cosmopolitan image and Noll, a classic "Aussie battler" from a small country town. When Sebastian and Noll showed up for their respective a cappella tryouts, both chose material that would become musically central to their respective campaigns. Each audition was a kind of televised virgin birth captured in its entirety and repeatedly recapitulated in longer, fuller versions as each singer grew in formal stature. These reiterations were crucial in building the reputation of each as a credible candidate for musical celebrity. Of particular interest here is what each singer brought with them into the audition room for their introduction to the Australian public. Each brought distinct styles of singing that started a chain of associations that continue to define their public images.

For the singer who would eventually become Australia's first "Idol," Guy Sebastian's voice received as much comment as his hair at his original audition. However, the focus on Sebastian's appearance was not simply an expression of superficiality. The young singer's hair became a synecdochical trademark of what briefly became one of the most identifiable brands in Australian popular music. Sebastian's afro-like hairstyle was used to link him with the African-American derived singing styles and genres he excelled at presenting. From the beginning, his musical style was founded on complex patterns of melismatic vocal invention familiar to fans of R. Kelly and Boyz II Men. Blessed with a clear vocal timbre in the upper reaches of the alto range, he also sported a strong, full falsetto and the occasional dip into the upper tenor range. His vocal style, however, was only rarely coded through associations with the contemporary style of African-American male soul or R&B singers. It was never demonstrative of the explicitly sexual modes of musical expression associated with those genres' most prolific performers. Instead, Sebastian went out of his way to affiliate himself with a varied group of female singers such as Beyoncé Knowles and Christina Aguilera, again with only the occasional hint of the explicitly sexual mode of musical expression of these performers. The producers highlighted the musical training he received in his Adelaide branch of the Assemblies of God church, a cousin of the Hillsong Church, an institution famed for its "rock concert" style services. Sebastian's repertoire choices and performance style were of a piece with his personal style. Each gradually grew into a crucial part of a regime of earnest self-expression that shaped his "Idol Journey."

In his initial audition, Sebastian chose "Ribbon in the Sky" by Stevie Wonder, giving "Idol's" producers their first opening to compare Sebastian to the Motown legend, an affiliation that framed Sebastian's continuing output well after the contest was complete (Scatena, 2003/4:81). Sebastian entered the audition room with a nervous smile on his face and walked quickly and somewhat uncomfortably to the parquet flooring in front of the "Idol" logo used for the audition. He wore what became a familiar costume, a patterned t-shirt and jacket combination, in this case a fuzzy suede jacket that protected him against the chilly Adelaide autumn he experienced while in the queue outside. The immediate remark from Dicko was obvious: "That's quite a 'fro you've got going there. Is that bed hair?" to which Sebastian jokingly replied "No, it's from the electric socket," breaking the heavy tension with his brilliant smile. Sebastian sang eight lines from "Ribbon in the Sky" and proved that he had no musical reason to be nervous. Sebastian sang using a clear tone that he often held back in his throat to produce a slight nasal sound that he cunningly contrasted with his full voice in dramatic fashion, often texturing his cadences with a strong vibrato. Sebastian was able to structure his two-minute presentation using reasonably precise intonation, implying an open harmony at the end of line four while closing it appropriately by landing on the tonic at end of line eight. He further structured his performance with a series of melismatic phrases, one running the down entire length of the diatonic scale, the other ranging down the scale then leaping well above the pitches he used for the main melody. These busy phrases of passing notes used to deliver maybe one or two syllables were precisely placed, completing line one in a five note burst and leaving line four hanging with a subtle eight note descent, the dynamics of which diminished gently to end the phrase without implying any harmonic closure. In lines three and seven he provided virtuoso passages of fifteen to twenty notes which he blended seamlessly into the powerfully sung tagline, "There's a ribbon in the sky for our love." The reactions of the judges were of immediate and unabashed praise. Dicko said simply, "Head and shoulders, the best voice we've heard today." Marcia Hines became visibly emotional, sputtering out a long series of short chopped phrases of exultant, incoherent adulation that continued after Sebastian had left the room. Mark Holden said, "That's times three." Interestingly, this unambiguous praise was never broadcast in full until Sebastian's The Winner's Story portrait appeared one week after the Grand Final, which gave these comments the uncanny ring of a foregone conclusion.

Noll chose for his audition the rock ballad "Hold Me in Your Arms" by Australia's Southern Sons. This helped the judges put Noll in a familiar frame with Holden telling him he could be the next Vince Gill. The comparison of new talent to old framed the extant credibility of this unfamiliar performer from the start. When Noll entered the audition room in Sydney, he appeared far more confident than Sebastian did. He wore a simple button down shirt with a wide collar and jeans, an outfit that would become a habit. Noll's biography took center stage during his audition. He was a farmer at the time of the contest, suffering through one of central New South Wales's worst droughts in living memory, working with his siblings to keep the family farm going after the death of their father. As Holden sympathetically noted, Noll "was carrying a load." Noll's story appeared in pieces throughout the competition and in full only after the contest was complete. During an unusually long conversation with the judges, Noll's calm description of how he dealt with his difficult circumstances, especially through his love of singing, obviously moved all three judges. His performance cemented their empathy (Australian Idol: Greatest Moments 2004, 2004).

Noll sang "Hold Me in Your Arms" in a slow and understated manner with little improvisation and only an occasional touch of vibrato, instead focusing on precise intonation in the melody, clear enunciation of the lyrics, and a slight upward tendency in the dramatic contour of his performance. He used a light, sweet tone without the scratchy texture he would employ later in the contest to great effect. Noll sang for nearly three minutes, giving the judges several verses and two choruses. In the first two verses, he barely expanded beyond the range of a perfect fifth while the first chorus ranged only slightly higher. In the final verse, Noll intensified his singing, took the melody to its highest point and then slid easily downward in pitch, volume, and intensity into the final chorus, finishing with a subtle slowing of tempo and a brief flourish in the final few notes. He used a slight contrast in tempo and dynamics to add to the power of the song. The lyrics resonated with his life story, infusing his performance of a song which describes love as a refuge from the trials of the world with a deep emotional appeal. The resonance between the two was so great as to fuse singer and song. Noll wisely avoided any hint of showmanship or attempts at virtuosity, allowing his unadorned vocal lines to cast a spell over three judges who couldn't help but send him on to the next round. Their praise was strong, but respectful, with Dicko telling Noll that he sang "with an absolute joy inside him" that he communicated through his performance. All three judges noted what an unexpected pleasure it was to hear him sing, with Mark Holden summing up the performance simply as "an extraordinary moment."

As noted in Chapter 6, one of the most difficult challenges facing contestants is to emerge from the first three rounds of the competition establishing themselves with some identifiable "X factor" while still adhering to the increasingly particular demands of the show. In the case of Sebastian and Noll, each found their distinction through contrasting means. Sebastian defined his performances through his gymnastic R&B-styled reinterpretations of classic songs such as "What a Wonderful World" and "When Doves Cry" while Noll displayed a steady reliability in his straightforward presentations of classic rock and power ballads by familiar stalwarts such as Bon Jovi, Foreigner, and Australia's Jimmy Barnes. In each case, "talent" was a broad concept, relating not only to the qualities of each singer's voice and presentation skills, but to their ability to respond to the requirements of the contest as a demonstration of the strength of their inner resources and fidelity to the work ethic required to become an "Idol." Talent was routinely described as the most significant marker of each contestant's real self. It was measured in the extent to which each could summon, on command, the power to make the most of their opportunities as they appeared, specifically by "connecting with the audience" by "communicating emotions" through music. This was made clear during each singer's initial audition. The temporally limited and heavily contextual forces of the contest exerted a powerful influence over these two singers' most important performances.

Sebastian grabbed one of his earliest opportunities to capture such a moment as he used contextual forces produced by the contest to his benefit. During the "Vocal Boot Camp," the three days of intense competition following the initial auditions, Sebastian used his final solo performance of the weekend to demonstrate, not only his vocal ability and his ability to engage an audience, but the one skill upon which he would rely throughout the contest, the ability to craft and capture a moment. Sebastian's innovative a cappella version of "Somewhere Over the Rainbow," "grabbed the judges' attention from the very first note," according to Andrew G's overawed voice over (*Australian Idol: The Winner's Story*, 2003). From his first few notes, Sebastian dramatically enhanced his status in the competition. He began by transforming the familiar melodic leap between the first and second syllables of the song into a dynamic and subtly adorned demonstration of his vocal range and power. He leapt a full step over the target note and gently landed on it, holding it for nine seconds, gradually increasing the rate and strength of his vibrato as he sang. The move captured the attention, not only of the judges, but of his assembled fellow contestants who cheered and clapped for him. He then delivered the next several lines in the highly adorned manner he preferred, offering no clear tempo, speeding up or slowing down his delivery for dramatic effect, allowing each line to end with irregular and indeterminate pauses, heightening the uncertainty as to what he might be planning next. He improvised heavily, even adding a scat riff on the word "blue" in the phrase "skies are blue," enticing the judges and drawing a beatifically appreciative smile from the usually stone-faced Dicko. Sebastian had so entranced the room that, as he began to sway and sing in a heavy see-saw rhythm as he sang the lines "Someday I'll wish upon a star," accenting the second and fourth beats of each measure with his voice and body, his compatriots in the audience began to clap along with this new tempo. This freed the singer, allowing him to throw in a few more scat phrases running up and down an improvised blues scale, emphasizing the flat seventh in his explosive melodic outline. The audience and the judges erupted in applause before he had even finished. In what was to become a familiar reaction, Sebastian simply walked off stage with barely a hint of acknowledgement that he had done anything worthy of note. He seemed to implicitly realize that such acknowledgment was unnecessary.

Both singers performed fairly well between the boot camp and middle rounds of the "Final 12," with neither being seriously threatened with expulsion. Each appeared to be working with producers to establish clear pop star personae amid the cacophony of a contest, the profile of which had been growing exponentially as it reached its more consequential phases. Sebastian and Noll continued impressive runs of success as other high-profile contestants disappeared. Noll in particular was proving to be an appealingly steady complement to Sebastian's inventive and dramatic reinterpretations of a range of familiar songs. Sebastian repeatedly proved his musical worth by personalizing a wide range of distinct songs, from the triumphant power pop of John Farnham's "You're the Voice" to the classic sentimentality of Bryan Adams's "Everything I Do" to an unusually mournful version of "When Doves Cry." Sebastian always sang confidently, fitting himself into one wardrobe package after another, moving easily around the stage to work the studio audience, without any obvious rhythmic or social inhibition. He always inhabited the small "Idol" stage as if he belonged there. By contrast, throughout the third round and even well into the "Final 12," Noll departed little from what was clearly becoming a formula. Whether he was performing "Let it Be," "When a Man Loves a Woman," or "Livin' on a Prayer," Noll's voice, wardrobe and bodily movements rarely changed. Whether it was "'70s Night," "Soul and R&B Night," or "Beatles Night," his voice always exhibited the same clear tone and slightly raspy texture. He almost always wore collared shirts with two buttons undone and loose jeans. He moved uncomfortably, often appearing to have little idea what to do with the hand that wasn't holding the microphone. Despite their contrasting styles, each found their respective moment of truth in the "Final 12" when staring the very real possibility of elimination in the face.

Two weeks before "Big Band Night," the formula that got Noll noticed started to falter. He was one of the bottom three vote-getters on "'80s night." At the end of the evening he stood onstage to await his fate, the uncertainty of which was unprecedented for his otherwise successful campaign. His performance of "Livin' on a Prayer," a seeming cinch given his previous choices of repertoire, had failed to lead him to safety. He survived, but only just. After a one-week reprieve, Noll reacted to the uncertainty surrounding his candidacy by giving his only display of the entire contest in which he departed from the familiar conventions he had embraced by performing a rousing rendition of "New York, New York." Noll emerged from backstage smiling confidently, wearing a tuxedo with an undone bow tie hanging loosely around his neck, his shirt open to its standard depth; the only period item missing was a cigarette. The familiar strains from the horn section began, emanating from what had grown during the "Final 12" into a very big band indeed. Noll appeared relaxed and happy, singing in his trademark style, clear and unadorned, hugging the lower register of his still limited range. Unusually, Noll brought free and expansive physical movement to his performance. This proved to be an exciting supplement to his strong, precise attack on a melody defined by a series of subtle melodic contours. Noll slowly strutted across the stage during the verses, snapping his fingers with wide, exaggerated motions, gesturing broadly to illustrate a line or two. At one point, in an unusually cheeky move, he introduced "Idol's" Musical Director John Foreman to the crowd as if both were on stage at The Sands. During the half-tempo finale, Noll roared each line, but with exacting intonation and dance moves that channeled Elvis's stint in Vegas far more than Sinatra's. He finished the final cadence with an unusually tuneful and judiciously adorned vocal passage, rising slightly above the tonic before landing on it with a soft thud. The crowd and the judges gave him a standing ovation. Dicko captured the moment by saying, "we said tonight was about crowd pleasing and I think this is one very pleased crowd." The performance set Noll up for his chance at the Grand Final in style.

When Sebastian took to the stage the following week on "'60s Night," his campaign for the "Idol" crown was in serious trouble. While he had made it to the final four without even a minor stumble, the previous week's performances on "Big Band Night" placed him in the bottom two. He stood on the brink of what would have been a shocking elimination. His performance of "Climb Ev'ry Mountain" was subsequently characterized as his "do or die" performance. Host Andrew G. introduced Sebastian by telling the viewers that the audience favorite was preparing to sing a tune from the 1965 musical The Sound of Music, lately made relevant again by Christina Aguilera. The choice of this song was clever. Sebastian had already been at pains to establish himself as a "spiritual" person. Given his musical training in the Assemblies of God church, this potentially odd song choice sat well with his gradually evolving "Idol" persona. Nor was the explicit association of Sebastian with Aguilera an accident. Sebastian was setting in stone his musical profile, defined from the first by his obvious enthusiasm for the florid R&B vocal stylings he used to rework every song he performed. The mere choice of "Climb Ev'ry Mountain" helped create a strong sense of semiotic unity before a note had been sung. The choice of this song referenced both Sebastian's piety and his style of vocal performance, marked as it was by extensive melismatic invention set within familiar melodies. The smirking tone and false surprise of the host's introduction set up Sebastian very well. He stepped on stage to perform a song which was framed as a brave choice, given its origins, but also a deeply personal choice because of the singer's public persona. Given the fragile status of his claim to the title of Australian Idol, the drama of the moment was surely going to reach a fevered pitch.

Sebastian's histrionic performance had few musical similarities with the original version of the song, relying instead on the vocal fireworks and familiar dramatic contours of contemporary R&B as embodied in Aguilera's version, complete with the gospel inspired overtones that define contemporary forms of the genre. Sebastian modestly took center stage wearing a white cotton suit and patterned t-shirt. He had a full "pop" orchestra behind him complete with a small backing choir. He began the first verse singing quietly, but with a full tone as the song's harmonies were outlined only by a piano. When he arrived at the second verse, a substantial string section entered, shortly thereafter anchored by a muted brass section, a heavy, but restrained bass line, drum kit, and timpani. Sebastian's truncated version of the song moved quickly through a second verse which expanded the dynamic range of the song as the orchestra swelled louder then eased into a swirling bridge section which landed Sebastian back on the song's signature lines. He and the orchestra then took these lines to ever-increasing heights, with the backing chorus repeating them several times in an extended final chorus shaped by Sebastian's idiosyncratic and improvisatory variations on the theme. The dramatic contour of the song was one constant, upward trajectory. The real drama exuded from the final verse which was embroidered with extensive melismatic vocal improvisations punctuated by the orchestra's thumping notes of the final line presented in a pounding unison. The middle four notes of the six syllable tagline, "un-til-you-find-your-dream," were all heavily accented, except for the final word, before which the orchestra came to a full stop as Sebastian hit and held the expected high note. The audience exploded in appreciation as the orchestra completed the cadence underneath. Before the harmonic resolution was complete, the studio audience, already cheering loudly, leapt to their collective feet in frenzied applause as the final notes receded into the din. Sebastian wiped away a tear, briefly turned his back to the cameras, composed himself, and bravely accepted the effusive praise of the three judges and the audience. This one moment was later credited not only with winning Sebastian the contest, but with supplying him with his entire career (see Australian Idol: Greatest Moments, 2004, 2004; Australian Idol: The Winner's Story, 2003).

These two "Final 12" performances were nothing if not well timed. Occurring in the final two programs before viewers were to decide on the finalists, Sebastian and Noll were heavy favorites to go through to the Grand Final. When the third contestant also vying for the honor was forced to pull out due to health complications with her vocal cords, Noll and Sebastian were free and clear. As they faced off in the seemingly superfluous "Showdown" episode, a week before the finale, each reverted to type. Noll performed Jimmy Barnes's Australian pub rock anthem "Workin' Class Man" in work boots, white singlet and jeans while Sebastian also played to his strengths, bringing down the house with a sassy rendering of Beyoncé Knowles's "Crazy in Love," clad in a fur coat, faux nose ring, and a massive pair of sunglasses. It was hard to miss the playful, albeit ham-fisted, attempts at costuming. The actual showdown was a central event in the eventual outcome of the contest. Both contestants were asked to perform the song written especially for the show, "Angels Brought Me Here." The song favored, in every way, the singer with the greater vocal range and clarity of emotional expression. In a moment of supreme, and possibly strategic, serendipity, its theme suited Sebastian's repeated evocations of his increasingly public Christianity. Sebastian performed the song with verve and confidence while Noll clearly struggled at the outer range of his abilities. The "Showdown" confirmed what Sebastian and "Idol's" producers had been trying to demonstrate as far back as the "Vocal Boot Camp"; he had always been the one to beat. As predicted by all and sundry, the Grand Final was both Sebastian's coronation and his coming out party, not simply as an "Idol" but as a thoroughly tempered, authentic pop star. As such, it is important to understand how the Grand Final set both Sebastian and Noll up for the futures long promised to them.

The materials that would help each singer realize those promises were the two songs most prominently featured in the nearly-three-hour spectacular that was the Grand Final. As noted in the previous chapter, the Grand Final of Australian Idol is better understood not simply as a celebration of one singer's achievement or as the culminating event of the series, but also as a central strategic transition visibly shepherding two contestants from the demands of a somewhat dubiously regarded singing contest to the more reliable and familiar trappings of musical celebrity. The Grand Final performances themselves were shaky and unpredictable. Noll sang another Australian classic, Moving Pictures' 1980s power ballad "What About Me?," without the clarity and power displayed in his previous performance of the song from "Australian Made" night during the "Final 12". He seemed unsure of where exactly he was supposed to stand, often hitting his marks slightly late. Sebastian performed "Angels Brought Me Here" seconds after he was announced as the winner. He was weepy and distracted. He began the song seated on the edge of the stage, singing to a small coterie of young women gathered between the front row and the stage itself; he appeared exhausted. His voice cracked at key moments and he missed several high notes quite badly, seemingly overwhelmed by his moment. The numerous reiterations of his triumph that followed over the next two years rarely included this performance, relying instead on the moment at which his triumph was confirmed. Given their quality, it is perhaps understandable that the producers left the actual performances from Grand Final night out of future publicity campaigns. But their Grand Final agenda was not confined to guiding viewers through their final votes. The Grand Final was also crafted to produce the first two singles of Australian Idol, the two musical symbols intended to confirm the show's ability to produce real pop stars. Neither singer ever sounded as good as on their respective "debuts." Both songs were clearly calculated to capitalize on each singer's "Idol Journey."

"Angels Brought Me Here" remains one of the most successful strategic decisions of any season of Australian Idol, quickly outgrowing the contest to become Sebastian's signature song. Singer and song became permanently wedded almost immediately after the song's release with "Idol's" producers relying on the familiarity consumers had with Sebastian and with a song in which the expected dramatic contours of contemporary R&B were perfectly confirmed.[4] The first lines could not have been more suited to the moment they implicitly chronicled. Sebastian's vocal line begins with a soft, low alto evoking earnest affection with the words "It's been a long and winding journey, but I'm finally here tonight." The lyrics walk a subtle line between telling Sebastian's story and the more universal story of finding a glorious triumph in love. At the same time, the song is heavily inflected with religious imagery. Phrases like "sunset of your glory," "my dream came true when I found you, my miracle … feels like I've been born again" and "you're the answer to my prayers" all carefully

---

4   For an illustrative example of how "Angels" hews very closely to the familiar contours of contemporary R&B, the structure and dramatic contour of the song matches Christina Aguilera's "Voice Within" almost exactly, right down to each section's length as well as their order.

mimic the conventions of Christian pop with Sebastian singing an apparent love song, while the object of his affections remains artfully ambiguous.

The song begins with only voice and keyboards which display a bright, bell-like texture on top with a smooth, full lower register churning along in an implied mid-tempo groove. There remains a great deal of open space in the texture with the keyboards striking only on the first beat of each measure in the first verse then echoing deep into the background. The rhythmic template of the song is established from the start with heavy on-beat accents. The second verse adds light rhythmic clicks and pops in the percussion as the pre-chorus grows with a full, but quiet rhythmic backing added through layers of instrumentation in the middle and lower ranges, including a bass playing mostly root notes, a guitar outlining the harmonies with arpeggios, and smooth, synthesized string sounds filling in the chords. There is a slight pause before the chorus when a heavier bass and clearer rhythm in the keyboards and guitar begin. The first chorus ends with a brief floating pause accented by wind chimes before the third verse begins. The third verse adds a full drum kit with bass drum, hi-hat, and rim clicks. There is only one verse in this section of the song before the pre-chorus enters. Sebastian's vocal range expands upward as he sings the same pre-chorus materials in the higher octave he used for the first chorus. The compressed structure and increasing vocal intensity push the momentum of the song forward. The second chorus adds harmonies in the backing vocals singing in a rhythmic unison with main vocal line in the first half, then moving into a subtle call and response in the second. In the second chorus, we hear the solid crack of a snare drum for the first time. The song then moves to the minor subdominant with new bridge material, as the forward momentum moves on unperturbed. While the full band plays the bridge, the following pre-chorus is an immediate contrast as the drums, bass, and guitar drop out, leaving only the voice and keyboards to recall the bright, open texture of the introduction. Another floating pause sets up an abrupt half step modulation upward and we are set for the climactic series of choruses to follow. Sebastian sings the final choruses in a predictably dramatic fashion, hitting the highest note of the song at the start to the second of the final set of choruses. The tune continues with the backing vocals carrying the song until Sebastian returns with a minor variation of the chorus to conclude. The guitar, bass, and drums drop out and the nearly forgotten opening texture returns as the harmony gently descends through a minor subdominant passage ending with a dominant to tonic resolution.

Nearly every choice Sebastian made during the contest confirmed his bent as an interpreter of songs popularized primarily by American women. "Angels Brought Me Here" presented fans with Sebastian's own claim on the tradition. The song is dominated by smooth textures in the foreground with a rhythmic background ranging from slight to strong which never completely takes over the role of driving the song. Sebastian's voice never concedes any space to the backing arrangement. The spotless production, computer driven studio techniques, and careful use of layered instrumentation allow Sebastian's vocal personality to predominate. The long upward tilt of the song is built layer by layer as each section gives us some new sound, or just as effectively, briefly takes familiar sounds away. Sebastian uses his voice in perfect accord. His improvisations are held in check until the final chorus and his intonation is flawless, no doubt assisted by the latest vocal smoothing technologies.

He was able to invest an entirely formulaic structure and inconsequential lyrics with a greater sense of propulsive drama than they might otherwise have warranted.

"Angels Brought Me Here" is a concise encapsulation of the pop star persona Sebastian painstakingly crafted during Australian Idol. The success of "Angels" was due in large part to the strong thematic resonance between Sebastian's life story and his "Idol" story, so carefully managed by the producers of the contest. Following his crucial "back from the brink," "do or die," bottom three experience in the "Final 12," when Sebastian presented his stirring version of "Climb Ev'ry Mountain," he returned to his favored material after forays into musical territory in which he often appeared lost. He cleverly chose Knowles's "Crazy in Love" after "Climb" as an upbeat proclamation of his potential as a pop star. But Sebastian's feminine mystique went well beyond his repertoire. His bright, easy smile, devout virginal Christianity, and sweet speaking voice formed the foundation of his pop star personality. His image included a penchant for soft, white mesh clothing, increasingly extensive adornment through all manner of jewelry and lithe dance moves supplemented with a seemingly constant touching of audience members in the front rows. His off-stage personality was free and easy, but he could slide into earnest, televised emotional admission at a moment's notice. Sebastian straddled a very public line between accessible public pop star and private devotee of Jesus and gospel inflected R&B. Sebastian's Australian and Malaysian origins, gorgeous mop of teased, kinky hair, and associations with specifically African-American styles explicitly marked him as a glowing example of Australian cosmopolitanism, safely feminized and removed from any hint of aggression or controversy. Sebastian's claims to some credible measure of musical celebrity rested on the conjoining of his persona and this song, fused at the moment of triumph during his last moments on the "Idol" stage.

Noll's first single was a slick version of "What About Me?," a song described as an alternative national anthem by host Andrew G. The song also capitalized on a strategic fusion of singer and song through a musical familiarity Noll had already crafted during the contest. This much less celebratory song exemplifies the expected structure and dramatic contours of the power ballad, a form Noll championed during the contest. The conventions of the form were confirmed by Noll's sweet voice and sturdy intonation during the early verses which evolved through a raspy build-up to climax in the strong, long, held notes of the final choruses. The song evoked the well-trodden ground of Noll's rural struggles. "What About Me?" begins with a narrative frame which places the singer as a chronicler of those struggling outsiders most often referred to in Australia as "battlers." The first lines are unambiguous. "There's a little boy waiting at the counter of the cornershop," and "they never ever see him from the top." As "he gets pushed around, knocked to the ground," the boy's response is the simple, oft-repeated cry, "What About Me?" The second verse outlines a similar tale of struggle. The singer makes a few demands of the high and mighty: "Take a step back and see the little people. They might be young but they're the ones that make the big people big." Each evocation of the "battler" ends with the same question. Noll is the outsider hero, demanding a fair go for his people. The final verse presents a note of near despondency as Noll sings, "And now I'm standing on the corner, all the world's gone home." The narrative climaxes only with a slight pause for hope. "I guess I'm lucky, I smile a lot," says the narrator, "but sometimes I wish for more than I've got." Given his own struggles, it is not a substantial journey from singer to song.

The music has all the attributes of a classic power ballad, but with a dramatic contour exactly mirroring Sebastian's "Angels." The song begins with a lone piano outlining the harmony of the bridge, easing into the first verse as synthesized strings briefly add to the texture. The voice and piano are drenched in echo but remain clear and up front in the mix. The producers have not sacrificed the attack of the piano notes or the texture of Noll's voice, but instead created a huge space behind them. Bright, but subtle percussion sounds mark the spaces between the chords and echo off into the deep background. The first chorus swells only slightly adding a thicker texture in the piano as the synthesizers re-enter underneath. As the next verse begins, a full band enters quietly with drums and synthesized strings holding the middle range over a subdued bass line. The song pauses briefly as Noll sings the tagline and then the full band suddenly thuds in, complete with power chords on a strong, slightly distorted guitar and a synthesized string section creating a thick, but not overcrowded texture. During a brief bridge section, the backing band pushes the momentum somewhat by expanding the dynamic range with a walking guitar line that buzzes through the rising root notes of a harmony while the string sounds also add a rising figure, both fading out as Noll gives us one more verse which reverts to the opening texture of a lone piano and voice. The pre-chorus enters for the last time reprising the harmony of the second half of the verse. The full band re-enters, hitting on the last eighth note of four and the first beat of the next measure in unison. The rising string figure returns and a heavy power chord on the dominant in the guitar line brings the band to a sudden stop as Noll intones "What About Me?" in a slightly drawn out triple meter, landing on "me" just slightly before the down beat of the first measure of the final set of choruses as the band enters full force. The song stomps through two choruses, the last of which repeats the vocal melody and harmony of the last measure of the chorus three times before returning to the quiet texture of the opening to close the song, with the now subdued cry of "What About Me?" repeating mournfully three times.

Noll remained comparatively opaque throughout the contest, but that was a huge part of his charm. His vocal range is not as wide as Sebastian's while his vocal timbre is just as clear and light but with only the occasional hint of vibrato or melisma. Instead, Noll centered his singing on the presentation of strong, unadorned vocal lines accenting the clarity of the melodies rather than making cluttered forays in and around familiar tunes. Nor did he make use of the dips and slides characteristic of the country singers to whom he was often compared. Instead, he relied most heavily on the solid, straight, held notes of power pop so perfectly exhibited in "What About Me?". His careful use of a scratchy, raspy texture in his voice in particularly dramatic verses and the high notes of the final choruses of most of the songs he performed during the contest added to the sense of personal expression in his performances, although Noll seemed careful not to be too expressive. Notably, his performances were almost entirely bereft of the rhythmic use of his body. Most often, he stood almost stock still, perhaps swaying slightly, apparently even poking fun at his penchant for bodily stiffness with a particularly clunky swing of his hips at the end of his rendition of "New York, New York." The producers routinely associated Noll with singers such as Bryan Adams and Richard Marx and not without reason. His clearly chosen local affiliations were too traditional "Aussie pub rock" as his performance of the sacred "Workin' Class Man" showed. However, Noll's version of pub rock was shorn of those untoward elements of aggression or controversy that have long characterized the form, a process of cultural sanitization akin to Sebastian's.

Noll's self-presentation was homologous to his singing style. He was a taciturn constant in the various "Idol" programs, calmly winding his way through a thickly crowded series of events with a subtle charisma that was rarely the subject of particular attention. He tended towards black t-shirts and jeans. His quiet, but strong presence was credited to his origins in the New South Wales country town of Condoblin. Importantly, Noll's campaign was far more associated with the trials of his working life than any of the other contestants. He was seen as a kind of throwback to a brand of classic Australian masculinity summed up in the words "good Aussie bloke." He presented himself as a remarkably sympathetic figure who rarely spoke of his troubles unless prompted and never appeared to require any special treatment. This, combined with his emotional, anthemic remake of "What About Me?," made him the performer of the year for those living in Australia's struggling, shrinking, oft-forgotten bush towns (see Miller, 2003; Phillips, 2004).[5] The song put him in the forefront of a tradition of Australian rock singers that had fallen into disuse in recent years and made him a hero to many a "tweener" less interested in the international style of R&B employed by Sebastian.

Each singer was an important catalyst for their gradual branding that began with their initial auditions. "Idol's" producers did not invent either singer's talent as each performed within themselves to make a strong impression in their original auditions. Both appeared humbled by their initial success. The ways in which each contestant's original audition was framed in the tightly-scripted televised versions of the early rounds of the contest depended on what each brought with them into the audition room. Both brought strong voices and definitive expressions of their public musical selves. These foundations changed little during the long contest. Instead, a musical context was constructed around each performer using familiar expectations already attached to their chosen genres. Near constant narrative retellings of each singer's "Idol Journey" helped to mark each singer retrospectively as a saleable commodity creating foregone conclusions out of those many months of trial and doubt. But the producers were never credited with these narrative interventions on the behalf of each singer. Instead, the producers created a context in which each could fill in the blanks left by their subtly stylized introductions to Australian television audiences. Both singers were shaped to represent much of what it means to be Australian, and an Australian pop star, in ways that were far more complementary than they were competitive. Sebastian was routinely held up as a representative of urban, multicultural Australia. His wardrobe choices played on notions of ambiguous sexuality and his evident joy and humility made him a pleasant, popular, non-threatening performer. Noll was the embodiment of the bedrock values of country Australia, which are, of

---

5   Over ten thousand people trekked to Condoblin for a special ANZAC Day concert by Noll, representing almost three times the town's resident population ("NSW homecoming hero," 2004).

course, often held up as the symbolic foundations of the entire nation. His story was beautifully clear. He had a hard go, but never complained. He was in many ways, an explicit embodiment of that most Australian of cultural characters, the battler.

However, if we accept the proposition made in the previous chapter that audience investment had to eventually rest not only in individual contestants, but in the show itself, we can see how the synergy of Sebastian and Noll placed a definitive stamp on the entire first series of Australian Idol. It was the ways in which this synergy was constructed and circulated through the expansive "Idol" medium that allowed the producers to claim that the program came to represent all of Australia, from city to country. The sharp contrast in background and experience between the two finalists played on vague notions of "togetherness" and "diversity" while papering over some fairly significant social cleavages in the wider society. In this respect, "Idol" proved itself to be incapable of explanatory nuance not restricted to an individual's life history and ignorant of cultural politics that were not resolutely affirmative. Clearly, the concerns of the producers lay closer to home. "Idol's" producers were primarily concerned with managing ideal consumer relationships removed from the complexities of cultural life, not actual social relationships enmeshed in the ambiguities of an increasingly divided country. Without Sebastian, perceptions of the program as a provincial talent show would have persisted. Without Noll, the constant, ringing complaints describing Australian Idol as a sell out to the multinational music industry would have resonated far more widely. The competition between these good natured, attractive performers made the Grand Final one of the highest-rating television programs in Australian history (Dale, 2003b).

The Threat of the Assembly Line

Between the end of series one and the start of series two, Australian Idol was said to have copped a significant level of abuse both from inside and from outside the music industry. The stinging rebukes to the contest were alleged to have come from industry executives and musicians alike. The purported attacks provoked a press campaign bent on defending the show and its impact on the Australian music industry, a rear guard action that lasted well into the second series. The most public dust-up was attributed to the fact that the show's "beacons of popularity," three of the top four finalists from series one, were "snubbed" at the 2004 Australian Recording Industry Awards (ARIAs). The nominations, voted on by a select group of artists, producers, and industry executives, failed to place any of the first crop of "Idols" in the top five of any of the "more prestigious" award categories, such as "Best Song," "Album of the Year," or "Breakthrough Artist" (Toy and Connelly, 2004). Instead, the three contestants from series one were nominated only for categories based on single and album sales, several of which they won. The "snub" was attributed to "elitism" and "snobbery" on the part of unidentified "music purists" who attached a "stigma" to the contest, a point driven home through unattributed claims that "Idol" "is reviled by those who believe its pre-packaged format undermines the promotion of more authentic music" (Jinman, 2004b; Chalmers, 2004b).

Despite the fact that "Idol's" public defenders didn't identify any specific critics (McMenemy, 2004), the publicity campaign combating this distressing "undercurrent of disdain" (Chalmers, 2004b) for the show was indicative of the theme that would come to define the second series. The second series of Australian Idol played out the tension between the two most visible forms of the contest's primary currency: credibility. This currency was measured both in terms of the hard facts of record sales as well as the broader more ambiguous category of popularity, described in Chapter 5 as a kind of hegemonic brand power. For the show's producers, it was not enough to measure the reach of "Idol" merely through the cold tabulations of units moved. "Idol's" producers craved what a political scientist might call "soft power," measured in terms of cultural influence. This more subtle demonstration was made through many not-so-subtle attempts to frame the second crop of "Idol's" as unique "role models," meeting the challenges of the contest by adhering to a familiar model of musical celebrity: someone willing to work hard to make the most of their opportunities by using their innate talent to communicate genuine emotions through music. The producers sought out academics and youth workers for media campaigns designed to frame "Idol" not simply as a compelling singing contest, but as an expression of "our basic humanity." "Idol," said one, gave the public an opportunity to watch the talents of ordinary people "unfold in the raw." Another commentator said he "would pour scorn on anyone who tries to belittle Australian Idol." He argued that the contestants "are fantastic role models in the sense they've had a goal, developed a strategy and gone for it" (Jinman, 2004b). The implicit conflation of the contestants, their talent, and the workings of the contest itself was a common rhetorical move not confined to the extensive media campaigns defending the show. Almost as if by design, the full range of argument put forward by "Idol's" diverse advocates obscured the exact nature of the contest's pervasive machinations, all of which were geared towards removing any taint of manufacture from the contestants. And yet, throughout the second series, these routine protests against "Idol's" critics paradoxically served only to reveal, not erase, the extensive scaffolding on which each "Idol's" televised pedestal rested.

As with series one, the construction of each contestant's "Idol" persona was founded on the materials gathered from their original auditions. For Casey Donovan, Australia's second "Idol," and Anthony Callea, the runner-up, the evolving meanings of each singer's candidacy were shaped in specific relation to the ways in which the materials gathered at each singer's original audition were presented and re-presented in increasing detail throughout the contest. Donovan's initial audition only rated a passing glance when first broadcast, presented in a sequence with several other Sydney-bound singers. Callea was treated more generously. His audition was framed by host Andrew G's conspiratorial whisper into the camera, "I think he's gonna do all right." Described as a "professional" singer and voice coach, Callea was confident and self-assured. Donovan, described simply as "16 years old," appeared to be extremely shy and uncomfortable. Yet, these two contrasting styles of self-presentation were unified by the narrative trajectory each singer's story took afterwards. Donovan was said to have emerged from her shell during the contest, while Callea was said to have become less "plastic" and more himself, themes reiterated countless times. Both singers were perceived to have achieved the necessary ends of honest self-expression through similar means, but starting from positions of polar opposition. The assured Callea gradually overcame the perceived barrier of excessive precision to enhance his public displays of emotion. The insecure Donovan shed her "protective mask of death metal clothing" and "bugger-off attitude" to connect with viewers to claim the ultimate prize (Jinman and McIntyre, 2004). The success of each was largely attributed to their respective acts of self-realization through self-transformation. At the hearts of these model stories are two repertoires connecting singer to song, contestant to contest, and "Idol" to audience.

The Semi-Professional and the "Ugly Ducking"

As noted earlier, Casey Donovan did not arrive for her a cappella audition looking the part of an "Idol," nor did she display any particular zeal for the prospect. Instead, she wore a gray cotton tracksuit top fully zippered up, board shorts, thickly striped knee-high socks and mismatched converse runners. Her black, knotted, partially dreadlocked hair hung over the sides of her face. But it wasn't just her attire that marked her as an unlikely "Idol." Donovan is also what several journalists referred to as "today's plus size diva." She was hailed, often patronizingly, as a triumphant agent in the fight against stereotypical models of beauty simply because of her body type (ibid.). When she arrived at her audition, it was difficult to see her as anything other than what she was, a 16-year-old girl who seemed uncomfortable in her own body. She often looked at her feet and mumbled brisk answers to the judges' searching questions. However, her singing voice and repertoire choices had almost no obvious connection to her clothing style or her understated demeanor. She sang in the familiar "Idol" style, relying primarily on strongly expressive renditions of rock and pop ballads, wisely eschewing anything by her two favorite bands, Incubus and Nirvana. Despite often distorting her intonation by oversinging passages of high notes, she could perform with both power and subtlety, visibly moving audiences and judges alike throughout the contest with her almost nakedly emotional style.

In the full version of her audition, not broadcast until a few days after the Grand Final on *Australian Idol: The Winner's Journey*, the contrast between Donovan's self-presentation and performance style was painfully clear. The halting Q&A with the judges, also not originally broadcast, was unusually poignant. Broadcast after her fresh triumph, the dissimilarities between the concurrent images of the stumbling auditionee and the newly charismatic "Idol" were readily apparent. However, her ability to perform was not in doubt. Donovan performed a few verses from "A Million Tears" by Kasey Chambers. The song is pure misery, describing the visceral sense of distress evoked by the song's narrator on meeting a former lover in public. Donovan began with the lines, "All my life, I've welcomed pain," presented in a husky, powerful alto. She stayed very close to the original melody, adding almost no ornamentation. Each line was sung without a clear tempo, with noticeable pauses making each phrase seem self-contained. Donovan only changed her dynamic level once, as she increased her volume dramatically and without warning to hit the high notes of the distinctly separated lines "I'll drink to the madness," and "that made me this way." The judges' praise was unabashed. Marcia Hines told Donovan that

"Kasey would be proud of you" and Mark Holden concurred. Hines then continued, saying "You really felt those lyrics; you've lived that." Dicko was only slightly more circumspect, suggesting, while "you haven't got a perfect voice by a long shot … you can communicate a song like that incredibly well," adding later, "you fascinate me." Marcia Hines then leapt in again giving Donovan some carefully considered advice: "When you're a performer, especially with a voice like that, girlfriend, you got nothing to apologize about. You came in here looking at your feet. I don't ever want to see you do that again." As Donovan comically walked out taking abnormally high steps, the judges burst out in laughter while still continuing to praise the young singer's emotionally charged rendition of a song that speaks to a kind of maturity and adult weariness her overwrought performance lacked.

Callea sang "Wishes" by Human Nature, an Australian boy band which peaked in the mid 1990s. In terms of demeanor and bearing, Callea appeared the consummate professional. Dressed in a bomber jacket, t-shirt, and jeans, the diminutive singer had his dark hair arranged in jagged, gel-covered, spikes running over the middle of his head from front to back; his skin appeared wet with a thin sheen of perspiration. Between the shine of his jacket, hair, and skin, Callea appeared to have been dipped in a light coat of varnish. He entered the audition room confidently and with great ease, smiling slightly and answering the judges' queries without the slightest stumble. He appeared serious, but not intimidated. When he began singing, he displayed a smooth lower range alto and easy bodily motion, crafting a clear tempo through his singing and by moving enough to hint at dancing while not actually doing so. This gave his performance a kind of studied casualness. He began on the second verse in which the narrator is asking for yet another chance at forgiveness. Callea worked his way through the third verse with complete confidence as well. Bravely, Callea also presented the fifth verse, essentially a vocal solo without much in the way of lyrical content, then concluded with the second verse again. This gave him an opportunity to display a style of vocal singing clearly taken from the boy band tradition of the mid to late 1990s. His vocal range was much broader than Donovan's and he used his pitch and dynamic range to great effect. He also ornamented his singing heavily during the nearly wordless fifth verse and presented his notes with an almost classic pop clarity in the other sections. The contrast was effective. The judges' praise was unambiguous although not demonstratively enthusiastic. Mark Holden and Marcia Hines made unusual admissions, both noting that they had seen Callea perform several times and that he had made an impression on each of them. Holden, in particular, praised the singer's commitment. Dicko asked simply, "What do you think it takes to win this competition?" to which Callea confidently and unhesitatingly responded, as if on cue, "determination and belief in yourself." Dicko then told the singer that he had, "the best voice we've heard today, absolutely." Continuing in an unusually even and business-like tone, Dicko suggested that Callea was "maybe a bit too plastic; you need roughing up a bit to give you an edge." After being waved on to Sydney, Callea formally shook hands with each judge and exited. The entire audition felt like a pleasant, routine banking transaction (Australian Idol: Series Two, July 14, 2004).

When each singer returned for the "Vocal Boot Camp," their stories picked up where each had left off. Casey was asked to clean up a bit and Anthony was asked to get a little dirty. Neither singer had any serious trouble during the boot camp, and while each received only moderate attention, they both moved into the "Semi-Finals" with ease. Both were among the least controversial choices made by the judges, despite the work Hines and Holden had to do on Dicko to let Donovan through. However, in the round of 30 the two singers' paths diverged immediately and dramatically with Callea failing to be voted through while Donovan was the recipient of unusually fulsome praise from the judges; the praise was definitive for a "Semi-Finals" performance. In both cases, the fates of both singers were said to hinge on the perceived earnestness of their expression, or lack thereof. However, it was not immediately clear why Callea was considered "plastic" while Donovan was thought "real." As will become clear below, while the musical justification for these distinctions is thin at best, the contextual forces surrounding each contestant's performances preceding the "Final 12" put a definitive stamp on their larger meanings within the contest.

Callea had the mixed fortune of being the first performer to grace the mini "Idol" stage in the "Semi-Finals". He was obviously nervous with co-host James Mathison noting that Callea's left leg was vibrating intensely as the singer sought to compose himself before performing. When he arrived on stage to perform a truncated arrangement of Robbie Williams's "Angels," Callea was all confidence. He said he chose the song because he thought "it would connect with a wide range of audiences, young and old," but incongruously described the choice as "a bit of a risk." His performance was polished and clean, with perfect intonation and enunciation. Wearing a simple, crisp, white collared shirt, and jeans, he began his performance standing at the back of the small stage holding the microphone in his hands. He sang the first two lines in near identical fashion in the lower end of his alto range with a slight breathy sound around the edges of his voice. He ended the lone verse with a quiet, but strong note held for two full bars. He affected an easy transition to the pre-chorus through a subtle drop-off in intensity. When delivering the words "I'm loving angels instead," Callea used little ornamentation and employed a descending melodic figure allowing his voice to almost trail off in volume and strength. This set up the chorus nicely. Again, Callea held his fire somewhat, delivering the two halves of the chorus with little melismatic excess, instead giving the camera a sly look before hitting his high note. The most mannered part of his short performance was the delivery of the tagline which Callea stretched and adorned, altering his pace to erase the strong tempo he had established previously, dragging out the word "instead" to the breaking point, forcing the backing band to noodle a bit too long on the final chord. As he sang, Callea continuously used his body and his hands in a continuous fit of professional expressiveness, swaying easily and without any visible discomfort. During his performance, the singer gradually moved forward to the front of the stage almost without ceremony. He timed his approach masterfully to make his arrival at the front of the stage coincide with the high note which ended the chorus. It was clear that, despite the lack of a studio audience, Callea was still working the room. He looked into the camera only when it panned by him and otherwise appeared to be gesturing to a non-existent front row (Australian Idol: Series Two, August 8, 2004).

The judges' response was nearly identical to their response to his original audition, despite the fact that over a month of real time had passed between the two. Mark Holden called his performance "first class" but wanted "a touch of the devil" from Callea. Dicko, as usual, had the most colorful reaction. While praising Callea's "absolutely rock solid performance," he warned the singer that "at this stage of the competition, this is where you have to engage the Australian public and they're going to demand a bit more personality … a bit more bacteria, to show what you're all about and bit more of an edge." Dicko's comments poured out in one long sentence that ended with the pithy phrase, "at the moment you look more like an Anthony Callea semi-realistic action figure than you do the real person" (ibid.). Callea looked both confused and bemused as he left the stage. On the live verdict show the next night, the Australian public "agreed with Dicko" and did not send Callea through (Australian Idol: Series Two, August 9, 2004).

Donovan had an easier time making it through the round, appearing in the middle of the final group of ten, a group that was far less able than Callea's. She chose "Here's Where I Stand," originally performed by Tiffany Taylor in the film *Camp*. Donovan wore a long, dark skirt with a subtle print in purple and black, with a multi-layered black blouse and a heavy array of black beaded necklaces. She made a point of noting that she carried her good luck charms with her on stage, two small fake mice and a plastic spider. They received almost as much attention as she did, until she started singing. Donovan stood in the middle of the stage behind the microphone stand and moved little during her performance. She began singing in a clear and calm manner, with a slight smile, swaying only slightly. The short first verse was followed by an equally short pre-chorus, each line delivered without ornamentation, using solid intonation and clear enunciation. The first chorus used the same harmonic and melodic materials as the verse and Donovan delivered them with increased strength, but without much in the way of drama. She saved the drama for the bridge and the final chorus. As she sung the bridge, Donovan increased the intensity of her delivery and moved up in power and range. She landed on the highest note she had sung to this point and held it as the band modulated up a full step underneath. She then sang "Here's-where-I-stand" hitting every note hard, displaying a lack of control and maturity in her voice as her power overcame her intonation forcing her slightly off pitch. She completed the second chorus and added a minor flourish at the end. She had not moved during the performance and had her eyes closed during the most dramatic parts of it. Style aside, Donovan's performance was almost exactly the same as Callea's in terms of dramatic contour, tempo, vocal technique, and the use of carefully timed melismatic ornamentation. Musically, there was little to choose between them, with the possible exception of Callea's far more precise intonation and control (Australian Idol: Series Two, July 21, 2004).

Donovan said she chose "Here's Where I Stand" because "it's just basically saying, here's where I stand, this is who I am." The judges picked up on the theme in their effusive praise after she was finished. Marcia Hines told Donovan that her "voice comes from this place within and that is such a gift," while Dicko told her, "there's something about you that's deeply special." He told her that her song choice was perfect and "I believed every word." Mark Holden could barely control himself. At the end of a series of stuttering half sentences he gave her his patented "Touchdown" maneuver in which he leaps out of his chair, winds his right arm around in a windmill motion and yells "Touchdown" while pointing at the performer. This had never been done in the "Semi-Finals" and clearly works better with a live studio audience in tow as it is intended to move voter sympathies. Holden later said, "it was stunning to see her open her soul." Donovan was the first go through to the "Final 12" from her group (Australian Idol: Series Two, August 22, 2004).

Meanwhile, Callea had to return one more time to that little "Idol" stage to take one last shot at the "Final 12" in the "Wild Card" show. In his pre-show interview, Callea said he had taken the judges' criticisms to heart. "I just don't want the performance to look so polished," he said, choosing the Hoobastank song "The Reason" to show the judges that he could "jump out of his comfort zone." Interestingly, his "Wild Card" performance was little different from his "Semi-Finals" performance. He again looked visibly nervous before taking the stage, this time wearing a patterned t-shirt and jeans. The song displayed almost the exact same tempo and instrumentation as his version of "Angels." The only difference was the immediate entry of the rhythm guitar and drums, although both were lightly played and sat well in the background. Callea's voice was again marked by the familiar breathy texture as he began singing quietly in his lower register. The only obvious difference was his use of a microphone stand placed in the middle of the stage. Callea presented the first two lines of the song in identical fashion and leapt into a surprisingly clear and well-tuned falsetto in order to raise the intensity slightly before going into the chorus. As the chorus began and he sang the lines "the reason is you" for the first time, he grabbed the microphone from its stand as if overcome by the moment. As he kept singing, raising his tone, pitch, and intensity, he flipped the microphone from hand to hand and pointed into the close-up camera as he hit the words "the reason is you" for the last time. He concluded this very brief version of the song with the line "I'm sorry I hurt you" delivered in the same tone as he used at the start of the song, this time offering his big, sad, dark eyes to the camera (Australian Idol: Series Two, August 30, 2004).

The judges were perfectly clear about why they thought this performance had been a dramatic improvement over Callea's "Semi-Finals" presentation. Marcia thanked him for listening to the advice she and her fellow judges gave him after previous performances and thanked him "for showing us your spirit and your soul … That's the most I've ever seen you," she concluded. Mark called it a breakthrough while Dicko said, in characteristic fashion, "Who are you and what have you done with Anthony? The Anthony I've seen up to now has been a life support system for a dodgy hairdo." The compliments continued to flow the next night when the judges became positively nurturing. After putting Callea through as their first "Wild Card," Marcia said the best part of his struggle for her was that "you learnt something. Your humility showed through and you showed us who you were," as if they had planned it that way. The rhetoric surrounding the "Wild Card" show was primarily aimed at justifying the role the judges played in usurping the power that was supposed to reside in the "Australian public." Mark Holden cited a singer from series one, Cosima Devito, who just happened to have the number one hit in Australia that very week and had also survived the "Wild Card" process. He noted, "this is the time when you've just got to let all your demons, all your love, all your pain, whatever it is that you need to lift off, you've got to lift off." The materials needed for lift off were of ambiguous character. As each judge stated repeatedly, this contest was not just about singing well, it was also about "connecting with the Australian public" (ibid.).

Donovan "connected" simply by being straightforward in her style of presentation. The fact that she often allowed her emotion to overpower her ability was a virtue in this context. It demonstrated an earnest enthusiasm for self-expression that defined her as a performer. It also suited her often teenage-themed, angst-laden material extremely well. In choosing "Here's Where I Stand," she evoked much of the song's original context and emotional impact. The original, performed by Tiffany Taylor in the film Camp, provided a triumphant conclusion to the story of an overweight teenage girl whose parents had her jaw wired shut to keep her from overeating. The obvious connections to Donovan were clear, but implicit, addressed obliquely in what Dicko called "a remarkable song choice." Callea found his professionalism, undeniable stage presence, and near perfect tone, texture, intonation, and expression to be obstacles in the quest for honest self-expression. It was unfortunate that he chose a Robbie Williams song which was seen as an easy choice. Worse than his song choice, however, was his perceived overreliance on a set of musical tools that were apparently insufficient in the pursuit of authentic musical celebrity. The dynamic between the "ugly duckling" and the "semi-professional" defined the rest of the contest for these two singers as each struggled to meet the judges' often vague and contradictory expectations by placing themselves somewhere between technical perfection and histrionic self-expression.[6]

For Callea, the moment in which these two forces met was on "Idol's Choice" night in the fifth week of the "Final 12". It was the first night on which the full "pop" orchestra was present and it marked the moment at which Callea emerged as a legitimate hope for the Grand Final. In the four weeks prior, Callea had not struggled, but neither had he distinguished himself. He had presented an interesting range of material, none of which seemed necessarily intended to satisfy the judges' admonitions to reveal more of himself. His previous weeks' performance on "Disco Night" was a sunny rendition of "Car Wash" which saw Callea wearing big mirrored sunglasses, a hooded sweatshirt with cutoff sleeves and jeans. Prior to that he performed a sassy version of "Gimme Some Lovin'" on "'60s Night." Callea was very much a stylistic chameleon, whose changes in vocal style matched his repertoire as seamlessly as his changes of wardrobe.

When he walked on stage to perform "The Prayer," a hit for Celine Dion and Andrea Bocelli, the dramatic context was markedly similar to that which surrounded Guy Sebastian's performance of "Climb Ev'ry Mountain." But there was no sense that Callea was facing a "do-or-die" moment. Callea had already faced his "Idol" abyss only a few weeks earlier when he was not chosen by the voters to continue into the "Final 12". Having survived as a "judges' choice" during the "Wild Card" program, he often noted how the experience made him realize how delicate his status was from that point on in the contest. Claiming every performance as his "last

---

6   The term "ugly duckling" was applied to Donovan by her father as her triumph was unfolding in real time right behind him. The moment was captured live at the Opera House and was chronicled in *Australian Idol: The Winner's Journey* (2004).

chance," Callea never wavered during the Finals, never landing in the bottom three and making it through to the Grand Final, thereby reclaiming the public support he had previously been denied. It was his performance of "The Prayer" that put him over the top. It changed perceptions of his candidacy for many of the same reasons Sebastian's performance changed his. Again, we find that this was due in part to a similar sense of semiotic unity joining together the singer and the song. Callea's "Italian roots" were on repeated display during the round of 30 and the "Final 12," embodied in his large supportive Melbourne family and his famous description of himself as "just a short little wog" (Australian Idol: Series Two, August 26, 2004). While his small stature and remarkably rich voice stood him in stark contrast to the other male contestants, it was Callea's ability to perform both parts of "The Prayer," singing Dion's part in English and Bocelli's in Italian, that lent credibility to his song choice. More important, this helped frame Callea's performance as a form of deep, personal expression because, at this point in the contest, there was still little indication that he was anything more than an unusually polished, semi-professional singer.

Callea walked on stage, modestly dressed in a light colored sweater with a white shirt underneath and a dark suit jacket over the top. The song began with a solo piano outlining the harmonies of the main verse as Callea quietly sang using the same breathy, low alto he had used so well in his previous performances. A solo violin entered into the background to supplement the piano, just before the full orchestra entered to fill out the second verse. Callea's singing was as finely controlled and tuned as any performance he had given. The first verse ended with a strong held note that perfectly resolved this section of the song. He began the chorus, sung in Italian, with a stronger more powerful sound, an increase in the speed with which he delivered his notes and a remarkably clear and precise delivery of a comparatively complex and difficult melody. The orchestra gradually swelled the dynamic range of the song through each distinct section of the chorus. Deep and heavy brass and percussion parts entered, the drums thudding on two and four offering the first distinct beat in the song. Callea then delivered a second climax, reaching and holding the high notes of the final chorus. At this point the orchestra and the singer held the moment with great solidity, both coming to a full stop several seconds later. A brief pinprick of silence was followed by a quiet harmonic resolution over which the singer provided a subtle, clear falsetto to finish with an understated flourish. The crowd and the judges leapt to their feet for an extended standing ovation, the longest of the series to this point.

The performance was as memorable as any produced by the show and Callea appeared to control every second of it. His vocal performance was probably more assured than any other from the second series, both technically and dramatically. His intonation and enunciation were nearly perfect, a fact highlighted by the song itself and by the fact that this consummate stage performer stood in one spot during the entire performance. Dicko, as usual, provided the defining response. After remaining visibly speechless for a long time, he seemed to sense that anything substantive or critical he might have to say would be superfluous. Instead, he said simply, "that is the finest performance I have seen on that stage over the last two years." This was followed by another roar from the audience, praise Callea accepted with visible humility.

Callea continued to expand his range and repertoire as he completed his seven "Final 12" performances without ever slipping into the relegation zone. The next week, on the "Beatles Special," he performed a rousing version of "I Saw Her Standing There" and followed this on "'80s Night" with a pedestrian version of Foreigner's "I Want to Know What Love Is." Callea continued to rely on the professionalism and stagecraft that had been the source of so much strife for him in the early rounds, giving assured versions of "Fever" and "Route 66" on "Big Band Night" and a wildly ornamented rendition of "Bridge Over Troubled Water" on "'70s Night." While he was able confidently to reinvent himself on a weekly basis by inhabiting a wide range of musical costumes, he was still relying on the same set of performative tools and gestures that had failed to win him the public support required to enter the "Final 12" in the first place. By surviving right to the end, he highlighted an odd paradox of "Idol." Callea had devoted himself to a competitive singing career since his early teens, winning enough talent shows and singing competitions to buy a luxury BMW sedan which he lovingly washed during his first televised portrait during the "Semi-Finals." Callea's "authentic" self that he displayed on Australian Idol was that of an ambitious semi-professional singer with the ability to use his voice and stage presence to capture a moment by "communicating emotions through music." It was exactly his ability to transform himself every week that allowed him to survive the taxing trials of the "Final 12," yet this is also what made him appear disingenuous. Despite the fact that he had six more nights of performing to survive following his breakthrough with the "The Prayer," just to get to the Grand Final, and despite the fact that the competition was fierce, Callea was never really pressed to surpass "The Prayer." And in many ways he didn't. He presented the song as his signature tune on Grand Final night and it was the first single he recorded after the contest was complete, eventually becoming the fastest-selling single in Australian music history (Moran, 2005).

Donovan's "Final 12" experience could not have been more different. Her repertoire was more thematically unified, her performance style and image more uniform, and the response from voters more ambiguous. She faced elimination three times after receiving one of the three lowest vote tallies on three separate nights. Yet the themes that defined her performances in the early rounds of the competition were only amplified throughout the "Final 12". Her repertoire and performance style marked her as honest and her repeated forays into the danger zone of elimination only confirmed this by demonstrating her unwillingness or inability to change her persona to please a fickle public. Donovan sang songs that expressed a defiance to the pain others might cause, such as "Beautiful" by India Arie, "The Special Ones" by George, or "Take Me As I Am" by Vanessa Amorosi. Stylistically, it gradually became clear during the "Final 12" that she was on her most stable ground when singing power ballads or straight ahead rock songs like Cheap Trick's "The Flame," "Don't Speak" by No Doubt, and "Somebody to Love" by Jefferson Airplane. She even shoehorned songs like "Eleanor Rigby" and "You're So Vain" to fit the mould. Donovan's route through the "Final 12" also seemed to be the most volatile. She was often relegated to face elimination after strong performances and famously received the highest vote tally of the week after performing "Eleanor Rigby," despite the fact that her performance fell apart completely when she forgot the words and stopped singing altogether. In every case, however, the judges were conspicuous in their support of her candidacy, defending her failures and extolling her triumphs.

Donovan's most important triumph was her performance of "You're So Vain," which, while not her best, was surely her most effective. Occurring during week ten of the "Final 12," there were only three contestants left and Donovan had placed in the bottom three the previous week. This was her last chance to make the Grand Final and she was not well placed to do so. Yet she entered the stage walking almost casually and began singing while still ambling forward. She wore yet another variation on the uniform she had been wearing since her couture conversion during the "Vocal Boot Camp": a dark skirt, layered black top, and a heavy complex of necklaces. Her voice was clear and solid, although as the melody went down on the line "you had one eye in the mirror" the last syllable completely disappeared. Donovan appeared to move easily and time her increases in vocal intensity and strength extremely well. As she moved into the chorus through the last two key melodic lines of the pre-chorus, she sped up her delivery, noticeably leading the band into the chorus. At the end of each chorus she hammered the words "Don't you, don't you, don't you?" with a power that was familiar from her previous performances, but nicely controlled in this one. By the end of her shortened version of the song, Donovan had transformed the easy sway of the introduction into an accusatory retort to some imagined slight. By the end she was glowering at the camera as she spit out the end of the chorus two final times. After she finished, the mood of the crowd and the judges was positively buoyant. Marcia Hines said, "every girl in here knows exactly what you are talking about" while Dicko delighted everyone when he remarked, "there's a guy at home who's testicles are shriveled right now." It was Donovan's primary champion, Mark Holden, who seemed to have missed the convivial vibe entirely as he pounded his desk rhythmically and yelled, "there is only one Casey Donovan and she will be compared to nobody." He then wound up his right arm for another in a series of "touchdowns" given to the singer. The next night, Donovan was voted through to the Grand Final receiving the highest number of votes.

This Grand Final was not the foregone conclusion experienced a year earlier. Donovan was certainly the crowd favorite and the judges' praise for her had taken on the tone of a campaign in the final few weeks leading up to the conclusion of the series. Also, the first original single for the series, "Listen With Your Heart," was far more suited to Donovan's "Idol Journey" than Callea's, especially given her weekly thematic refrain of the importance of surmounting life's obstacles. But both finalists were more than capable of delivering the song with the requisite measure of credibility. During the "Showdown" episode which brought the "Final 12" to a close, both Callea and Donovan relied on the familiar moves that had brought them to this point to present strong versions of the song.

The Grand Final to the second series of Australian Idol aimed to outdo the previous year's festivities and did so, if only in the seemingly endless procession of famous faces, performances, and the seemingly interminable wait for a verdict. The show was over three hours long, sending large sections of the Australian public scrambling for their video recorders after sending their disappointed children to bed. The full membership of the "Final 12," joined by Guy Sebastian and Shannon Noll from the first series, kicked off the show proper with an incongruous rendering of

"Waltzing Matilda" replete with the best R&B ornamentation the finalists could muster. Donovan performed "Symphony of Life," an upbeat mid-tempo ballad by Australia's Vanessa Amorosi and Callea followed with yet another version of "The Prayer." Each used their last opportunity to exhibit their skills by reminding voters of the heady days of weeks one and six respectively. When Donovan won, she reacted with an engaging mix of disbelief and tears, hugging Callea who also seemed unusually thrilled. When she said she didn't know how to start her new song, Callea helpfully reminded her of the words with a level-headed grace that endeared him to many.

The commercial release of Donovan's version of the song is a familiar example of contemporary balladry sitting firmly in the middle of the "Idol" canon. It aptly fulfils the vague, thematic function of a series signature song. The message was familiar, neatly summed up by lines such as "When you can't find your way through the night" and "When you can't find that path that leads you on and you don't know which road to choose, that's when you've got to listen with your heart." The song begins with a gently orchestrated major key progression which presents the central melodic fragment from the chorus played on a piano backed with a synthesized string section and a slight vocal invocation over the top. The first verse has only vocals, a computerized acoustic guitar sound playing arpeggios, and a smooth, phased synthesizer playing a light eighth note pattern with accents emphasizing the off beats while holding down the tempo. The drum and bass kick in strongly to lead into the chorus, but both pull back immediately after it starts. Donovan's voice is almost absurdly smooth, with a near total lack of texture to it. Her intonation was clearly perfected by various kinds of studio wizardry and soaked in reverberation to the point where it was hard to recognize those imperfections which defined her performances during the contest. The chorus has two halves to it, the second distinguished by a brief moment of melodic soaring in the vocal line. The chorus is then followed by a reprise of the material from the introduction. The second verse is largely the same as the first as the strings drop back out and a light, but solid percussion line re-enters, supplemented by a hint of electric guitar. The second chorus thickens the texture of the song by adding a backing choir which takes the vocal lead as Donovan responds using the space and freedom afforded her, but also being placed much further back in the mix. The same interlude as before reappears and brings the chorus to a solid and complete resolution on the tonic. The song then moves to the minor subdominant for a bridge as the intensity of the song increases, the dynamic level rises and the texture begins to thicken. The rhythm section emerges more solidly from the back of the mix and Donovan hints at the awkward, growling, uncontrolled vocal power she often displayed during the show. As the bridge builds, the song moves through a half-step modulation upwards and then everything comes to a full stop for an instant. The choir recites the tagline and Donovan and the full band re-enter to respond in kind. Then, they deliver the fullest rendition of the chorus at the end of which Donovan hits the high note on the last word of "and your heart will bring you home." She offers us a descending passage over one more iteration of the central harmonic progression of the chorus which slides easily into the final iteration of the concluding passage of the chorus. It is, in a word, textbook.

The second series of Australian Idol has since come to be defined by the dramatic inversion of the relationship between the two finalists. Donovan's version of "Listen With Your Heart" was released immediately on her ascension, but was widely perceived to be a "failure" (Chartsong Productions, 2004b). It is not entirely clear why a double-platinum single and album would be regarded as unsuccessful except for the fact that Callea's unprecedented success with his version of "The Prayer" followed shortly after Donovan's single came out, but before her full album was completed. Guy Sebastian even publicly questioned whether the choice of "Listen With Your Heart" was appropriate for Donovan. He suggested that it didn't fit her "dreadlocks and grunge" image. "I don't know if people were voting for Casey to get 'Listen With Your Heart,'" said Australia's first "Idol", going on to suggest that Donovan "find out who she is" in order to resurrect her career (AAP, 2005). While Callea has since gone on to find success rivaled only by fellow runner-up Shannon Noll, Donovan has not enjoyed anything near the success enjoyed by the other "Idols". Her formal association with "Idol" ended in July 2006 when newspapers reported she was dropped from the record label associated with the show, Sony-BMG. The label claimed that they simply didn't have time for her. An unnamed family friend claimed that she had been dropped as early as March 2006 "after they strung her along for a long time" (Sams, 2006). By mid 2006, Donovan was "considering offers from at least two independent labels," around the time Callea's second album was being recorded. On a website posted by her management agency, an old biography still reminded us of the familiar story of Casey Donovan even as that story was reaching its dismal conclusion:

> Casey Donovan was never expected to win Australian Idol. From the outset she was the outsider. Neither contrived, media savvy, Hollywood glam or predictable, Casey was always exactly who she is: herself. Raw, messy, vociferous, vulnerable and determined, Casey Donovan was different to the other contestants. She was incapable of self-betrayal and she could never sell out (Harbour Agency).

Despite Donovan's perceived lack of success, the second series of Australian Idol still produced a few new stars, even if its once brightest had dimmed considerably.

Conclusion

The stories of Australia's first two "Idols" and their respective runners-up vividly demonstrate how the transformation of ordinary people into credible pop stars depends centrally on the contextual forces created by the show itself. The paradoxes that make these transformations possible are legion. The producers and representatives of the show have been very aggressive in defending the show against charges that the "Idols" are "manufactured," claiming instead that hard work, talent, and that special something are enough to make the contestants legitimate musical celebrities. These claims, made repeatedly and vociferously, are put forward even as endless hours of footage of the very means of manufacture themselves go to air week after week. During the six months of the contest we are given access to intimate footage of make-up and styling sessions, photo shoots, vocal workshops, and public appearances in which people who can't quite believe what is happening to them often act like the very fans who have come to see them. We hear the suggestions and support of the vocal coach and the gentle coaxing of the musical director. We see the judges taking a contestant or two aside to give them a bit of advice on their appearance or their attitude. And yet, despite the hundreds of people working behind the scenes to pull this often daring form of television off every week, we are still asked to ignore these machinations, or at least, not to see them for what they are.

The paradox that "Idol's" materials must be directed to resolve requires masking the obvious simultaneity of the contestants' work at self-fashioning with the industrial production of their pop star personae. We are constantly having our attention drawn to the former specifically by distracting us from the increasing presence of the latter. The constant attempts by the show's producers to collapse the inherent and necessary distance between ordinary person and real pop star is doomed to fail precisely because it is exactly this distinction between these two modes of expression that the show is dedicated to producing. This is where the producers create and exploit the visceral and undeniably emotional impact the show has on so many people, the payoff that keeps them tuning in and voting week after dramatic week. The most visible and affecting displays of emotion are produced by the contestants achieving their dreams by rising to meet challenges they didn't know they could conquer by summoning resources they didn't know they had or by failing to meet expectations despite the best of intentions and the most arduous of efforts.

This is what made Anthony Callea's success in the contest so compelling. Callea was not the type of ordinary person the show needed. He was already well-versed in the most common and successful modes of self-fashioning required for pop stardom and had already begun to inhabit the role of pop star well before he stepped before the cameras. This is precisely what was said to be holding him back. His lack of "bacteria," "edge," and "personality" were all euphemisms for his lack of the kind of "ordinariness" required of aspirant "Idols." Casey Donovan had edge to spare and was praised to the skies when her voice cracked or when she lost a bit of intonation, enunciation, or even entire verses. She was presented as too much herself to be anything else, a narrative that proved compelling enough for her to become the second "Idol," but was erased when she went into the recording studio to produce her first single. For Guy Sebastian, the shaping machinations of "Idol" proved to be a boon to a career that gradually grew into a trap from which he couldn't escape. The distinctive brand constructed around him during the first series could not be detached from its associations with the "Idol" brand as the two were symbiotically meshed. Shannon Noll, on the other hand, uneasily outgrew "Idol" in part because of the seamless integration of his own personal life experience with his "Idol" persona. Given that his life experience obviously pre-dated his participation in the contest, his pop star persona could survive being detached from the show whereas Sebastian's could not.

Australian Idol was created to facilitate strong long-term relationships between the show and its audience. The materials that form the sinews of meaning created by the show are the songs and performances through which the contestants "communicate emotions" which tighten these often less than resolute bonds. The narrative contexts into which these calculated, manufactured, but unpredictable moments of drama are set are designed to cement these connections. The life stories and "Idol Journeys" of the various aspirants give meaning to what might otherwise be merely a collection of unevenly performed cover tunes, but which become, in the context of the show, a substantive storehouse of aesthetic materials whose manipulation provides us with a reluctant recognition of the inherently manufactured nature of pop stardom and an earnest celebration of the hope for transformation upon which each candidacy rests; neither could exist without the other. In 2004, a significant number of Australians watched as a shy, angry, overweight, 16-year-old girl from a poorly regarded suburb southwest of Sydney became a confident, self-assured, and respected musician performing on the main stage at the Sydney Opera House. Is it any wonder that most of us didn't look too closely at the loud, cynical, calculating machine that made it all possible?

Conclusion

Why "Idol"?

Kids formats are coming up, especially as they involve merchandising possibilities …
I don't think they have been exploited enough (Jacob Houlind, Director of Sales, MTV
International).[1]

During the third and fourth seasons of Australian Idol, Kyle Sandilands, the radio
shock jock chosen to replace Ian "Dicko" Dickson as the nasty bastard on the
judging panel, stirred up outrage amongst the viewing public with many of the
barbed epithets he hurled at contestants. The judge Australian Idol's producers like
to describe as an unrepentant speaker of truth made several insulting references to
specific body parts of female candidates. Many accused him of perpetuating the
kinds of stereotypes said to be responsible for a growing crisis in body image
amongst Australian youth. The enmity Sandilands provoked, however justified,
seemed misplaced. After all, three of Australian Idol's main sponsors at the time
were McDonalds, Nestlé, and Maybelline. Each targets children with demonstrable
precision and unseemly abandon. They market make-up to "aspirational" eight year
olds, Happy Meals to four year olds, and a wide range of sugary beverages to all and
sundry (Ebenkamp, 2003; Pidd, 2007). The collective power of these corporations
to affect the body image, not to mention the actual bodies, of millions of Australian
children would seem to dwarf that of Sandilands, just as it dwarfs the power of the
many public interest groups and non-governmental organizations allied against their
more appalling market penetration strategies (Jimenez, 2007). Yet Australian Idol
has been immune to this kind of criticism. Those with whom they do business and
who pay large sums for the privilege have used the show to inoculate themselves
against any untoward advances of social conscience. They can claim great pride in
supporting Australia's youth as they pursue their dreams while no doubt remaining
content to train the next generation of consumers without regard for the growing
incidence of diabetes, anorexia, and obesity in young people that many have linked to
the unregulated marketing of food and beauty products to children and adolescents.
Those therapists and youth workers who "would pour scorn on anyone who tries
to belittle Australian Idol" have been nowhere to be found in this debate (Jinman,
2004b).

One of the reasons why Australian Idol hasn't been subjected to the kinds of
criticism as similar corporate marketing endeavors is the great joy and pleasure it
provides to so many. A wide array of viewers watches the show in massive numbers
both in earnest and irony. Large numbers of excitable youth overpopulate shopping
malls when "Idols" make a public appearance. They send single after single up the

---

1   Scott (2002).

charts, they scream and yell outside the Opera House during the red carpet walk leading into the Grand Final, they have continued to crowd the annual auditions in consistently increasing numbers across the country, and they provide a tremendous amount of informal, enthusiastic chatter on the internet and talkback radio in the weeks and months leading up to the final vote. The music industry more generally has escaped similar rebuke largely for the same reasons. The pleasure most people take in their products usually renders irrelevant criticism of the means by which those products are produced, distributed, and sold. But as the technological foundations of the music and entertainment industries shifted, so did their ability to assert any tacit and necessary association between the emotional investments fans make in music and the economic ones. And, as it turned out, the music industry didn't have any particularly persuasive arguments to offer its consumers as to why they should remain loyal, paying customers. So the music and entertainment industries reacted how most corporations react when their market share is threatened. They asserted their considerable economic and political power in a variety of highly consequential legal, political, and economic forums. They successfully transformed intellectual property law around the world to achieve the kinds of legal restrictions on the free flow of information that many believe will have serious and damaging long-term consequences for the use of the internet as a tool for democratic political, cultural, and economic development (Mann, 2000). Suggestions that these outcomes have been the result of "negotiations" between empowered consumers and a chastened industry resulting in some form of mutual benefit are at best fanciful.

Just as important, both industries used their extensive communicative powers to enforce their versions of the piracy story to underpin their accomplishments in the legislative sector. Evil pirates and misguided fans were blamed for the slump in album sales and layoffs at headquarters even as the music industry's own strategic planning was telling them about the remarkable potential of the online market in music. Independent researchers pointed out how hysterical and inaccurate many of their statistical claims were while others argued piracy increased sales enough to counter the illegal trade in song files. Still, only two months after the Australian Recording Industry Association's piracy investigators histrionically decried the "1 billion songs a year" traded online in Australia and the groups of teenagers tromping into record shops "to buy just one CD," its American counterpart abruptly declared victory (O'Grady, 2007). Mitch Bainwol, the RIAAs new CEO, stated that illegal file sharing had been "contained" through changes to copyright law, a US Supreme Court decision holding file-sharing services liable for the actions of their users, and the increasing number of legal music download services (Graham, 2007). Even the IFPI suddenly discovered that "digital is empowering the music consumer" (IFPI, 2007). This change in tactics marked an important shift in the coordinated, sometimes contradictory campaigns combating illegal file sharing. More important, these public relations campaigns have done their job. They have been mostly disciplined and reflected a level of strategic planning and adherence to the kinds of corporate practices that define contemporary global commerce. Many within the music industry have argued that it is their increasing fealty to these practices and strategies that have hollowed out the industry's ability to find and develop new talent. Others argue that the process of artist development simply had to change in the face of the many larger transformations in popular culture (Sanghera, 2002c).

The "Idol" phenomenon resolves this question quite inventively. It reflects the kinds of practices and strategic imperatives that define the forms of corporate globalization the music and entertainment industries have wholeheartedly embraced, in deed if not in word. It is a primary expression of a globally hegemonic culture of exploitative labor relations, intrinsic and reflexive consumerism, industrial synergy, cost-effective brand integration, and lax accountability. It is also an extremely clever response to the multifaceted existential challenges the music industry has been trying to face down since at least the mid 1990s. Its multiple revenue streams mean producers can worry less about fighting "pirates" and more about enticing "consumers." Its silvery sheen of public ratification skillfully conjures and quantifies the emotional investment made by the audience while simultaneously enhancing the value of their economic investment even when they don't appear to be buying anything. It is an exciting brand of television that achieves high ratings at low costs inspiring a clamor amongst advertisers to participate. The "Idol" brand exerts a hegemonic power within the realm of music television which has allowed it to reap vast amounts from merchandising and licensing deals. Finally, "Idol" has transformed the once risky and onerous process of acquiring and marketing new talent into the nearest thing one can get to a certainty in the music business.

"Idol" also shows us how the microscopic details of a familiar song delivered through a carefully mediated pop star persona set within the drama of a specifically contextualized performance is materially connected to the global branding empire that shaped and produced it. The connection is formed in the ways in which the meanings of those materials are produced to link performer to audience. The meanings of "Idol's" materials can only be specified as they move through "Idol's" painstakingly managed medium. Their meanings are specified as the audience's agency, incited through varied means and appropriated to serve increasingly specific ends, is channeled through "Idol's" numerous revenue streams, many of which don't require anything resembling a costed transaction. The fun and pleasure of this almost lurid process of creating a pop star is melded seamlessly into its multi-tiered commercial architecture. But this is not some grand Pavlovian exercise in coercing people to part with their time, attention, and money. The "Idol" medium is designed to produce exactly what we expect it to, formed as it is through our expectations as music consumers. This is why the "Idol" medium takes such an enormous amount of work to construct and maintain. The logistical heroics of the cattle-call auditions alone are impressive, undertaken on the road at transient venues, herding thousands through what is portrayed as a trying ordeal. The collection and editing of what is probably thousands of hours of footage over several months to firm up the claims of the overwrought scriptwriting of the introductory episodes has proven to be a compelling entrée to the competition for huge numbers of viewers. Further, the gradual coaxing of a metaphor-laced narrative from this jumbled complex of flawed auditions, emotive reaction shots, and what seem to be barely distinguishable contestants cannot be easy. Whittling down the crowd to a "Final 12," all of whom have a reasonable chance of winning, appears to proceed under its own steam, but the work rate of the extensive production team and aesthetically-minded coaching staff are presented to us as boundless. Manufacturing a pop star has never seemed so labor intensive as it does on "Idol." But this is the point. If they want us to believe in our "Idols," we have to believe in the way they were made.

There is a multitude of ways to study the music industry and music consumption. I am well aware I have only scratched the surface. I have framed this book throughout as a tightly focused examination of the ways in which specific kinds of consumer relationships are constructed and maintained socially, politically, technologically, and economically. The values and strategic imperatives of a now global consumerist economy govern the production, distribution, and circulation of a great deal of popular music. The planning regimes and grandiose gestures of so many self-proclaimed protectors of music do have their consequences. They forge a chain linking musicians to fans which inevitably shapes the sounds we experience, sometimes down to the most miniature aural detail. Yet the guiding principles and tasks which have governed corporate globalization and the rapid expansion of consumerism over the last several decades have found little expression in the work of the majority of scholars of popular music. Part of the problem lies in the inevitable chafing between the precepts and impositions of consumerism and the perceived validity and credibility of the music it produces. The debates about "authenticity" and "manufactured" pop, while purporting to be about the means of manufacture, have been almost obsessively concerned with the conditions of interpretation. Not all means of manufacture are the same, nor should they be rendered identically against the flat backdrop of academic populism. As large sectors of the music and entertainment industries become increasingly governed on terms once reserved for economists and advertisers, we will need to keep a closer accounting of their rapidly evolving mechanisms of consumption.

Bibliography

Agence France-Presse/Associated Press (AFP/AP). (2007). "Jumpin Jack flush, it's cash cash cash." Sydney Morning Herald, 26–28 January, p. 14.

Albini, Steve. (1999). "The problem with music." In Frank, T., and M. Weiland (eds). Commodify your dissent. New York: W.W. Norton, pp. 164–76.

Alderman, John. (2001). Sonic boom: Napster, MP3, and the new pioneers of music. Cambridge, MA: Perseus Publishing.

"American Idol and Elvis now owned by same company." (2005). FinancialWire, 2 May, p. 1.

Anderman, Joan. (2005). "Hey, hey, hey. The irresistible singable stick-in-your-mindable jingle." Boston Globe, 9 January, p. N1.

Anderson, Chris. (2004). "The long tail." Wired, 12(10). <http://www.wired.com/wired/ archive/12.10/tail.html>.

Anderson Tim. (2006). Making easy listening: material culture and postwar American recording. Minneapolis, MN: University of Minnesota Press.

Ang, Ien. (2003). "Culture and communication: toward an ethnographic critique of media consumption in the transnational media system." In Parks, L., and S. Kumar (eds). Planet TV: a global television reader. New York: New York University Press, pp. 363–75.

Angus, Ian. (1998). "The materiality of expression: Harold Innis' communication theory and the discursive turn in the human sciences." Canadian Journal of Communication, 23(1). Available at: <http://www.cjc-online.ca/>.

Anstey, Mike. (2007). "Jargon buster." Promotions and Incentives, January, p. 13a.

Antony, Rachael. (2003). "Culture police: logos." Big Issue, (180):8.

Appadurai, Arjun (ed.). (1988). The social life of things: commodities in cultural perspective. Cambridge: Cambridge University Press.

——. (1996). Modernity at large: cultural dimensions of globalization. Minneapolis, MN: University of Minnesota Press.

Armstrong, Stephen. (2006). "Bloggers for hire." New Statesman, 135(4807):26–7.

Associated Press (AP). (2005). "Sony-BMG Music settles Spitzer's payola probe." 27 July. <http://www.msnbc.com/id/8700936/>.

Aster, Andrea. (2002). "Music marketers go mobile." Marketing Magazine, 107(46):11.

Attali, Jacques. (1985). Noise: the political economy of music. Minneapolis, MN: University of Minnesota Press.

Atwood, Brett. (1997). "Web music sales expected to soar: report predicts $1.6 billion in revenue by 2002." Billboard, 109(25):6, 82.

——. (1999). "Study predicts a digital-download bonanza." Billboard. 111(17):3, 80.

Ault, Susanne. (2003) "For marketers, teens are a moving target." Billboard. 115(45):6, 61.

Australian Associated Press (AAP). (2005). "Guy's advice for Casey." The Age (Melbourne) 9 March. <http://www.theage.com.au/news/Music/Guys-advice-for-Casey/2005/03/09/1110316061768.html>.

"Australian idle craven image." (2003). Sydney Morning Herald, 22 November, p. 44.

Australian Idol: Greatest Moments. (2003). FremantleMedia Operations.

Australian Idol: Greatest Moments 2004. (2004). FremantleMedia Operations.

Australian Idol: Series Two. (2004). Produced by Grundy Television, a FremantleMedia Company. Broadcast on the Ten Network, Sydney. Broadcasts began 13 July.

Australian Idol: The Winner's Journey. (2004). Produced by Grundy Television, a FremantleMedia Company. Broadcast on the Ten Network, Sydney, 26 November.

Australian Idol: The Winner's Story. (2003). Produced by Grundy Television, a FremantleMedia Company. Broadcast on the Ten Network, Sydney, 21 November.

"Australian Idol to hit screens in mid 2003." (2003). eBroadcast.com.au. 29 April, Australian Idol Online. <http://www.australianidol.vze.com>.

Australian Idol: Up Close and Personal. (2004). Produced by Grundy Television, a FremantleMedia Company. Broadcast on the Ten Network, Sydney, 19 October.

Avalon, Moses. (2006). Confessions of a record producer: how to survive the scams and shams of the music business. San Francisco, CA: Backbeat Books.

Bach, David. (2004). "The double punch of law and technology: fighting music piracy or remaking copyright in a digital age?" Business and Politics, 6(2). <http://www.bepress.com /bap/vol6/iss2/art3>.

Bakan, Joel. (2004). The corporation: the pathological pursuit of profit and power. New York: Free Press.

Banerjee, Scott. (2004). "Web data: the new tool." Billboard, 116(41):1.

Barlow, John Perry. (1994). "The economy of ideas." Wired, 2.03. <http://www.wired.com/wired/archive/2.03/economy.ideas_pr.html>.

Barton, Mike. (2004). "Mobiles let customers call the tune." Sydney Morning Herald, 4–5 September, p. 5.

Beilharz, Peter (ed.). (2001). The Bauman reader. Oxford: Blackwell.

Bessman, Jim. (1994). "Firm turns fans into promoters." Billboard, 106(29):53.

Bishop, Jack. (2004). "Who are the pirates? The politics of piracy, poverty, and greed in a globalised market." Popular Music and Society, 27(1):101–6.

——. (2005). "Building international empires of sound: concentrations of power and property on the 'global' music market." Popular Music and Society, 28(4): 443–71.

Blackman, Guy. (2007). "Commercial kudos." The Age (Melbourne), "M," 8 April, p. 25.

Block, Valerie. (2002). "Ads change tune, give more bands their big breaks." Crain's New York Business, 18(46):4.

Boland, John. (2002). "Study: file sharing boots music sales." <http://news.com.com/ Study+sharing+boosts+music+sales/2100-1023_3-898813.html>.

Bolin, Rebecca. (2005). "EU calls the music industry a cartel." Law Meme, Yale Law School. <http://research.yale.edu/lawmeme/modules.php?name=News&file=article&sid=1453>.

Born, Georgina. (1993). "Afterword: music policy, aesthetic and social difference." In Bennett, T. et al. (eds). Rock and popular music: politics, policies and institutions. London: Routledge, pp. 266–92.

Botting, Caroline. (2006). "A dim harbour view." Inner City Courier, 122(15):8.

Brody, E.W. (2001). "The 'attention' economy." Public Relations Journal, 46(3):18–21.

Brown, Stephen. (1997) Revolution at the checkout counter. Cambridge, MA: Harvard University Press.

Bruno, Antony. (2006a). "Pandora's box." Billboard, 118(8):20.

———. (2006b). "Top execs cry for new biz models." Billboard, 118(11):12.

———. (2006c). "Dialing for gold." Billboard, 118(32):16.

———. (2006d). "Digital entertainment: digital music – The human touch." Billboard, 118(43):26.

Bulkeley, W., and W. Wong. (2003). "Six degrees of exploitation?" Wall Street Journal, 4 August, B1.

Burkart, Patrick. (2005). "Loose integration in the popular music industry." Popular Music and Society, 28(4):489–500.

———, and T. McCourt. (2004). "Infrastructure for the celestial jukebox." Popular Music, 23(3):349–62.

Burnett, Robert. (1996). The global jukebox: the international music industry. London: Routledge.

Burt, Tim. (2003). "More ways to flog a good tune." Financial Times, 1 July, p. 9.

Butler, Ben. (2003). "Hit & Ms." Big Issue, (178):9.

Campbell, J.E., and M. Carlson. (2002). "Panopticon.com: online surveillance and the commodification of privacy." Journal of Broadcasting and Electronic Media 46(4):586–606.

Carey, Alex. (1995). Taking the risk out of democracy: propaganda in the U.S. and Australia. Sydney: University of New South Wales Press.

Carluccio, J. et al. (2000). Turntablist Transcription Methodology. <http://www.battlesounds.com>.

Carroll, W., and C. Carson. (2003). "Forging a new hegemony? The role of transnational policy groups in the network and discourses of global corporate governance." Journal of World-Systems Research, 9(1):67–102.

Castelluccio, Michael. (2006). "The music genome project." Strategic Finance, December, p. 57.

Cavicchi, Daniel. (1998). Tramps like us: music and meaning among Springsteen fans. New York: Oxford University Press.

Chalmers, Emma. (2004a). "Music industry records sales high note." Courier Mail (Brisbane), 18 March, p. 7.

Chalmers, Emma. (2004b). "Pop stars or false idols?" Courier-Mail (Brisbane), 14 August, p. 31.

Chanan, Michael. (1995). Repeated takes: a short history of recording and its effects on music. London: Verso.

Chartsong Productions. (2004a). "Australasian record label update." 21 April.

———. (2004b). "Australasian record label update." 14 December.

Christman, Ed. (2001a). "The face of the industry as 2001 unfolds: album sales increase by 4% in 2000." Billboard, 113(2):1, 88.

———. (2001b). "SoundScan numbers show 0.35% of albums account for more than half of all units." Billboard, 113(17):66.

———. (2002). "One-stop status: how key liquidations and consumer shifts are affecting this once-thriving sector." Billboard, 114(11):86–7, 89.

———. (2003). "Sales down, retailers up." Billboard, 50(115):3.

———. (2005a). "Where are the hits: with U.S. sales down 7.6%, industry looks for answers." Billboard, 117(29):27–8.

———. (2005b) "SoundScan: entertainment spending up." Billboard, 117(37):16.

———. (2006a). "Top sellers bottom out: a historical low in smash hits." Billboard, 118(3):22.

———. (2006b). "Up front: special report–2005 sales data: long tail is wagging." Billboard, 118(11):9–10.

Clark, Drew. (2005). "The battle between tinseltown and techville." Washington Post, 10 April, p. B5.

Clements, Nicole. (2005). "The new rock stars." Sydney Morning Herald, "My Career," 18–19 June, p. 17.

Cochrane, Nathan. (2003). "Too much information." Sydney Morning Herald, 11 November, "Next," p. 5.

Coleman, Mark. (2005). Playback: from the Victrola to MP3: 100 years of music, machines, and money. Cambridge, MA: Da Capo Press.

Connell, J., and C. Gibson. (2003). Sound tracks: popular music, identity and place. London and New York: Routledge.

"Continuing to usher in the big awards." (2004). Canberra Times, 10 December, p. 11.

Cooper, J., and D. Harrison. (2001). "The social organization of audio piracy on the internet." Media, Culture and Society, 23(1):71–89.

Couldry, Nick. (2002a). Media rituals: a critical approach. London: Routledge.

Couldry, Nick. (2002b). "Playing for celebrity: Big Brother as ritual event." Television and New Media, 3(3):283–93.

Coultan, Mark. (2004). "Game for anything." Sydney Morning Herald, 22 May, p. 29.

———. (2006). "Meet the king of cashing in on fame." Sydney Morning Herald, 29–30 April, p. 28.

Cowen, Tyler. (1998). In praise of commercial culture. Cambridge, MA: Harvard University Press.

Crosley, Hillary. (2007). "Arrested development." Billboard, 119(14):24–6.

Currier, Terry. (2003). "How exclusives are killing retail." Billboard, 115(33):12.

"Cyber-pirate flaunts key to song files." (2003). Sydney Morning Herald, 29–30 November, p. 3.

Dale, David. (2003a). "Everyone's a critic." Sydney Morning Herald, 30–31 August, p. 32.

——. (2003b). "Keeping it short, sharp and simple wins the ratings war." Sydney Morning Herald, 1 December, p. 2.

Dannen, Frederic. (1991). Hit men: power brokers and fast money inside the music business. London: Vintage.

Davenport, T., and J. Beck. (2002). "The strategy and structure of firms in the attention economy." Ivey Business Journal, 66(4):49–55.

Davis, Susan G. (1999). "Space jam: media conglomerates build the entertainment city." European Journal of Communication, 14(4):435–59.

Davis, Tony. (2003a). "Stars in their eyes." Sydney Morning Herald, 1 November, p. 31.

——. (2003b). "Idol hands produce the goods." Sydney Morning Herald, 10 November, p. 6.

Day, Peter. (2003). "British entertainment guru enjoys record-breaking year." Knight Ridder Tribune Business News, 5 January, p. 1.

de Certeau, Michel. (1984). The practice of everyday life. Berkeley, CA: University of California Press.

Dennehy, Luke. (2003). "Entertaining Idol thoughts." Herald Sun, 9 June, Australian Idol Online. <http://www.australianidol.vze.com>.

DeNora, Tia. (2000). Music in everyday life. New York: Cambridge University Press.

DiCola, P., and K. Thomson. (2002). A report on the effects of radio ownership consolidation following the 1996 Telecommunications Act." <http://www.futureofmusic.org/resources/>.

Doss, Erika. (1999). Elvis culture: fans, faith, and image. Lawrence, KS: University Press of Kansas.

"Downloading 'myths' challenged." (2005). BBC News. <http://news,bbc.co.uk/go/pr/fr/-/1/hi/technology/4718249.stm>.

Drahos, Peter. (2002). Information feudalism: who owns the knowledge economy? London: Earthscan.

Drew, Rob. (2004). "'Scenes' dimensions of karaoke in the United States." In Bennett, A., and R. Peterson, Music scenes: local, translocal and virtual. Nashville, TN: Vanderbilt University Press, pp. 64–79.

——. (2005). "Mixed blessing: the commercial mix and the future of music aggregation." Popular Music and Society, 28(4):533–51.

Duany, A. et al. (2000). Suburban nation: the rise of sprawl and the decline of the American dream. New York: New Point Press.

Dudley, Jennifer. (2003). "Money to burn." Courier-Mail, 6 December, p. 31.

Ebenkamp, Becky. (2003). "T2: divide of the tweens." Brandweek, 44(26):18–19.

Edwards, Joseph. (1981), Top 10's and trivia of rock & roll and rhythm & blues. St Louis, MO: Blueberry Hill Publishing.

Eliezer, Christie. (2002). "Labels welcome return of Virgin megastores to Australia." Billboard, 18(114):39.

Elliott, R., and N. Jankel-Elliott. (2003). "Using ethnography in strategic consumer research." Qualitative Market Research, 6(4):215–23.

Elmer, Greg. (2004). Profiling machines: mapping the personal information economy. Cambridge, MA: MIT Press.

Emling, Shelley. (2004). "Ring tone millionaire dreams of soapies on mobile phone TV channel." Sydney Morning Herald, 31 January, p. 13.

Esse, Christopher. (1987). "Taped at retail." High Fidelity, 37, September, p. 14.

Ewen, Stuart. (1996). PR!: a social history of spin. New York: Basic Books.

"Excerpted written statements from work-for-hire hearings." (2000). Billboard, 112(24):97.

"Fall, mountians, fall." (1996). Rock and Rap Confidential, pp. 1–3.

Fantel, Hans. (2001). "Life begins at twenty: the compact disc celebrates a birthday." Opera News, 66(4):42–3.

Farrelly, Elizabeth. (2003). "A generic cityscape closes in." Sydney Morning Herald, 21 October, p. 13.

Featherstone, Mike, et al. (1995). Global modernities. Thousand Oaks, CA: Sage.

Fenster, Mark. (2002). "Consumers" guides: the political economy of the music press and the democracy of critical discourse." In Jones, S. (ed.). Pop music and the press. Philadelphia, PA: Temple University Press, pp. 81–92.

Fink, Robert. (2002). "Elvis everywhere: musicology and popular music studies at the twilight of the canon." In Beebe, R. et al. (eds). Rock over the edge: transformations in popular music cultures. Durham, NC: Duke University Press, pp. 60–109.

Fiske, John. (1987). Television culture. London: Methuen.

Fitzpatrick, Eileen. (2000). "Suits bring scour to file for bankruptcy." Billboard, 112(44):9.

——, and D. Reece. (1998). "On the net, marketing info. on viewers still in its infancy." Billboard, 110(47):88.

Fox, Barry. (2002). "Record labels to take 'viral' approach to PR." New Statesman, 175(2355):21.

Fox, Mark. (2004). "E-commerce business models for the music industry." Popular Music and Society, 27(2):201–21.

——. (2005). "Market power in music retailing: the case of Wal-Mart." Popular Music and Society, 28(4):501–19.

Frank, Thomas. (2000). One market under god: extreme capitalism, market populism and the end of economic democracy. New York: Doubleday.

Frew, Wendy. (2003). "Youth of today just doesn't watch enough TV." Sydney Morning Herald, 9 October, p. 27.

Frith, Simon. (1988). Music for pleasure: essays in the sociology of pop. Cambridge: Polity Press.

—— (ed.). (1993). Music and copyright. Edinburgh: Edinburgh University Press.

——. (2002). "Fragments of a sociology of rock criticism." In Jones, S. (ed.). Pop music and the press. Philadelphia, PA: Temple University Press, pp. 235–46.

——. (2004). "Essay review: reasons to be cheerful." Popular Music, 23(3): 363–72.

Future of Music Coalition (FMC). (2001). "Major label contract clause critique." <http://www.futureofmusic.org/resources.cfm>.

Gandy, Oscar. (1993). The panoptic sort: a political economy of personal information. Boulder, CO: Westview Press.

García-Canclini, Néstor. (2001). Consumers and citizens: globalization and multicultural conflicts. Minneapolis, MN: University of Minnesota Press.

Garofalo, Reebee. (1999). "From music publishing to MP3: music and industry in the 20th century." American Music, 17(3):318–54.

Garrity, Brian. (2003). "Music gets less space at Virgin." Billboard, 115(51):65.

——. (2006). "Editors try to stem their hype." Billboard, 118(24):65.

——, and E. Christman. (2003). "RIAA figures show continuing decline." Billboard, 115(37):7.

Garrity, B., and G. Mayfield. (2003). "Digital biz reaches two frontiers: digital singles nearing eclipse of hard copies." Billboard, 115(45):1, 50.

Gebesmair, A., and A. Smudits (eds). (2001). Global repertoires: popular music within and beyond the transnational music industry. Aldershot: Ashgate.

Gibson, Timothy. (2000). "Beyond cultural populism: notes toward the critical ethnography of media audiences." Journal of Communication Inquiry, 24(3): 253–73.

Given, Jock. (2003). America's pie: trade and culture after 9/11. Sydney: University of New South Wales Press.

——. (2004). "'Not unreasonably denied': Australian content after AUSFTA." Media International Australia, 111, pp. 8–22.

Gladwell, Malcolm. (1997) "Annals of style: the coolhunt." New Yorker, 17 March. <http://www.gladwell.com/1997/1997_03_17_a_cool.htm>.

——. (2001). The tipping point: how little things can make a big difference. Boston, MA: Back Bay Books.

Glaister, Dan. (2006). "Age no bar as baby boomers rock the music industry." Guardian Unlimited, 28 November. <http://www.guardian.co.uk/print/0,,329645858-110878,00.html>.

Gliddon, Joshua. (2003). "Facing the music." The Bulletin, 21 January, p. 68.

Goddard, Charlotte. (1999). "What's in store for music promotion?" Marketing, 9 December, p. 29.

Godin, Seth. (2001). Unleashing the ideavirus. New York: Hyperion.

Goldhaber, Michael. (1997). "The attention economy and the net." First Monday: peer-reviewed journal on the net. <http://www.firstmonday.dk/issues/ issue2_4/ goldhaber>.

Goodsir, Darren. (2004). "Retailers fear giant landlord in Pitt Street mall." Sydney Morning Herald, 4 September, p. 5.

Gorder, Don. (2000). "IAJE: Legal issues in jazz – Point: sound recordings now to works for hire." Jazz Educators Journal, 33(2):76, 78.

Goss, Jon. (1995). "'We know who you are and we know where you live': the instrumental rationality of geodemographic systems." Economic Geography, 71(2):171–98.

Gotting, Sean. (2003a). "Bubble-gum pop meets fast food for ad campaign." Sydney Morning Herald, 4 September, p. 5.

——. (2003b). "See me, feel me, touch me, buy me." Sydney Morning Herald, 4 September, p. 13.

Govenar, Alan. (1990). The early years of rhythm & blues: focus on Houston. Houston, TX: Rice University Press.

Gracyk, Theodore. (1996). Rhythm and noise: an aesthetics of rock. Durham, NC: Duke University Press.

Graham, Jefferson. (2007). "RIAA chief says illegal song-sharing 'contained.'" USA Today, 12 June 2007. <http://www.usatoday.com/tech/products/services/2006-06-12-riaa_x.htm>.

"Greed is bad." (2003). Rock and Rap Confidential, 198, pp. 3–4.

Greene, Thomas. (2006). "Piracy losses fabricated – Aussie study." <http://www.theregister.co.uk/2006/11/09/my_study_best_your_study/>.

Greider, William. (1997). One world, ready or not: the manic logic of global capitalism. New York: Penguin.

Griffin, Michelle. (2004). "Who's responsible? Viral advertising." Sydney Morning Herald, "48 Hours," 3–4 July, p. 2.

Grossberg, Lawrence. (1992). We gotta get out of this place: popular conservatism and postmodern culture. New York: Routledge.

——. (2002). "Reflections of a disappointed popular music scholar." In Beebe, R. et al. (eds). Rock over the edge: transformations in popular music cultures. Durham, NC: Duke University Press, pp. 25–59.

Hackley, Christopher. (2002). "The panoptic role of advertising agencies in the production consumer culture." Consumption, Markets and Culture, 5(3):211–29.

Hanman, Natalie. (2006). "Push comes to shove for boy bands." Sydney Morning Herald, 29–30 April, p. 38.

Hannerz, Ulf. (1992). Cultural complexity: studies in the organization of meaning. New York: Columbia University Press.

Hannigan, John. (1998). Fantasy city: pleasure and profit in the postmodern metropolis. London: Routledge.

Harbour Agency. <http://www.theharbouragency.com/artist-profile/casey-donovan>.

Haring, Bruce. (1996). Off the charts: ruthless days and reckless nights inside the music industry. New York: Carol Publishing Group.

——. (2000). Beyond the charts: MP3 and the digital music revolution. Los Angeles, CA: OTC Press.

Harvard Project on the City. (2000). Mutations. Bordeaux: Arc en rêve centre d'architecture.

——. (2002). Guide to shopping. London: Taschen.

Haslam, Dave. (1997). "DJ culture." In Redhead, S. et al. (eds). The clubcultures reader: readings in popular culture studies. London: Blackwell, pp. 168–79.

Hay, Carla. (2002). "'American Idol' weds reality TV and music." Billboard, 114:31 (3 August):1, 65–6.

——. (2003a). "'Idol' ups stakes for TV talent." Billboard, 115(17):1, 67.

——. (2003b), "Simon says …," Billboard, 115(26):1, 84.

——. (2003c). "Mix tapes rise from street as hip-hop promo, A&R tool." Billboard, 115(17):1.

Hayes, Simon. (2006). "Piracy stats don't add up." Australian IT, 7 November. <http://www.australianit.news.com.au/story/0,24897,20713160-15306,00.html>.

Head, Beverley. (2005). "Hip pocket rockets." Sydney Morning Herald, 11 May, p. 11.

Henry, Amy. (2003). "How buzz marketing works for teens." Advertising and Marketing to Children, April–June, pp. 3–10.

Henwood, Doug. (2003). After the new economy: the binge ... and the hangover that won't go away. New York: The New Press.

Hepworth, David. (2006). "Why 'Smash Hits' bubble burst." Sydney Morning Herald, 13 February, p. 14.

Herman, E., and R. McChesney. (1997). The global media: the new missionaries of global capitalism. London: Cassell.

Hiatt, Brian. (2006). "Rock and roll: 2005 year-end-report – Singles sales boom." Rolling Stone, 26 January, p. 14.

——, and E. Serpick. (2006). "Rock and roll: music tanks in 05 – Labels woes continue as album sales drop seven percent; digital singles sales surge." Rolling Stone, 26 January, pp. 9–10.

Hills, Rachel. (2006). "Access all areas." Sydney Morning Herald, "News Review," 7–8 October, p. 26.

Hipp, Brian. (2006). "Music Genome Project provides viable alternative for audiophiles on a budget." Herald (South Carolina), 30 January, p. 4B.

Hoggard, Liz. (2003). "Queen bee of buzz." Sydney Morning Herald, "Spectrum," 19–20 July, p. 8.

Holland, Bill. (1999). "In a flat market, CDs are on rise." Billboard, 111(35):100.

——. (2000a). "A legal primer on 'works for hire.'" Billboard, 112(4):122.

——. (2000b). "Artists, representatives speak out on new amendment." Billboard, 112(4):123.

——. (2000c). "Hearings sought on 'work for hire' law." Billboard, 112(5):9.

——. (2000d). "New work-for-hire law to be examined: subcommittee to hear witnesses." Billboard, 112(21):1, 112–13.

——. (2000e). "Work-for-hire repeal? RIAA's involvement goes back 10 years." Billboard, 112(31):1, 103.

——. (2000f). "Work-for-hire rollback proceeds." Billboard, 112(38):5.

——. (2000g). "RIAA royalty plan protested." Billboard, 112(44):9.

——. (2001a). "Govt., tech critics decry RIAA tactics." Billboard, 113(44):7.

——. (2001b). "RAC, RIAA clash over recordings' work for hire status." Billboard, 113(47):87.

Holmes, Peter. (2003). "Sound barrier: why the music industry is struggling to make money." Sunday Telegraph, 12 October, p. 1.

Holmes, Su. (2004). "'Reality goes pop!': reality TV, popular music and narratives of stardom in Pop Idol." Television and New Media, 5(2):147–72.

Homan, Shane. (1999). "Australian music and the parallel importation debate." Media International Australia, 91, 97–109.

Horner, Jim. (1991). "The case of DAT technology: industrial versus pecuniary function." Journal of Economic Issues, 25(2):449–57.

Iccarino, Clara. (2003). "Idol pleasures." Sun Herald, 2 June. <http://www.smh.com.au/ articles/2003/06/01/1054406069702.html>.

Idol House Party. (2004). Produced by Grundy Television, a FremantleMedia Company. Broadcast on the Ten Network, Sydney. Broadcast on September 1.

Imfeld, C., and V. Ekstrand. (2005). "The music industry and the legislative development of the Digital Millennium Copyright Act's online service provider provision." Communication Law and Policy, 10(3):291–312.

Immel, Mattais. (2006). "Two brands are better than one." Brand Strategy, 8 May, p. 11.

Inside Idol. (2004). Produced by Grundy Television, a FremantleMedia Company. Broadcast on the Ten Network, Sydney. Broadcasts began on 6 August.

International Federation of the Phonographic Industry (IFPI). (2004). The recording industry: commercial piracy report. London: IFPI.

——. (2005a). "IFPI news: quotes." <http://www.ifpi/org/site-content/press/200504/12p.html>.

——. (2005b). IFPI 05: digital music report. London: IFPI.

——. (2007). IFPI 07: digital music report. London: IFPI.

Janson, E., and R. Mansell. (1998). "A case of electronic commerce: the on-line music industry: content, regulation and barriers to development." ACTS/FAIR, Working Paper 40, Science Policy Research Unit, University of Sussex, March 1998.

Jeffery, Don. (1998). "Entertainment biz going to research like it's 1999." Billboard, 111(2):43.

——. (1999). "Muze survey details buying habits of kiosk users." Billboard, 111(26):74, 78.

——. (2000) "The evolution of e-music and its consumers." Billboard, 112(10):104.

Jenkins, H. et al. (eds). (2002). Hop on pop: the politics and pleasures of popular culture. Durham, NC: Duke University Press.

Jimenez, Cher. (2007). "Spilled corporate milk in the Philippines." Asia Times Online. <http://www.atimes.com/atimes/Southeast_Asia/IG25Ae01.html>.

Jinman, Richard. (2003). "You be the judge: how "Australian Idol" works." Sydney Morning Herald, 28 July. <http://www.smh.com.au/articles/2003/07/27/1059244486431.html>.

——. (2004a). "Inside the label babel." Sydney Morning Herald, 7 February, p. 31.

——. (2004b). "Listen to the beat of pop elitism." Sydney Morning Herald, 18 September, p. 5.

——. (2006). "Mapping an album's DNA." Sydney Morning Herald, 28 January, p. 33.

——, and P. McIntyre. (2004). "Forget the vote, the real winner of television's biggest show is Australia's youth." Sydney Morning Herald, 20 November, p. 4.

Johnson, Walter. (2003). "On agency." Journal of Social History, 37(1):113–24.

Jones, Steve. (2000). "Music and the internet." Popular Music, 19(2):217–30.

——. (2002). "Music the moves: popular music, distribution and network technologies." Cultural Studies, 16(2):213–32.

——, and A. Lenhart. (2004). "Music downloading and listening: findings from the Pew Internet and American Life Project." Popular Music and Society, 27(2): 185–99.

"Just exactly why do we need the music industry?" (2000). Rock and Rap Confidential, 175, pp. 3–4.

"Just exactly why do we need the music industry?" (2002a). Rock and Rap Confidential, 193, p. 3.

"Just exactly why do we need the music industry?" (2002b). Rock and Rap Confidential, 194, pp. 3–4.

"Just exactly why do we need the music industry?" (2002c). Rock and Rap Confidential, 197, p. 7.

"Kara, A., and E. Kaynak. (1996). "Markets of a single customer: exploiting conceptual developments in market segmentation." European Journal of Marketing, 31(11/12):873–95.

Kenney, William Howland. (1999). Recorded music in American life: the phonograph and popular memory, 1890–1945. New York: Oxford University Press.

Kipnis, Jill. (2004). "Labels get aggressive with DVDs." Billboard, 116(9):3, 75.

Kleinman, Mark. (2003). "Nestle agrees L6m ITV pop idol deal." Marketing, 30 January, p. 1.

Knight, Anneli. (2004). "No escape." Sydney Morning Herald, 3 July, pp. 6–7.

Kohler, Alan. (2003). "Google set to rewrite the rules of advertising." Sydney Morning Herald, 4 November, p. 21.

Koolhaas, Rem. Ed. (2000). Mutations. Bordeaux: ACTAR.

Koranteng, Juliana. (1993). "Advertising goes on record." Marketing, 4 March, p. 23.

Kretschmer, M. et al. (2001). "Music in electronic markets: an empirical study." New media and society, 3(4):417–41.

Lanham, Richard. (2006). The economics of attention: style and substance in the age of information. Chicago, IL: University of Chicago Press.

Lanza, Joseph. (1994). Elevator music: a surreal history of muzak, easy-listening, and other moodsong. New York: St. Martin's Press.

Larsen, Peter. (2003). "Idol riches lift the fortunes of Fox." Financial Times, 16 September, p. 15.

Leach, Elizabeth. (2001). "The vicars of 'wannabe': authenticity and the Spice Girls." Popular Music, 20(2):143–67.

Lee, Julian. (2004a). "Move over yuppies, a new tribe is born." Sydney Morning Herald, 18 February, p. 3.

——. (2004b). "Ad research gets up close and personal." Sydney Morning Herald, 15 July, p. 5.

——. (2004c). "Tracking the moods, hour by hour." Sydney Morning Herald, 15 July, p. 29.

——. (2004d). "Hello, I'm on the bus – texting for Pepsi." Sydney Morning Herald, 22 July, p. 25.

——. (2004e). "Stealth marketers ready to railroad the unsuspecting." Sydney Morning Herald, 24–25 July, p. 3.

——. (2006). "Plug us in and turn us on sonny." Sydney Morning Herald, 13–14 May, p. 29.

Lefebvre, Henri. (1991). The production of space. Oxford, Blackwell.

Leyshon, A. et al. (2005). "On the reproduction of the musical economy after the internet." Media, Culture and Society, 27(2):177–209.

Lichtman, Irv. (1998). "Comeback kids." Billboard, 110(24):45.

Locke, Christopher. (2001). Gonzo marketing: winning through worst practices. Cambridge, MA: Perseus Publishing.

Longhurst, Brian. (1995). Popular music and society. London: Polity Press.

Lowe, Sue. (2003). "That song's great: phone it to me." Sydney Morning Herald, 30 October, p. 3.

Malbon, Ben. (1999). Clubbing: dancing, ecstasy and vitality. London: Routledge.

Maley, J., and T. Davis. (2003). "Idol worship unearths three stars and a pot of gold." Sydney Morning Herald, 1 November, p. 3.

Manktelow, Nicole. (2004). "Wings clipped." Sydney Morning Herald, "icon," 24–25 April, p. 3.

——. (2005). "Through innocent eyes." Sydney Morning Herald, "icon," 25–27 March, pp. 6–7.

Mann, Charles. (2000). "The heavenly jukebox." Atlantic Monthly, 286(3), September, pp. 39–59.

"Marketing's ugly duckling." (2006). Marketing, 11 October, pp. 49–50.

Marsden, Paul. (2002). "Brand positioning: meme's the word." Marketing Intelligence and Planning, 20(5):307–12.

Marsh, Dave. (2002). "Just exactly why do we need the music industry?" Rock and Rap Confidential, 192, pp. 2–3.

——. (2000). "Meaner." Rock and Rap Confidential, 170, pp. 1–3.

Mayfield, Geoff. (2001). "A decade ago, SoundScan burst onto the scene." Billboard, 113(22):8.

McAllister, Matthew. (1996). The commercialization of American culture: new advertising, control and democracy. Thousand Oaks, CA: Sage.

McCourt, T., and P. Burkart. (2003). "When creators, corporations and consumers collide: Napster and the development of on-line music distribution." Media, Culture and Society, 25(3):333–50.

McCourt, T., and E. Rothenbuhler. (1997). "SoundScan and the consolidation of control in the popular music industry." Media, Culture and Society, 19(2): 201–18.

McGuigan, Jim. (1992). Cultural populism. London: Routledge.

McIntyre, Paul. (2004a). "It's a super size Mac attack." Sydney Morning Herald, 26–27 June, p. 49.

——. (2004b). "The big sell." Sun Herald Magazine, 26 September, pp. 30–31.

McLaren, Carrie. (1998). "Why is that man starting at me?" Stay Free! 15:51–2.

McLeod, Kembrew. (2005). "MP3s are killing home taping: the rise of internet distribution and its challenge to the major label music monopoly." Popular Music and Society, 28(4):521–31.

McMahon, Neil. (2007). "Your whole life is going to bits." Sydney Morning Herald, 14–15 April, p. 13.

McMenemy, Lauren. (2004). "Why Guy's pop is not worthy." Advertiser (Adelaide), 16 October, p. 48.

McRobbie, Angela. (1995). "Recent rhythms of sex and race in popular music." Media Culture and Society, 17(2):323–31.

"Memorex Moment." (2002). Rock and Rap Confidential, 192, pp. 3–4.

Miller, D. et al. (1998). Shopping, place and identity. London: Routledge.

Miller, Lisa. (2003). "A dusty town gathers to cheer its idol, Nollsy the Condo kid." Daily Telegraph (Sydney), 10 November, p. 3.

Moore, Allan. (2001). Rock: the primary text. Aldershot: Ashgate.

Moore, Molly. (2005). "U.N. body endorses cultural protection." Washington Post, 21 October, p. A14.

Moore, Robert. (2003). "From genericide to viral marketing: on 'brand.'" Language and Communication, 23:331–57.

Moran, Jonathon. (2005). "Getting fans to go for seconds." Townsville Bulletin, 19 March, p. 38.

Morris, Anthony. (2005). "The smell of success," Big Issue, (233):19.

Murfett, Andrew. (2006). "The home front." Sydney Morning Herald, 4–5 March, p. 31.

"Music piracy 'does hit CD sales.'" (2004). BBC News. <http://news,bbc.co.uk/go/ pr/ fr/-/1/hi/entertainment/music/3995885.stm>.

Needham, Christy. (2003). "Last blast for the music moguls." Sydney Morning Herald, 13 September, 25, p. 32.

——. (2004). "Now all the world's a stage." Sydney Morning Herald, 3–4 January, p. 15.

——, and R. Jinman. (2003). "Can't stop the music." Sydney Morning Herald, 22 November, p. 29.

Negus, Keith. (1995). Popular music in theory. Hanover, NH: Wesleyan University Press.

——. (1999). Music genres and corporate cultures. London: Routledge.

——. (2002). "The work of cultural intermediaries and the enduring difference between production and consumption." Cultural Studies, 16(4):501–15.

Neisser, Drew. (2006). "Tidal wave of brand democratization." Vital Speeches of the Day, 72(18/19):526–30.

Nelson, Joyce. (1989). Sultans of sleaze: public relations and the media. Toronto: Between the Lines Press.

New South Wales Government. (2000). Sharing Sydney Harbour: Regional Action Plan. Sydney: Dept. of Urban Affairs and Planning.

Nixon, Sherrill. (2006). "City braces for mall king's Pitt Street plan." Sydney Morning Herald, 17 February, p. 3.

——, and P. du Gay. (2002). "Who needs cultural intermediaries?" Cultural Studies, 16(4):495–500.

Norrie, Justin. (2007). "Mobile boom, computer doom." Sydney Morning Herald, 14–15 April, p. 13.

"NSW homecoming hero." (2004). Sydney Morning Herald, 1–2 May, p. 46.

Nunns, Stephen. (2002). "Good vibrations: ambience and alienation in the twentieth century." Journal of Popular Music Studies, 14(2):115–37.

Oberholzer-Gee, F., and K. Strumpf. (2004). "The effect of file sharing on record sales: an empirical analysis." <http://www.unc.edu/~cigar/papers/ FileSharing_ March2004.pdf>.

O'Grady, Anthony. (2007). "Pain of a music industry in transition." Sydney Morning Herald, 14 March, p. 13.

Olsen, Eric. (2002). "Slaves of celebrity." Salon.com. <http://www.salon.com/ent/ feature/ 2002/09/18/idol_contrcat/index.html>.

O'Rourke. Morgan. (2004). "Setbacks in the music piracy war." Risk Reporter, 51(6):9.

"Orrin G. Hatch: Top contributors." <http://www.opensecrets.org/politicians/ contrib.asp?cid=N00009869&cycle=2002>.

Owen, David. (2006). "The soundtrack of your life." New Yorker, 10 April: 66–71.

Paoletta, Michael. (2006). "Seeing the light." Billboard, 118(33):28.

Parks, L., and S. Kumar. (2003). Planet TV: a global television reader. New York: New York University Press.

Patterson, Orlando. (1994). "Ecumenical America: global culture and the American cosmos." World Policy Journal, 11(2):1–11.

Paulson, Tom. (2003). "For your information, there's too much of it." Sydney Morning Herald, 1–2 November, p. 19.

"Pay to play." (1996). Rock and Rap Confidential, 131, p. 2.

"Paying the cost to feed the boss." (2002). Rock and Rap Confidential, 190, pp. 2–3.

Peers, Martin. (2003). "The TV-Pop music connection – Fox's American Idol yields two hit records for BMG; some doubt trend has legs." Wall Street Journal, 15 April, p. B1.

Pendleton, Jennifer. (2003). "'Idol' a standard for integration." Advertising Age, 74(12):S2.

Pesselnick, Jill. (2001). "Music goes to college." Billboard, 113(37):27.

Petersen, Freya. (2003). "The show's over for pets caught up in fads." Sydney Morning Herald, 29 November, p. 11.

Petradis, Alexis. (2004). "Ring it up: there's money to be made from mobiles." Sydney Morning Herald, 28 May, p. 13.

Phillips, Liam. (2004). "Never mind the paddocks." West Australian (Perth), 29 July, p. 7.

Pidd, Helen. (2007). "Food manufacturers target children on internet after regulator's TV advertising clampdown." Guardian Unlimited, 31 July. <http://lifeandhealth. guardian.co.uk/food/story/0,,2138178,00.html>.

"Piracy makes up 11 pct of Australian music sales." (2003). Reuters News, 16 July, p. 4.

"Pop Idol rings up mobile revenues for Fremantle Media." (2003). Television Business International, 15(6):1.

"Pop Life." (1997). Rock and Rap Confidential, 147, p. 3.

"Pop Life." (2000). Rock and Rap Confidential, 173, p. 3.

Porter, Hugh. (2006). "Bands and brands." Time International, 26 June, p. 46.

Poschardt, Ulf. (1995). DJ culture. London: Quartet Books.

Poster, Mark. (2004). "Consumption and digital commodities in the everyday." Cultural Studies, 18(2/3):409–23.

Potter, Russell. (1998). "Not the same: race, repetition, and difference in hip-hop and dance music." In Swiss, T. et al. (eds). Mapping the beat: popular music and contemporary theory. London: Blackwell.

Purcell, Charles. (2003). "Buzz power." Sydney Morning Herald, "icon," 25–26 October, p. 8.

Quart, Alissa. (2003). Branded: the buying and selling of teenagers. London: Arrow Books.

Rifkin, Glenn. (1994). "With Garth Brooks help, McDonald's success at its first attempt to sell music with food." New York Times, 26 September, p. D7.

Robinson, D. et al. (eds). (1991). Music at the margins: popular music and global cultural diversity. Newbury Park, CA: Sage.

Rosen, Emanuel. (2000). The anatomy of buzz: how to create word of mouth marketing. London: Harper Collins.

Sams, Christine. (2004a). "Music giants to unite in $7bn merger." Sydney Morning Herald, 15 August, p. 15.

——. (2004b). "Sebastian not idle on criticism." Sun Herald, 26 December, p. S14.

——. (2006). "Discarded idol." Sydney Morning Herald. <http://www.smh.com.au/news/music/discardedidol/2006/07/16/ 1152988404930.html>.

Sanghera, Sathnam. (2002a). "Where there's a will." Financial Times, 2 April, p. 28.

——. (2002b). "Pop music's multimedia impresario." Financial Times, 7 September, p. 13.

——. (2002c). "Executives worry about piracy." Financial Times, 15 November, p. 28.

Sanjek, Russell. (1996). Pennies from heaven: the American popular music business in the twentieth century. New York: Da Capo.

Sawhney, Mohanbir. (n.d.). "Beyond relationships marketing: the rise of collaborative marketing." CRMToday. <http://www.crm2day.com/>.

Scatena, Dino. (2003/4). "New kid on the block." Rolling Stone: The Rock & Roll Yearbook, pp. 78–82.

Scherzinger, Martin. (2005). "Music, corporate power, and unending war." Cultural Critique, 60:23–67.

Schiller, Herbert. (1971). Mass communications and American empire. New York: Oxford University Press.

——. (1986). Information and the crisis economy. New York: Oxford University Press.

Schlosberg, Justin. (2005). "Who's paying for song Bribes?" CommonDreams.org, 4 August. <http://www.commondreams.org/views05/0804-30.htm>.

Scott, Kevin. (2002). "A licence to print money." Television Business International, 14(4):1.

Seabrook, John. (2003). "The money note: can the record business be saved?" New Yorker, 78(18):42–55.

Selsky, Deborah. (1990). "Compact discs now 26 percent of recorded music sales." Library Journal, 115(12):32.

Serpick, Evan. (2006). "Rock & roll: custom radio." Rolling Stone, 9 February, p. 20.

Shakur, Afeni. (1999). Dear 2Pac: fan letters, poems, art. Los Angeles, CA: Destiny Merchandising.

Shapiro, Samantha. (2007). "Hip hop outlaw (industry version)." New York Times Magazine, 18 February. <http://www.nytimes.com/2007/02/18/magazine/18djdrama.t.html>.

Shedden, Iain. (2003). "Music companies warned: 'adjust to survive'." Australian, 28 March, p. 19.

——. (2004). "Industry repudiates downloads research." Australian, 1 April, p. 12.

Sherman, Cary. (2000). "IAJE: legal issues in jazz – Counterpoint: sound recordings are already works made for hire." Jazz Educators Journal, 33(2):77–8.

Shields, Rob (ed.). (1992). Lifestyle shopping: the subject of consumption. London, Routledge.

——. (1999). Lefebvre, love and struggle: spatial dialectics. London: Routledge.

Silverstone, Roger. (1993). "Television, ontological security and the transitional object." Media, Culture and Society, 15(4):573–98.

Sisario, Ben. (2005). "Music industry financier buys 'American Idol.'" New York Times, 19 March, p. B9.

Solomon, Michael. (2003). Conquering consumerspace: marketing strategies for a branded world. New York: American Marketing Association.

"Sony and the poor boys." (1999). Rock and Rap Confidential, 164, p. 5.

Stahl, Matthew. (2002). "Authentic boy bands on TV? Performers and impresarios in The Monkees and Making the Band." Popular Music, 21(3):307–29.

——. (2004). "A moment like this: American Idol and narratives of meritocracy." In Washburne, C., and M. Derno (eds). Bad music: music we love to hate. New York: Routledge, pp. 212–32.

Stanley, Alessandra. (2003). "Here's reality: 'Idol' feeds hopefuls to a shaky music business." New York Times, 23 January, p. E1.

Stanley, T.L. (1995). "Brand builders." Brandweek, 27 February, p. 9.

Starr, L., and C. Waterman. (2003). American popular music: from minstrelsy to MTV. Oxford: Oxford University Press.

Steinberg, Brian. (2005). "Madison Avenue is getting the beat." Wall Street Journal, 23 March, p. B3.

——, and E. Smith. (2006). "Rocking Madison Ave." Wall Street Journal, 9 June, p. A11.

Sterne, Jonathan. (2006). "The mp3 as cultural artifact." New Media and Society, 8(5):825–842.

Stonehouse, David. (2003). "Price of glory." Sydney Morning Herald, "icon," 12–13 July, pp. 6–7.

——. (2005). "Searching for." Sydney Morning Herald, "icon," 18–19 June, 6–7.

Strauss, Neil. (1996). "Are the pop charts manipulated?" New York Times, 25 January, C15, p. 20.

——. (2000). "Out on the street, cyber and otherwise." New York Times, 4 May, p. E6.

Straw, Will. (2000). "Exhausted commodities: the material culture of music." Canadian Journal of Communication, 25(1). <http://www.cjc-online.ca>.

Sullivan, Andy. (2005). "Ringtones make sweet music for record label." Reuters, 24 June. <http://news.yahoo.com/s/nm20050624/tc_nm/>.

"Sydney auditions: conditions of participation in the Australian Idol audition." (2004). Australian Idol Online. <http://au.australianidol.com.au>.

Sydney Harbour Foreshore Authority. (2004). "What's on: Darling Harbour 2004." Darling Harbour: enjoy: play it your way. Sydney: Sydney Harbour Foreshore Authority.

Szalai, George. (2007). "Dialogue with George Sillerman." Hollywood Reporter, 26–28 January, p. 398.

Tatchell, Jo. (2005). "Together in electric dreams." Guardian, 17 January. <http://arts.guardian.co.uk/features/story/0,11710,1391951,00.html>.

Taylor, Chuck. (1998). "Paid play changing biz landscape." Billboard, 110(19): 1, 82–3.

——. (2001). "Preteens a lucrative, if vulnerable market." Billboard, 113(19):1, 5.

Teitelman, Bram. (2005). "Survey: CDs, radio rule." Billboard, 117(29):9.

"This software picks hits." Current Science, 90(4):12.

Thomas, Brett. (2003a). "Caught in the net." Sun Herald, "Sunday Metro," 6 July, p. 1.

——. (2003b). "False idols." Sydney Morning Herald, 20 July. <http://www.smh.com.au/articles/2003/07/20/1058639656075.html>.

Thompson, C., and Z. Arsel. (2004). "The Starbucks brandscape and consumers' (anticorporate) experiences of glocalization." Journal of Consumer Research, 31 (December), pp. 631–42.

Timson, Lia. (2006). "Burn, burn, burn." Sydney Morning Herald, "icon," 25–26 February, p. 3.

Tolson, Andrew. (2001). "'Being yourself': the pursuit of authentic celebrity." Discourse Studies, 3(4):443–57.

Tomlinson, John. (1991). Cultural imperialism: an introduction. Baltimore. MD: Johns Hopkins University Press.

——. (2003). "Media imperialism." In Parks, L., and S. Kumar (eds). Planet TV: a global television reader. New York: New York University Press.

Toy, N., and F. Connolly. (2004). "Home grown." Daily Telegraph (Sydney), "Sydney Confidential," 17 September, p. 32.

Toynbee, Jason. (2000). Making popular music: musicians, creativity and institutions. London: Routledge.

Turner, G. et al. (2000). Fame games: the production of celebrity in Australia. Cambridge: Cambridge University Press.

Turow, Joseph. (1997). "Breaking up America: the dark side of target marketing." American Demographics, 19(11):51–5.

——. (2000). "Segmenting, signaling and tailoring: probing the dark side of target marketing." In Anderson R., and L. Strate (eds). Critical studies in media commercialism. London: Oxford University Press.

Twitchell, James. (1999). Lead us into temptation: the triumph of American materialism. New York: Columbia University Press.

U.S. Department of State (USDOS). (2004a). "U.S. launches first investigation of online copyright piracy." Office of Public Affairs, U.S. Consulate General, Sydney.

——. (2004b). "U.S. releases 2004 report on intellectual property protection." Office of Public Affairs, U.S. Consulate General, Sydney.

——. (2004c). "Intellectual property rights linked to security, official says." Office of Public Affairs, U.S. Consulate General, Sydney.

——. (2006a). "Copyright protection vital to promoting cultural diversity." Office of Public Affairs, U.S. Consulate General, Sydney.

——. (2006b). "Intellectual property expert discusses copyright protection." Office of Public Affairs, U.S. Consulate General, Sydney.

——. (2006c). "U.S. praises Pakistani protection of intellectual property." Office of Public Affairs, U.S. Consulate General, Sydney.

von Seggern, John. (2002). "Music file-sharing: impacts on the music industry." <http://www.digitalcutuplounge.com/newsite/jvs_papers/file_sharing_report2002.htm>.

Wallis, R., and K. Malm. (1984). Big sounds from small peoples: the music industry in small countries. New York: Pendragon.

Walsh, Chris. (2006). "SONY BMG, Pandora strike U.K. license." Billboard, 118(49):19.

Warren, Rich. (1998). "The future of home recording." Stereo Review, 63(1):67–71.

Weaver, Jane. (2006). "Downloads to save music biz: pay services will help industry recover, new report says." MSNBC Interactive. <http://www.msnbc.msn.com/id/3073260/>.

Werde, Bill. (2004). "Rock & roll: P2P gets profitable – former Napster, Grokster bosses go to work for the majors." Rolling Stone, 963 (9 December), p. 36.

"What is fair market share?" (2006) Billboard, 118(10):10.

Williamson, J, and M. Cloonan. (2007). "Rethinking the music industry." Popular Music, 26(2):305–22.

Wilson, Richenda. (1999). "Commercial sounds." Marketing Week, 22(14):47.

Winseck, Dwayne. (2002). "Illusions of perfect information and fantasies of control in the information society." New Media and Society, 4(1):93–122.

World Idol. (2003). FremantleMedia Operations. Broadcast on Ten Network in Australia on December 26, 2003.

Wright, Gerard. (2004). "Music: the caffeine of love." Sydney Morning Herald, 11–12 September, p. 35.

——. (2006). "Look what they've done to my song." Sydney Morning Herald, 4–5 March, p. 31.

Zak, Albin. (2001). The poetics of rock: cutting tracks, making records. Berkeley, CA: University of California Press.

Zuel, Bernard. (2004). "Mergers strike a blow for independents." Sydney Morning Herald, 29 September, p. 16.

——. (2006). "Charting downloaded music tells us nothing new." Sydney Morning Herald, 10 April p. 3.

Discography

Big Mama Thornton: Hound Dog/The Peacock Recordings. (1992). Los Angeles: MCA Records. MCAD-10668.

Big Mama Thornton with the Muddy Waters Blues Band–1966. (2004 [1966]). Arhoolie Records. CD 9043.

Elvis' Golden Records. (1958). RCA Records. PD85196.

Elvis in the 50s. (2002). London: BMG UK. 74321944249.

Just As I Am. Guy Sebastian. (2003). BMG Australia. Cat. #82876587792.

One Determined Heart. Paulini. (2004). Sony Australia, Cat. #5176962000.

That's What I'm Talking About. Shannon Noll. (2004). BMG Australia, Cat. #82876594852.

The Chess Story: From Blues to Doo Wop. (1992). Charly Records. CD INS 5033.

The R&B Box: 30 Years of Rhythm and Blues. (1994). Los Angeles: Rhino Records. R2 71806.

When the Sun Goes Down: The Secret History of Rock & Roll. (2002). New York: RCA Victor/BMG. 09026-63986-2.

Filmography

Hype! (1996). Fabulous Sounds. NW1159.

Scratch. (2001). Darkhorse Entertainment. DVD07301.

Index

active audience theory 6, 7, 11, 80
Adorno, Theodor 7, 91
Aesthetics 3, 33, 35, 90, 104, 107
 and analytical categories 11, 37
 and the Idol phenomenon 51–2, 96,
  100–101, 110–12, 114–17, 124, 127,
  154
 and piracy 50–51
 in popular music analysis 35–8
 and the medium and materials of
  popular music 39–50
Alderman, John 55, 57–8, 60–61
ambient media 77, 85–6, 89, 101
American Idol 106, 108
Anderson, Chris 71
Anderson, Tim 2, 5
Ang, Ien 6
'Angels' 138
'Angels Brought Me Here' 134–5, 137–8
anti-piracy campaigns 2–3, 59, 78
Appadurai, Arjun 19, 33
ARIA Awards 140
artistic medium 38–40
Attali, Jacques 1
attention economy 6, 12–13, 21–2, 75–7,
  81–2, 85, 101, 121, 157
Australian Idol 13, 51, 106, 118–20
 aesthetics 51–2, 96, 100–101, 110–12,
  114–17, 124, 127, 154
 and branding 106–7, 101, 114
 contestants 51, 95, 97, 99, 100, 103–21,
  123–8, 131–2, 134–5, 139–41, 148,
  150, 152–3
 pop star personae 101
 core relationships 98, 100, 117, 124–7
 cross promotion 3, 13, 98, 101, 112
 Final 12 109
 Grand Final 107, 116, 119, 130, 135,
  147–50
 'Idol House Party' 117
 Initial auditions 107–12
 'Inside Idol' 105, 115, 117, 119–20,
  126–7

 judges 95, 100–101, 103, 108–10,
  112–13, 115–16, 119–21, 123, 126,
  130, 131–4, 142–8, 150, 153
 narrative 3, 51, 96, 103–9, 111, 114–16,
  120, 121, 124–5, 127–8, 137, 139,
  141, 155, 157
 Producer auditions 111, 126
 product placement 99, 116
 Semi-Finals 114–18
 Showdown 134
 sponsorship 108, 116
 'Up Close and Personal' 117, 127
 Vocal Boot Camp 103, 112–14
 voting 95, 99, 106, 115, 117–18, 152–3
 Wild Card 115–16, 146–7
 'Winner's Journey' 119, 123–4, 142
 'Winner's Story' 130–31, 134
authenticity 36, 103–5, 121, 124, 134, 140,
  147, 149, 158

Bakan, Joel 5
Barlow, John Perry 79–80
Bear Stearns 99
blogs 8, 22, 86–8
BMG 67, 83, 107, 152
Born, Georgina 7
branding 12, 22, 57, 96–9
 and popular music 72, 75–7, 83–8
 theories of 82
 value of 12, 13, 75, 96–9
Burkart, Patrick 2, 57
Burnett, Robert 7
buzz 87–8

Callea, Anthony 110–11, 116, 125, 141–54
Carey, Alex 2
cassette format 59
celebrity 20, 101, 103–5, 118, 120–21, 126,
  129, 135, 137, 141, 147
Chanan, Michael 8, 58
CKX 99
'Climb Ev'ry Mountain,' 133–4, 137
Coleman, Mark 8, 58

compact discs (CD) 19, 28–34, 55
  adoption of 59
  development of 58–9
  sales of 4, 39, 59, 62, 66–73, 82, 84–5,
    87–8, 91, 97, 101, 105, 107
consumer agency 4–10, 14, 20–21, 25–6,
    28, 34, 80, 100, 112, 127, 157
consumer culture 6, 8–14, 18–22, 30, 32, 34,
    81, 86, 88, 102, 115
consumer ethnography 86–7
consumer information 12, 17–18, 23, 27, 32,
    34, 70, 73, 77–80, 86–7, 89–90
consumer resistance 6, 9, 14, 28, 43
consumer surveillance 24–5, 73, 81
consumption 1–14, 17, 35–42, 51–2,
    56–8, 69, 71–3, 75–81, 86–91, 97–8,
    101–2, 117, 158
  acts of 19–34
  mechanisms of 1–14
  spaces of 19–34
coolhunting 22, 86–7
copyright law 11–12, 24, 60–66, 79, 156
corporate globalization 6, 10, 14, 96, 98,
    101
  and consumer culture 17–18
  and the music industry 3–4, 58, 101
Couldry, Nick 101, 107
Cowen, Tyler 5, 8
cross-promotion 3–4, 12–13, 85, 98
cultural populism 2, 5, 102, 158

Dannen, Frederic 59
Davis, Susan 28
demographics 8, 17, 22–3, 27–30, 32, 71,
    80, 82, 86
deregulation of capital markets 98
digging 49–50
Digital Audio Tape (DAT) 59
Digital Versatile Discs (DVD) 1, 69, 88, 101
Dirt Cheap CDs 32–4
disintermediation 66
DJs 48–50, 79
Donovan, Casey 119, 123–5, 141–7, 149–54
Drahos, Peter 4, 58

Elmer, Greg 22
entertainment industry 1, 4–6, 8–9, 11–13,
    18–32, 56–9, 63, 69–72, 76–8, 82–8,
    98, 101, 156–8

Ewen, Stuart 2

file sharing 3, 12, 56, 60, 63, 67–8, 78, 84,
    156
Fink, Robert 42, 44–5
Fiske, John 5, 8
Frank, Thomas 5–7, 80–81
Frankfurt school 7, 80
Frith, Simon 5, 8, 12, 50
Fuller, Simon 13, 95, 99–100, 103, 123

Gandy, Oscar 21, 23
Garofalo, Reebee 57–8, 71
geodemographics 12, 88
Gibson, Chris 7
Gladwell, Malcolm 22, 81, 87–8
globalization 1, 6, 10–14, 18–22, 157–8
  and consumer culture 11, 17–19
  and finance capital 98
  and the music industry 10–14, 26, 31–2,
    95–8, 102
Goss, Jon 25, 27
Gracyk, Theodore 6, 11, 35, 39, 41–3, 47–8
Grossberg, Lawrence 5, 35–7, 42, 50

Hannigan, John 28
Haring, Bruce 57, 59, 61, 98
Harvard Project on the City 17, 21, 24, 27,
    75
Henwood, Doug 18, 58, 75–6
Herman, Edward 58, 98
'Here's Where I Stand' 145, 147
'Hold me in Your Arms' 130
'Hound Dog' 42–4, 46, 52

intellectual property 4, 12, 21, 51, 56,
    58–61, 78, 101, 156
International Federation of the
    Phonographic Industry (IFPI) 60,
    68–9, 78, 156

Johnson, Walter 7
Jones, Steve 2, 24, 66, 68

Last.fm 89–90
Lefebvre, Henri 26
Leyshon, Andrew 2, 23
'Listen with Your Heart' 150, 152
Locke, Christopher 80, 89

long tail markets 71–2

McDonald's 82, 108, 155
McGuigan, Jim 2, 7
Mann, Charles 4, 8, 12, 55–6, 61–3, 68, 156
manufactured pop 124
market research 8–9, 27, 55–6, 68, 73, 82, 85–6, 99, 156
market risk 4–5, 9, 11, 13, 18, 57, 62, 67–8, 73, 85, 91, 96–7, 99, 102, 115
marketing 2, 4, 9, 12–13, 22, 24, 29–30, 66, 73, 75–6, 79–89
    peer-to-peer 22, 78, 81, 86
    tipping point 81
    viral 9, 12, 22, 75–6, 81, 88
    whisper 81
    word of mouth 81
Maybelline 99, 115, 155
'Million Tears, A' 142
mobile phones 22, 83–4, 86, 88–9, 101
Moore, Allan 37
Moore, Robert 76
MP3 3, 22, 69, 75, 84, 88
    development of 55–6
MP3.com 63
Music Genome Project 90–91
music industry 1–14, 20, 23, 25–30, 34, 56–61, 63–73, 76–80, 82–91, 96–107, 121, 128, 140, 156–8
    and contracts 61–6, 84–5, 125
    and copyright 11–12, 24, 60–66, 79
    definition of 2
    disintermediation of 66
    distribution systems of 9–10, 25, 40, 56–8, 61, 67–8, 70, 73, 78, 84
    globalization of 1–5, 18, 26, 58–60, 63, 68, 77, 95–8, 100–101, 102, 128, 156–8
    and merchandising 4, 30, 32, 121, 155, 157

Napster 3, 66
Negus, Keith 2, 5, 7, 10, 71
'New York, New York' 132–3
Noll, Shannon 109, 119–20, 128, 130–34, 137–40, 155

ontology of popular music 11, 35–7, 40, 47–50

Otis, Johnny 44–5

Pandora.com 90
payola 67
Peer-to-peer networks 69, 78, 81
    marketing on 86
piracy 2–4, 12–13, 22, 24, 35–6, 50–51, 60–63, 66–9, 78, 156–7
    and record sales 68
playlists 90
Pop Idol 106
popular music 1–3, 5–14, 23–4, 33, 35–43, 52, 96, 105, 124, 128, 158
    genres of 34, 36–7, 39, 91
    medium and materials of 38–52, 58–78, 91
    and ontology 35–7, 40, 47–51,
    and retailing 1, 23, 28–34, 66–7, 70, 72, 86
Potter, Russell 7
'Prayer, The' 147–52
Presley, Elvis 42–6, 76, 99, 133
promotional cultures 3, 9, 12, 21, 35, 43, 46, 51, 85, 88, 101

R&B 42–6, 120, 129, 133, 135, 137, 151
'Reason, The' 146
Recording Industry Association of America (RIAA) 60–61, 63–9, 72, 156
    and piracy 60–61, 66–9
    and work for hire 63–6
relationship mining 86
'Ribbon in the Sky' 129
ringtones 22, 89
risk management 4, 13, 18, 57, 62, 67–8, 73, 85, 91, 96–7, 99
royalties 62–3, 66

'Scratch' 47–8, 50
Sebastian, Guy 124–5, 129–40, 158, 153
Sillerman, Robert 99
Solomon, Michael 5, 75, 80
song placement 22
Sony 60–61, 82, 90
Soundscan 12, 69–72
Stahl, Geoff 108, 118, 121, 124
street teams 88
Sydney 19, 26, 28–32, 75, 81, 118, 128, 143, 154

as fantasy city 28, 30
Opera House 106, 116, 119, 156
and shopping 30–32

Thornton, Big Mama 42, 44–5
Tomlinson, John 19, 58
Toynbee, Jason 7–8, 27, 40
trendspotters 8, 87
Turner, Graeme 2, 21
Turntablism 47
tweeners 22, 99, 139
Twitchell, James 5, 8, 18

United States Department of State (USDOS)
     58, 60

United States Supreme Court 4, 156
Universal Price Code 17, 80–81

video games 4, 22, 83, 85, 101
Virgin Megastore 19, 30, 42–3

'What About Me?' 137–9
Winseck, Dwayne 18, 57, 73
'Wishes' 143
World Economic Forum 4
World Idol 95–6, 109
World Trade Organization 59

X factor 118, 131